D1300317

Technical Analysis Tools

Also available from
Bloomberg Press

Investing in Hedge Funds:
Revised and Updated Edition
by Joseph G. Nicholas

Hedge Fund of Funds Investing:
An Investor's Guide
by Joseph G. Nicholas

Market-Neutral Investing:
Long/Short Hedge Fund Strategies
by Joseph G. Nicholas

Hedge Fund Risk Fundamentals:
Solving the Risk Management and Transparency Challenge
by Richard Horwitz

———————

A complete list of our titles is available at
www.bloomberg.com/books

ATTENTION CORPORATIONS

This book is available for bulk purchase at special discount. Special editions or chapter reprints can also be customized to specifications. For information, please e-mail Bloomberg Press, press@bloomberg.com, Attention: Director of Special Markets, or phone 212-617-7966.

Technical Analysis Tools

Creating a Profitable Trading System

MARK TINGHINO

BLOOMBERG PRESS
NEW YORK

© 2008 by Mark Tinghino. All rights reserved. Protected under the Berne Convention. Printed in the United States of America. No part of this book may be reproduced, stored in a retrieval system, or transmitted, in any form or by any means, electronic, mechanical, photocopying, recording, or otherwise, without the prior written permission of the publisher except in the case of brief quotations embodied in critical articles and reviews. For information, please write: Permissions Department, Bloomberg Press, 731 Lexington Avenue, New York, NY 10022 or send an e-mail to press@bloomberg.com.

BLOOMBERG, BLOOMBERG ANYWHERE, BLOOMBERG.COM, BLOOMBERG MARKET ESSENTIALS, *Bloomberg Markets,* BLOOMBERG NEWS, BLOOMBERG PRESS, BLOOMBERG PROFESSIONAL, BLOOMBERG RADIO, BLOOMBERG TELEVISION, and BLOOMBERG TRADEBOOK are trademarks and service marks of Bloomberg Finance L.P. ("BFLP"), a Delaware limited partnership, or its subsidiaries. The BLOOMBERG PROFESSIONAL service (the "BPS") is owned and distributed locally by BFLP and its subsidiaries in all jurisdictions other than Argentina, Bermuda, China, India, Japan, and Korea (the "BLP Countries"). BFLP is a wholly-owned subsidiary of Bloomberg L.P. ("BLP"). BLP provides BFLP with all global marketing and operational support and service for these products and distributes the BPS either directly or through a non-BFLP subsidiary in the BLP Countries. All rights reserved.

AutoCAD is a registered trademark of Autodesk, Inc.
COMEX is a registered trademark of the New York Mercantile Exchange.
CQG, and CQG Trader are trademarks of CQG, Inc.
Excel, Microsoft, MSN, Office, Windows, and Windows Vista are registered trademarks of Microsoft Corporation.
Google search is a trademark of Google.
Java and RCG Onyx are trademarks of Sun Microsystems.
Market Profile and Liquidity Data Bank are registered trademarks of the Chicago Board of Trade.
Sesame Street is a registered trademark of Sesame Workshop.
WINdoTRADEr is a registered trademark of WindoTrader Corporation.
X-Trader and X_Study are registered trademarks of Trading Technologies.
Yahoo! is a registered trademark of Yahoo! Inc.

This publication contains the author's opinions and is designed to provide accurate and authoritative information. It is sold with the understanding that the author, publisher, and Bloomberg L.P. are not engaged in rendering legal, accounting, investment-planning, or other professional advice. The reader should seek the services of a qualified professional for such advice; the author, publisher, and Bloomberg L.P. cannot be held responsible for any loss incurred as a result of specific investments or planning decisions made by the reader.

First edition published 2008
1 3 5 7 9 10 8 6 4 2

Library of Congress Cataloging-in-Publication Data

Tinghino, Mark.
    Technical analysis tools : creating a profitable trading system / Mark Tinghino. -- 1st ed.
    p. cm.
  Summary: "Technical Analysis Tools gives readers an arsenal of technical analysis tools. From a brief discussion of fundamental analysis to an in-depth discussion of technical analysis and the author's own cycles method, readers will find time-tested approaches to technical analysis. They'll learn how to determine which technique is best for them in this hands-on guide. Helpful appendixes are included" –Provided by publisher.
    Includes bibliographical references and index.
    ISBN 978-1-57660-248-5 (alk. paper)
    1. Investment analysis. I. Title.

HG4529.T56 2008
332.63'2042--dc22   2007045459

Acquired by Stephen Isaacs

To Carol

Contents

Part One

Technical Analysis Trading Arsenal

Part Two

Putting It All Together

Foreword

When my friend Mark Tinghino requested that I contribute a foreword for *Technical Analysis Tools*, my first thought was why he and the editors at Bloomberg Press for that matter were bothering with another book on this topic. As the discussion of price trend analysis in general, and technical analysis in particular, has expanded across time into such a crowded body of knowledge, it was reasonable to question what else even as talented an analyst as Mark could possibly add. Yet, as I was aware of Mark's background as well as his devotion to the craft, the least I could do was take a look.

The manner in which he develops his major themes and specific insights inspired me to ensure potential readers of this fine work understand that it contains essential further knowledge for those at an entry or intermediate level of trend analysis experience. Of course, even sophisticated analysts are also likely to gain from his interesting perspective, as well.

In essence, *Technical Analysis Tools* quickly progresses from a foundation of basics to a broad, balanced review of primary techniques and important related topics. It delivers a wholly productive focus on both analysis methods and practical considerations. These range from risk management to the importance of employing a multifaceted approach.

Consolidating this type of broad view into an understandable and readily applied approach is why, among other books which claim to afford their readers this luxury, *Technical Analysis Tools* truly earns its subtitle: *Creating a Profitable Trading System*. In many circles, "trading system" has come to mean automated algorithmic black boxes. However, the most enlightened and successful traders, investors, and technical mentors have always advocated a "systematic" approach to market analysis. As challenging an endeavor as successful trading or portfolio management has always required extensive insight and rigorous discipline to succeed; the black box fascination is merely the most extreme manifestation of removing the emotional component.

An article I penned quite a few years ago, "The Importance of Balance,"[1] is subtitled "Why the Major Classes of Technical Indicators Are Best Viewed in Conjunction and Across Time Frames." Prior to full exploration of that topic, I reference a quote from the ancient Chinese spiritual and philosophical guide to life, the *I Ching*: "In danger, all that counts is really carrying out all that has to be done—thoroughness—and going forward, in order not to perish by tarrying in the danger."[2]

That Asian focus is consistent with Mark's avocation of studying Eastern philosophical systems, which is a natural extension of formal education in philosophy with a specialization in the philosophy of science. All of which was instrumental in directing his initial market perceptions and extended professional training away from routine acceptance of "classical" technical analysis indications to broader themes and cycles as the most effective manner to construct a successful system. Only after that intellectual exploration did he return to consideration of what was truly useful from the classical indications and techniques. As well as any specific techniques, this provides analysts, traders, or investors the advantage of drawing upon those broad perspectives in *Technical Analysis Tools* in ways that best suit their individual style.

Enriching the initial market "landscape" discussion of chart analysis with the importance of a cyclical view is extremely important. Certainly the study of chart patterns that include understanding trends, trend lines, and price channel activity is essential. That is historically the basic language and conceptual foundation upon which further expertise is built. Yet Mark benefits his readers with the added perceptions that stem from the experienced analysts' awareness that all price movement takes place in the context of various forms of cycles; this is one of the most powerful differences between tactical tricks and the sort of systematic approach required for true sophistication.

Mark's discussion of alternative methods also is very important. It addresses many popular techniques' strengths and weaknesses, and how they fit in with the most critical major insights. In that regard, many of the market analysis techniques that some have taken as primary frames of reference were never intended

---

1. Alan Rohrbach, "The Importance of Balance: Why the Major Classes of Technical Indicators Are Best Viewed in Conjunction and Across Time Frames," Rohr International (1996).

2. Richard Wilhelm, trans. (Chinese into German) and Cary F. Baynes, trans. (German into English), *The I Ching, or Book of Changes*, 1st ed., Bolingen Series XIX (Princeton University Press, 1950), p. 115.

as such. As far back as Welles Wilder's articulation of the Relative Strength Index and other indicators in *New Concepts in Technical Trading Systems*,[3] the creators of those techniques cautioned that they were effective only as indications of potentials that required confirmation from subsequent price activity. Along with Mark's extensive review of risk management, his focus on confirmation is another important aspect of the effective systematic approach that he has managed to compress into this concise and balanced volume.

All of which is enhanced that much further by Mark's proprietary view of cycle analysis. He accurately notes that viewing markets as wave phenomena is significantly better as a metaphor than as an explicit system. Some interesting insights have surely evolved from rigid systematic wave analyses. Yet, for the most part, there is quite a bit of debate whether this is a matter of form over function. In most instances, it has led to more contention than clarity, as the specific implementation always seems to be highly subjective.

The true benefit for his clients and the readers of this book is more how the general wave concept encouraged Mark's intense interest in cycles. Quickly realizing that even highly successful analysis of occasional ultra-long-term cyclical trend reversals could not be the basis for active market analysis, he has expanded those initial compelling insights into an active approach to short-term cycle analysis as well. He is also always very clear that effective risk management requires discipline in the application of all technical analysis. More so than quite a few other proponents of that specific form of analysis, he aggressively applies that to cycle analysis as well.

Good trend analysis mentors or technical analysis authors are like good storytellers. They provide enough background to infuse meaning and vision into what can otherwise be boring rudimentary expression of simple techniques. A forceful focus on critical fine points accompanied by useful anecdotes and sidebars are all essential for meaningful technical texts. That is especially so for the explicit yet expansive concepts of price trend analysis. Although many narrowly defined courses and books admittedly provide useful insights, Mark has gone well beyond that in articulating the rich context that experienced analysts appreciate is necessary to fully illuminate this multifaceted subject.

---

3. J. Welles Wilder Jr., *New Concepts in Technical Trading Systems* (Trend Research, 1978); an example of at least one of Wilder's more prominent techniques in conjunction with confirmation from chart activity is on page 70.

I thank Mark for asking me to express how this work combines perspective, techniques, and balance in a manner rarely seen in highly specific technical volumes in any field. It is an excellent addition to the broad body of price trend analysis knowledge. While it will provide some readers with strikingly new insights, in my humble view it will also significantly assist experienced analysts and investors in achieving more cohesive and systematic application of their existing expertise.

ALAN ROHRBACH
President, Rohr International, Inc.

Acknowledgments

Special thanks are in order to Alan Rohrbach for writing the foreword and his generous assistance on structure and flow of topics; to Neal Weintraub, Lan Turner, and Barret Fiske for allowing me to paraphrase portions of their work on seasonal spreads; to Erika and Chris La Pelusa for their hard work on researching fundamentals of the copper market and preparing the first draft for that section (and their willingness to temporarily step outside of their chosen genre of fiction); to Patrick Spears for imparting his wisdom about trading discipline and assessing risk versus reward; to Michael Esposito for his assistance with the appendix on financial reports, and to Jeffrey Fillian for his assistance with the appendix on trading software. Thanks to Stephen Isaacs of Bloomberg Press for championing the book, to David George and Evan Burton for work on the graphics, to Kelli Christiansen of Bibliobibuli for developmental editing, and to JoAnne Kanaval and the Bloomberg editorial staff for putting on the finishing touches. Thanks to Terry Liberman and Jim Dalton for their insights on Market Profile. Thanks to Larry Rosenberg for his encouragement. Thanks to Aaron Reinglas and Curt Zuckert for help in gaining access to source materials from the CME library. Thanks to Vipul Shah for his collaboration over the past two decades and his insights on interest-rate cycles. Thanks to Frank Skorski for his kind and patient mentoring when I first started trading futures. Thanks to Jorin Daleanes and Craig McWilliams for collaborating on research into and real-time testing of trading strategies. Last but not least, thanks to Carol, my significant other, for balancing my technical bias with her penchant for keeping a close eye on market forces and fundamentals.

Introduction

Technical analysis has come a long way in the past few decades, and today traders of every level make the most of this very useful tool. So, this book is for institutional traders and individual investors alike. Although it takes you through the basics from square one, as well as covering advanced topics, it also offers some unique insights based on my work on cycles for timing trades on evaluating market news, which is not something you will find in most other books available on technical analysis.

I begin with a discussion of fundamental vis-à-vis technical analysis, including the historical causes of technical analysis overtaking fundamentals as the preferred approach among professional traders and money managers. I then cover the essentials of reading price charts, followed by adjunct tools such as indicators and Market Profile for assessing volume. To that solid foundation, I add my cyclical model, which I use as an overlay on standard technicals for precise timing of trades. Finally, I discuss building a complete trading program and sound money management principles.

To date no analyst has been able to accurately forecast market prices 100 percent of the time. Armed with massive computerized number-crunching and modeling capabilities and futuristic neural nets, current state-of-the-art analysis still falls short of National Weather Service meteorological forecasts, which are generally extremely accurate for three days into the future. The difference lies in cause-and-effect factors. Wind vectors and ocean currents are juggernaut forces that are not easily swayed from their course of movement, whereas markets consisting of mass auctions involving a multitude of humans making trading decisions based on emotions and occasionally reason are subject to winds of commerce that can be very fickle indeed.

Like millions of butterflies with fluttering wings, traders, when observed in real time, seem to embody jumbled chaos that only rarely coalesces into some semblance of order that allows one to tie a rise or dip in prices to a set of clearly identifiable statistics of supply and demand. Sudden spikes in intraday price levels often can be seen following major economic reports, but they rarely have any follow-through, and the price settles back into the typical narrow trading range before the end of the regular session. With these spikes, it's as though the markets were a hornet's nest, and the Brownian motion of the swarming winged insects gets temporarily disrupted as they fly into a fleeting frenzy. On the other hand, markets do make huge moves from time to time. Savvy traders who are prepared to capitalize on such larger swings can make huge profits when they get on the right side of the move and have the bravado to ride out the roller coaster without jumping off prematurely. Not-so-savvy traders can rack up unnerving losses when they see a big move get underway, proceed to jump in just before a correction, get whipsawed and shaken out of their positions, and end up kicking themselves when the market turns right around and heads screaming back in their direction as they stand on the sidelines dumbfounded and frustrated. (That is assuming they actually get an order filled and don't end up chasing the market with limit orders that fail to get matched under fast market conditions.)

Designing a killer trading system is only half of the equation. Following that system according to your preset rules is the other piece of the puzzle. Without that premise, the whole thing falls apart, and what should be a smoothly running machine ends up a jerky, out-of-control monster that causes money to spill out of your trading account and into the hands of professional floor traders, specialists, market makers, and large institutions. Curve fitting your analysis is the deadliest of sins. It is the ultimate vanity: the belief that your own conception is superior to the reality of market turbulence that is ready to strike like a Category 5 hurricane on the ill-prepared.

An interesting fact about traders is that they have an entirely different mindset from those who are purely investors. An investor likes to buy and hold, collecting dividends or accrued interest and hoping for some additional rate of return when, for instance, their shares of stock increase in price over periods of years or even decades. By contrast, a trader has a take-the-money-and-run attitude with the goal of parlaying a series of (one hopes) successful trades into a sum of money that is many times the original amount in the trading account. Trading then becomes a business, just like any other type of business. Although to the casual observer it may seem that a trader is engaged in a hobby that either increases the trader's net worth or decreases it, a serious trader puts in many hours of preparation studying markets, researching price data and (with many of them) charts, and planning specific trading strategies.

I have never worked on an exchange floor. I have visited traders in the pits in Chicago and taken a few cursory glances at the seemingly haphazard flow and execution of buy and sell orders, but that is not quite the same thing as transacting business in such an environment. I have always traded from "upstairs," armed with up-to-the-second charting software containing all sorts of specialized studies. Some floor brokers find trading in the pits virtually impossible and prefer trading from off the floor, because it is too difficult to assess price action from that vantage point. Other traders have had the opposite reaction, going through a period of adjustment when they leave the pits and can no longer assess the order flow firsthand. They devise other means of making their assessments, which are an integral part of their trading decisions.

Twenty years ago, I used to trade at home with electronic quotes and charts, but I still had to call my broker to get any orders executed. Today, it is an entirely different world. I get real-time quotes and charts and execute trades over a high-speed Internet connection, and need to pick up a phone only when there is an outage. My preliminaries and equity runs come by e-mail prior to the next day's trading session. It is a solitary pursuit.

Anyone who wants to graduate from amateur to professional trader needs to view trading as a business just like any other type of enterprise. There are costs of doing business, and there are inherent risks. There are matters of accounting and taxes and disaster recovery plans. There is a minimum investment in terms of time and capital to make any business a success, even if there is a sound business plan in place.

The message for my readers is that if they proceed methodically with a sound plan, they can be successful as traders. In the absence of such discipline, they may get lucky, but will lose in the long run, for the odds are against them. They basically have two choices: 1) Find a system devised by someone else and trade it mechanically, or 2) do their own homework and devise their own system.

In the first case, they run the risk of most systems in that the systems tend to run hot and cold. Once they start losing money, they will tend to abandon the system and look for another one, ultimately becoming system hoppers and never succeeding in the long run. My opinion is that most people are better off tailoring a system to their own needs and their own trading style based on their unique personality. What works for one person may not work for another. Jack D. Schwager interviewed many prominent successful traders for his book, *The New Market Wizards* (HarperCollins, 1992), and it is striking how very different each of them is from the others featured in those pages. One common trait they share, however, is that they are self-made and self-sufficient. They are true mavericks. My hope is that each person who reads this book will be inspired to find his own path to success and sufficient confidence to be able to actually follow that path without deviating. Overcoming fear is a critical factor in all endeavors, but it is particularly critical in the arena of trading. Having a plan that you have constructed on your own can go a long way toward instilling confidence, and may get you through the inevitable losses along the way that take the faint of heart out of the game for good.

The chapters that follow provide some valuable information for any prospective trader regarding time-tested approaches to technical analysis, such as Market Profile, which many floor traders and institutional money managers have utilized for over two decades. Although the scope of this book does not allow for an exhaustive treatment of any specific method, my objective is to provide some insight to guide the reader in selecting one or more avenues of research.

Technical Analysis Tools

Technical Analysis Trading Arsenal

CHAPTER 1

Approaches to Market Analysis

The discipline of price forecasting has undergone a sea change over the past three decades. Prior to the 1970s, conventional wisdom dictated reliance upon factors of supply and demand, or the market fundamentals, as the one tried-and-true methodology for forecasting prices. Looking to price charts and technical patterns and levels for future price projections was considered by most market professionals to be a mere oddity. Since then, however, there has been a shift in attitude toward charting.

A number of factors have played a role in that shift. The inflationary trends and floating foreign exchange rates of the early 1970s and, later in that decade, desktop computer software for price charts and technical analysis contributed to the change. Unlike during the prior two decades wherein trends could be more easily forecast from the available data on supply and demand and historical correlations between those fundamentals and price changes, the fundamental approach to analysis became less than reliable as a methodology. The 1950s and 1960s were, however, decades characterized by stability and a lack of inflation.

Furthermore, international faith in the greenback was undermined by the Federal Reserve's maneuvering to counteract the negative influences of war debts coupled with the rescinding of the policy of guaranteeing U.S. currency with gold and efforts to stabilize foreign currency exchange rates. Prices were affected by influences both inflationary and deflationary and a looming energy crisis revolving around crude oil.

A natural outcome of those shifts in the economic climate was the dramatic rise in volatility across all market sectors, which was fueled by fluctuations in the dollar and inflationary forces rather than actual supply and demand. The bubble in agricultural markets during that period is a prime example. Classical fundamental analysts were extremely vexed by the violent upheaval in the wake of those phenomena.

Market analysts were finally ready to embrace the technical approach. Unable to rely solely upon fundamentals to account for the price swings that were occurring on a regular basis, they could no longer ignore technical analysis as a means of assessing trends and risk. Markets were either reacting in far greater measure than supply-and-demand factors would indicate or not reacting enough to those factors. Technical analysis had finally entered the mainstream after decades of holding a marginal status.

Today, technical analysis is as ubiquitous as desktop and notebook computer technology. The access to technology was part and parcel of the triumph of the technical school of thought, which emphasizes price action rather than fundamentals of supply and demand. What was once a laborious process involving painstaking updating of price charts with graph paper and pencil along with manually executed mathematical calculations is now accomplished with the click of a mouse button. Gathering months or years worth of daily open, high, low, and close price data, let alone accumulating data on intraday prices, used to be a monumental task. With the software available today, which is affordable for even the most modest trading budget, every tick can be included as part of the analysis. That has opened up a whole new vista of analytical algorithms on high-frequency data.

The complexities of a global market have served to increase exponentially the number of variables of a fundamental assessment. Factors and events have a direct effect on many markets in a concrete and observable manner—things as diverse as interest-rate policies of Japan's central bank, Environmental Protection Agency (EPA) restrictions that cause oil refineries in the United States to shut down, a burgeoning middle class in India with newly acquired disposable income, newly built Chinese factories that trigger a skyrocketing demand for raw materials such as copper and steel, or even a freak ice storm that wreaks havoc on citrus groves in California. Such events may disrupt market cycles and, as a result, affect fundamental analysis.

The concept of market cyclicality involving bull markets that alternate with corrections and bear markets is nothing new. Just as economists and fundamental analysts study business cycles that affect various industries, technical analysts often take a cyclical view of the markets. There has been a major problem with prevailing cyclical models: Timing market tops and bottoms based on regular cycles can work consistently over a period of years or decades, but it eventually breaks down as the price swings get out of sync with a specific periodicity that has for the most part been artificially superimposed upon the raw data. Such approaches are just as much mental constructs as are chart patterns and wave counts. They are an attempt to distill order from chaos. Benoit Mandelbrot,

IBM fellow at Yale University and considered the father of fractal geometry, points out a number of shortcomings with those models in his book *The (Mis)Behavior of Markets*.[1] According to his mathematical analysis, the model that in reality best fits the data in the case of financial markets is one that also fits turbulence in air or water currents. The consequence of reliance upon such flawed approaches is that the trader runs the danger of being caught in unexpected volatile swings that could swiftly wipe out any realized gains in a portfolio in the virtual blink of any eye.

Following market cycles, though, can be a useful tool in the technical analysis arsenal—when used correctly. With proprietary research of hundreds of cycles that have proven consistently reliable over three decades of price data (as opposed to cycles studied by other researchers), we can formulate and incorporate a new cycle model into a technical trading strategy. The cycle analysis itself is a timing mechanism, but buy and sell indications come from assessing overall market strength or weakness, just as any technical indicator designed to measure overbought/oversold conditions can do with varying levels of reliability depending on trending versus trading markets. In order to forecast a potential reversal in price direction on a cycle boundary, there needs to be some clear direction of an existing trend. A market that is trading sideways or with ambivalence about whether the bulls or bears are in charge is not one that is going to generate clear indications.

The cornerstone of all technical analysis is the price chart. For the inexperienced trader, however, trying to make sense of a typical chart is akin to reading tea leaves. Chartists hone their craft over many years, and recognition of recurring patterns comes from having seen them over and over again. Indicators are meant to supplement the chart patterns rather than dictate market forecasts on their own. They distill some information from price data that are used to construct the graphical representation of prices.

The technical analyst does not have an easy task ahead of him. If it were as simple as learning some techniques and tools and then applying them to various markets, there would be droves of self-made billionaires walking around, and mutual funds would have 1,000 percent annual rates of return year in and year out. The other piece to the puzzle, money management, is far more crucial to

---

1. Benoit Mandelbrot and Richard L. Hudson, *The (Mis)Behavior of Markets: A Fractal View of Risk, Ruin and Reward* (Perseus Publishing, 2006).

achieving consistent investment results, and even the best real equity curves of the top-performing professional money managers have unsightly declines when market turbulence has taken its toll. There is a steep learning curve on the theoretical side, and then another one on the practical side as the student ventures into unfamiliar territory by jumping into the fray. My hope is that this book will provide a good foundation, so that no one jumps without a parachute.

My work on cycles is philosophically akin to the total body of work on the subject: using cycle boundaries to find price extremes in the form of highs and lows that resemble peaks or valleys on price charts. The specific approach is slightly different, however, in that cycles external to financial markets are researched with the object of discovering any correlations with market major and minor tops and bottoms. There are hundreds of cycles utilized in the proprietary model, which in practical application involves overlying the cycle boundaries on charts with vertical lines, which is identical to approaches of other cycle researchers. The cycles are of varying length, from a year or two in the case of the short ones to decades in the case of the longest ones. So, rather than starting with price data to discover cyclicality, I have started with cycles found in phenomena external to those data sets and then matched them statistically to price swings.

Whether or not there is some genuine cause and effect, such as the link between lunar cycles and ocean tides, is basically irrelevant, although scientists might find investigation along such lines fascinating. What is actually important is whether they are correlated closely enough to be useful in combination with other approaches to analysis such as fundamental and technical tools; and I am firmly convinced they are, after observing their performance utilizing more than thirty-five years of historical price data for analysis, and, even more important, having actually utilized them to some extent to trade in real time for the past twenty-three years. The model also seems to dovetail well with Mandelbrot's fractal framework, which also is all about timing. In a sense, it could be argued that the correlations are also with those fractal volatility packets that coincide with significant price swings. Just like fractal analysis, cyclic analysis of markets is still in its infancy, and visionary researchers of the future should provide the rest of us with some astounding revelations about cyclicality in markets.

Yet, based on only what we know today, with correlation to selective other methods to reinforce effective trend analysis and risk management, cycles can be a powerful analytical tool. Using cycles provides strong natural discipline that is based on both economic and technical rhythms and tempos, and restrains the inherent emotional responses that are sometimes fostered by the actively evolving signals from other methods. Cycle analysis helps traders or investors focus on the periods of greatest importance to the price trends. In addition to maintaining a structured trend perspective, another benefit is the degree to which that structure restrains the tendency toward overactive trading. It also reduces the novice analyst's tendency to become confused by overly complex systems incorporating too many approaches, classically referred to as analysis paralysis.

Although employing some range of multiple technical indicators across varied time frames is necessary to determine optimal times and prices for potential trend decisions, the key remains selectivity, choosing those tools wisely to suit the style and goals of the individual analyst or investor. Creating an optimal system requires enough familiarity with the strengths and weaknesses of each trend analysis method during different market phases to best benefit the analyst. The extensive descriptions and assessments of the highly varied approaches reviewed in this book and the limited considerations on how they complement each other are designed to enhance that pursuit.

In addition to fundamental and technical schools of thought, there is a third approach with respect to picking stocks, as espoused by Jim Cramer of CNBC's *Mad Money*.[2] It is a type of analysis that he refers to as "commonsensical," a "buy and homework" method as distinct from the orthodox "buy and hold" philosophy of investing. That commonsensical analysis is specifically designed for private speculators (although it served Cramer well as a hedge fund manager, so it would apply to institutional traders as well), and it provides a set of rules for timing the acquisition and liquidation of shares with the optimum risk/reward ratio. It is an approach to analysis that is of particular significance for the asset classes of equities, bonds, and (yes, sometimes the right place to stand temporarily is on the sidelines) cash. Cramer demonstrates how it trumps both the technicals and (at times) fundamentals in the case of individual stocks. With respect to that superiority of technique, it is important to understand the difference between the stock market and other markets such as futures and spot currencies (Forex).

The fortunes of a company are subject to variables that can spell unforeseen financial disaster and a decimation of share prices that could end at zero. A commodity, interest-rate instrument, or stock index, on the other hand, is not

---

2. James J. Cramer, *Jim Cramer's Real Money: Sane Investing in an Insane World* (Simon & Schuster, 2005).

going to go below a certain threshold at which the price is discounted beyond the bounds of reason. If there is a bumper crop in wheat, for example, the over-supply may depress wholesale prices, but it is not going to eliminate the underlying demand for the grain as long as there are humans on the planet who need to eat. An individual wheat farmer may be forced into bankruptcy in the event the declining margins do not at least cover the cost of living, but wheat production will still carry on. Also, companies, unlike commodities, need to be competitive and able to weather business cycle downturns. Stocks also differ from other asset classes in that they represent the underlying value of companies only to the extent that they are priced accordingly, and that is often not the case as exaggerated or unfounded rumors knock down the stock prices of otherwise sound businesses, or speculative bubbles inflate share prices to completely unsustainable levels. The application of technical analysis should take into consideration the asset class under analysis. In the case of equities, it will often have to play second fiddle to commonsensical analysis.

Although technical analysis today is favored by many if not most traders, fundamental analysis still has its place when it comes to market analysis and price forecasting. But technical analysis paints a picture that, in many ways, fundamental analysis cannot. The next chapter takes a closer look at fundamentals.

CHAPTER 2

Fundamentals: Navigating the Labyrinth

Forecasting prices is a daunting task, but an even more formidable exercise is analyzing all of the various factors of supply and demand. The situation has been exacerbated in recent decades by the emergence of the world market with all its intertwining interconnections that create a mind-boggling tangle. Prices of crude oil and metals skyrocketed in the beginning of this new millennium, but they also saw some major corrections following each new high. Analysis of supply and demand alone is not as effective as technical levels in explaining the countertrends within the major uptrends in those markets.

Copper and the Mobius Strip of Supply and Demand

First, consider one particular global commodity market: that mainstay of the Bronze Age, copper. Increased Chinese demand for industrial metals, which was fueled by accelerated building of factories to respond to the global hunger for cheap goods, caused copper futures prices to quintuple from 2002 to 2007, as shown in **Figure 2.1** on the following page. That's the simple explanation. When discussing the bull market on copper on a fundamental level, there is no definite end to the factors that influence its market value. Chasing down a solid point of origin for why copper has been such a hot commodity for the past decade is like peeling away the layers of an onion only to find another whole onion at the core. One industry leads to another in an unending trail.

Within this Mobius strip are the answers to why copper has had a nearly unprecedented run in this commodities bull market. For thousands of years, copper has been a primary ore mined for the production of functional and decorative items in many different arenas such as weaponry, tools, utensils, plumbing and electrical components, and wiring. Today, the trend continues.

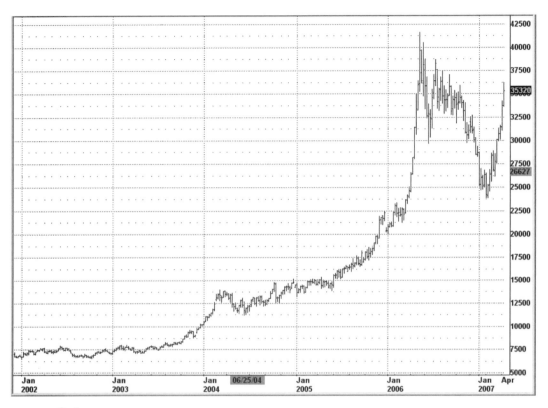

FIGURE 2.1

Copper Futures, 2002–2007

Source: eSignal

Demand

China is the world's largest consumer of copper, using 3.72 million tons in 2006. AME Mineral Economics research forecasts China's portion of world consumption for 2008 to be 22.8 percent, all of Western Europe's portion to be 21.7 percent, and the U.S. portion to be 13.4 percent.[1] There are many reasons for China's hefty demand for the nonferrous metal. Most household appliances today carry the ubiquitous "Made in China" label. The quest for understanding

---

1. http://www.ame.com.au/guest/cu/strategic.htm.

the growth in the copper market could almost end at this ever-familiar sticker, which is seen on just about anything that either plugs into an electrical socket or runs on batteries. The real focus, however, goes beyond China's exports to its own national consumption of copper.

As Simon Hunt, director of commodity consultancy Simon Hunt Strategic Services (UK) Ltd., stated at the GaveKal Conference in November 2006, there are four main fields of use for copper in China, which contribute to 77 percent of its consumption. The four areas are: magnet wire, building wire, power cables, and air conditioning/refrigeration tubes. Discussed below are two of those four areas addressed by Hunt.

Magnet Wire

The wire that is used to bring power to appliance motors is magnet wire made from refined copper. Over the past decade, production of magnet wire increased by 17 percent annually. This spike is accredited in part to China's growth in the production of electrical appliances. As listed on China's National Bureau of Statistics website, total retail sales for electric appliances increased 22 percent in 2006.

Magnet wire finds even more uses—from electronic sensor coils to clutch-and-brake coils—in China's automotive industry, which is soaring as well. According to PanAsianBiz.com, China produced 7.28 million vehicles in 2006—an increase of 27 percent. Automotive sales jumped 25 percent from the previous year, totaling 7.22 million vehicles sold. China's export of automotive goods alone accounted for more than $25.5 billion in sales.

Another leading user of magnet wire is China's transformer industry. The figures depicted in the abstract of a report titled "China Transformer Industry Report, 2006–2007," by Frank Fang, senior analyst for Research Connect, show that in the first half of 2006, production value rose 19 percent, with an average sales rate up to 96.49 percent. According to statistics from select transformer enterprises, the average profit margin rose 2.1 percent from 2005, making a 23 percent jump during the first half of 2006.

The catalyst for this increase was a national power shortage China experienced between 2000 and 2005. This crisis resulted in steady progress for the power industry, which caused an increase in investment in power. By 2007, China had become the world's third-largest electronics market, with growth exceeding any other producer's. However, the competition in this market is particularly intense, and unlike the electrical appliance and automotive industries, transformer production is a prime example of where supply of copper is exceeding demand.

Fang also wrote in his report that the transformer industry was currently plagued by increased costs. Some degree of overcapacity can provide a competitive edge to a company in that industry, however, oversupply of copper transformer components is apparently dogging those companies even further. That is evidenced by intensified competition in the marketplace, products that are homogenous, and a scattering of supply sources.

Current global supplies of transformers greatly outstrip demand. Foreign enterprises have increased production in China since the 1990s, lured by low labor costs, high quality, and tax incentives. They are also aggressively acquiring existing Chinese companies in the transformer industry, and that activity is expected to accelerate.

Building Wire

During the past decade, the use of building wire has seen an increase of 14 percent annually. Domestically, China's housing market is booming. In 2001, the cost of houses in China leaped 2.5 percent from the previous year. On Monday, July 23, 2001, the *China Daily* cited the National Bureau of Statistics of China, stating that the price of a house built for middle- and high-income home buyers averaged 2,368 yuan (U.S. $285) per square meter for the first five months of that year, up 200 yuan over the same period in 2000. Then, in 2004, despite China's efforts to slow the rising prices of homes (which included the central bank raising the benchmark interest rate by 0.27 percentage points with the hope of dissuading people from putting money into property), the market continued to grow. Talk of a bubble burst began to spread. By the end of November of that year, price elevation rose to 12.5 percent year-on-year.

Unfortunately, 2005 showed a darker reality than the hopes expressed four years earlier by Xie Jiajin, director of the Real Estate Department under the Ministry of Construction. At that time, Xie said that, "Generally speaking, the whole real estate market in China has entered a vibrant period and I think it will last for a relatively long time." In the October 19, 2005, edition of the *New York Times*, it was reported that Shanghai had more than four thousand skyscrapers and expected to build another one thousand by 2010. Not more than twenty years ago, there was virtually no housing construction or office building planned. According to CLSA, a brokerage house specializing in the Asia-Pacific region, China is expected to see 75 million more farmers moving to cities by 2012, culminating in perhaps the largest mass migration in history. If only half of the 75 million farmers were to purchase homes, with each home requiring approximately four hundred pounds of copper to construct (based on U.S. figures), that would equal 15 million tons of copper spread out over that five-year span.

With so much money being made in China's housing and development market, and despite the fears that the bubble may burst, it appears that there's something of a gold fever spreading. To quote the *New York Times* 2005 article, "Rising prices have created a circuslike atmosphere in parts of China. Real estate fairs are mobbed, land speculation is rampant, and some poor farmers dream about converting their wheat fields into the next Beverly Hills."

Even American firms are jumping at the opportunities developing in China. Goldman Sachs and Merrill Lynch have entered into the real estate race, along with Morgan Stanley, which acquired about $700 million in commercial real estate in Shanghai. Similar trends are seen in Beijing as well.

The development boom taking place in China is the primary motivation in China's quest for more natural resources. The Chinese need raw materials to build and energy to power—both of which heavily rely on copper.

Riding on top of this surge are the preparations for the 2008 Olympic Games, which will be held in Beijing. Major construction projects in development to host this event are putting additional strain on the supply of water and power—and driving up the demand for copper.

The United States (whose own housing market is in a decline) provides a good example of the trends that affect the supply and demand of copper on a global level. On a domestic level, there are common reasons for the normal fluctuation in the demand for copper throughout the year. Weather is a prime example.

According to ISRI's February 23, 2007, *Friday Report*, as a result of more favorable climate conditions, construction is heaviest between the months of May and September. This is called a "construction surge." Outside this period, demand for copper rises without a match in consumption, creating an imbalance on the supply-and-demand scale. As the warmer months pass and supplies diminish, the scale equalizes. A secondary demand surge occurs again with "first notice day" with the July High Grade Copper Contract, which extends into early September, again tilting the scale.

Globally, this scale is bigger, more sensitive, and has a wider range of circumstances weighing on its balance. And like the above-mentioned example, there is a regular ebb and flow of copper worldwide that keeps the equilibrium stable.

But because China has driven copper into a bull run in the commodities market, that equilibrium has been disrupted. It's akin to the United States bolstering its supply of copper to meet the needs of the upcoming fair-weather construction surge, only to find that the warm months never pass, and construction will continue indefinitely.

Supply

Currently, China is the world's largest copper-consuming country, making it the heavyweight on the supply-and-demand teeter-totter. In 2002, China surpassed the United States in consumption, and based on graphs configured by the AME Mineral Economics firm, projections show that in 2008 China will consume 22.8 percent of the world's copper supply—1.1 percent more than Western Europe and 9.4 percent more than the United States.

Wading through this rocky sea of speculations, conjecture, and contradicting figures, it is unclear whether the demand for copper has entirely tipped the teeter-totter to the demand side. What is certain, however, is that the world's copper supply is taking a massive hit from China, and suppliers are reacting.

Chris Curfman, president of the global mining division at Peoria, Illinois-based Caterpillar Inc., has noted that the growth in the demand for copper is "testing the limits of a lot of capabilities"[2] of suppliers. With China's demand exhausting older and, at one time, plentiful mines, mining companies such as BHP Billiton are spending more on exploration and are pushing away from Chile (the world's largest copper producer) into riskier territory for new copper prospects. Moving into harsher environments of Africa and politically unstable parts of Asia and Mongolia will mean more frequent disruptions in production in the mines and will effectively raise the price of copper, which already is continually rising due to diminishing supplies.

According to the London Metals Exchange (LME), as of early 2007, there was a global inventory of 178,075 tonnes of copper stockpiled in warehouses. This figure puts some copper manufacturers at a meager three-day supply as opposed to the normal fourteen-day supply. The deficit at the time of this writing implies that the price of copper would have to drop substantially before it would be financially advantageous for a restocking to occur to equalize supply.

---

2. http://www.bloomberg.com/apps/news?pid=20601087&sid=auIDFMGiOLiE&refer=home

This is forthcoming, according to Eduardo Titelman, executive vice president of the Chilean Copper Commission.

Titelman's optimism is shared by many in the mining industry. Despite the risks, mining companies worldwide, like BHP Billiton, are increasing production to meet the strong demand from China. Codelco, the biggest copper-producing company in the world, is expected to increase its output to 19 percent by the beginning of the next decade. Additionally, Phoenix, Arizona-based Freeport-McMoRan Copper & Gold Inc. projects an increase in copper production of 18 percent by 2009, and Southern Copper Corp., also based in Phoenix, plans to see a 14 percent jump by the same year. Even China is gearing up its domestic production, opening new mines to help stabilize the supply deficit.

But the worldwide effort to meet the rising demand for copper comes with problems that threaten to keep the price of copper high or, at the very least, slow its descent. Peter Kukielski, chief operating officer for Teck Cominco Ltd., said in an interview, "You have restraints on the supply side, and while the demand side stays strong and those restraints exist, the price will stay high."[3]

The restraints Kukielski referred to may be similar to those detailed in the March 19, 2007, issue of *Behre Dolbear Global Mining News*. In one article in this edition, it was reported that for Antofagasta PLC, owner of three copper mines in Chile, supply "remains vulnerable to declining grades and other constraints including equipment availability, labor shortages, and power and water supplies." Rio Tinto, one of the world's leading copper-producing companies, shares similar constraints. In another article of the same edition, Paul Skinner, Rio Tinto's chairman, remarks that, "A number of constraints, ranging from shortages of key consumables, like truck tires and explosives, to the tight supply of skilled technical managers and tradesmen, have limited the growth of new production capacity." It is in these last two quotes that the Mobius strip folds back on itself, and we come full circle to understand why copper has had such a successful run in this commodities bull market.

The Unique Nature of the Copper Market

The unique aspect of the nonprecious metal commodities is this: unlike many other commodities such as corn, wheat, cotton, and the like, it takes nonprecious

---

3. http://apareena.arvopaperi.fi/forum/search/msg/id=sf/msg=4627641/; quoted from a Bloomberg article from March 30, 2007.

metals to mine nonprecious metals. The clue to this phenomenon in the preceding paragraph is that both Antofagasta and Rio Tinto expressed concerns over shortages surrounding equipment availability, power and water supply, truck tires, and explosives—all of which use copper either as a component or an adjunct to processing. Like many other nonferrous metals mined, copper, in part, is a self-generating commodity.

Of course, this self-propulsion can be a double-edged sword. Copper production needs to keep up with its own consumption, and when a rapidly growing heavyweight like China enters the picture and consumes a big chunk of the world's supply, it tips the scale and hikes prices, making it even more difficult for mining companies to acquire their own share needed to keep up with the strong demand.

This very demand is what could keep copper on its bull run through the decade. And although supply is struggling to keep up with the demand, it will continue to press forward to meet the challenge. As the old saying goes, "Where there's a will, there's a way." Right now, in the world of copper, China is that will.

So, given all of the complexities of just a single market like China, it is a monumental task to pin down the factors of supply and demand in order to utilize fundamental analysis to devise a workable trading strategy for copper futures. That is where technical analysis comes to the aid of the trader. Adding market timing via multiple cycles to the mix is like icing on the cake, as will be evident from the chapters that follow.

Major Trend Influences from Money

Technical analysis is not carried out in a vacuum. Low volume and virtually moribund volatility that sets in hours (and sometimes even days) before the release of an important economic report is evidence of traders of every plaid standing aside, if not actually flat,[4] until the numbers come out; and the reaction follows with a flurry of orders (or lack thereof, depending on what the prior expectations are and how much the numbers deviate from those expectations). Technical tools provide long or short biases and key price levels, but making the connection between important events and price action in advance is another matter altogether.

---

4. Having no position in the market, either long or short.

Many forces can cause distortions in price levels that are not all in kilter with fair value based on supply and demand. Large hedge funds, for example, can drive a stock price down sharply when many of them unload shares en masse. A frenzy of buying activity that causes a stock price to shoot up dramatically in a single session might be due to what's been dubbed the "Cramer Effect": Jim Cramer making favorable remarks about the company in question on his CNBC show *Mad Money*. By and large, the majority of forces that move markets are those that have very-near-term effects, and the market usually returns to its prior level. Having examined factors of supply and demand in the copper market, let us next consider how access to capital affects prices.

The Nature of Money

Market forces that cause long-term price trends are far worthier of a trader's attention than the short-term swings. Understanding the nature of money is undeniably essential to gaining valuable insights about the cost and flow of money and inflationary trajectories, which are literally omnipresent undercurrents of the economic milieu. Money has its own supply and demand fundamentals (which affect the cost of borrowing capital) independent of the factors of supply and demand of financial markets. Insights into market price trends are gained by a firm grasp of interest-rate cycles. Money is printed and coined by the government mints, but what determines how much currency the mint churns out every year? What makes a dollar worth a dollar and valid for a purchase of any item on the shelf of a dollar store? What would our society be like without it as a convenient medium of exchange? Hard currency is no longer the primary tool for purchases. It has been supplanted by electronic impulses between point-of-sale devices in retail locations and financial institutions. Cash is now an invisible phantom represented by bits and bytes in the database of some bank's computer servers tied to other bits and bytes that represent the owner of an account whose identity is now more valuable to a thief than the cash in the potential victim's wallet by virtue of the line of credit linked to those very bits and bytes percolating in silicon wafers and semiconductors.

The standard measure of money supply is the various aggregates, M1, M2, M3, and L. M1 is the most liquid repository, as it is the sum total of all cash and checking accounts (a check being a viable substitute for hard cash that is immediately spendable, a form of currency in its own right). M2 is M1 plus the sum total of bank and credit union savings accounts and time deposits plus money market funds. M3 is M2 plus M1 plus large-denomination instruments such as CDs of $100,000. L lumps together the other three aggregates with the remaining liquid assets including T-bills, commercial paper, U.S. savings bonds, and some other instruments.[5] All of those pools are exclusive of money tied up in illiquid assets such as real estate, as well as all of the money in equities and margin accounts. These auxiliary reservoirs are subject to rapid evaporation, due to the risk factor, as opposed to the other more stable aggregates.

Although the demand for money is variable—it ebbs and flows depending on money's cost (interest rates for borrowers)—the supply of it is pretty much fixed. The mint is not in a position to increase wealth simply by printing extra twenty-dollar bills. Wealth, after all, is based on real assets such as land and natural resources. The type of currency used to measure wealth is immaterial. Currency is a type of marker, just as chips at a casino are. Chips are just pieces of plastic good for use only at the tables and the cage on the gaming floor. They are tokens of actual cash.

Money in its various forms simply flows from one pool to another. When stock prices are in a nosedive, money naturally flows out of equities and into money market deposits and debt instruments like bonds. When stocks are in a charging bull rally, money naturally flows from other sources into equities. The overall wealth in the nation is not increased because Google stock triples in value, nor is it increased if the Dow Jones Industrial Average and S&P 500 indexes post 5 percent gains. Those are just paper gains. They do not represent actual increases in wealth.

Those paper gains are not the equivalent of the Louisiana Purchase of 1848, for example, which greatly extended U.S. territory and added to the national real estate holdings. Approximately 530 million acres were purchased from France for three cents per acre in a broad expanse of territory in the central region of the current United States that includes the Midwestern breadbasket states. One does not even need to reach for the pocket calculator or open up a Microsoft Excel worksheet to calculate how much such an asset has appreciated in value over the past one hundred and sixty years. Irrespective of the increase in price per acre, the underlying worth of the fertile land on which food crops are grown and through which runs the mighty Mississippi River is an undeniable constant.

---

5. William Greider, *Secrets of the Temple: How the Federal Reserve Runs the Country* (Simon & Schuster, 1987), pp. 57–58.

Inflation and the Value of Money

Inflation is the monster that gobbles up retirement savings and weakens the purchasing power of the workforce. Pay increases lag behind the rate of increase in retail prices and cause real earnings to drop over time rather than increase, resulting in a drop in consumer confidence, as money that would otherwise be spent on luxuries is earmarked for basic necessities instead. Inflation is such an ever-present eight-hundred-pound gorilla that the U.S. Federal Reserve Bank began a series of measured increases of the discount rate by 25 basis points at regular intervals at the end of former Fed chairman Alan Greenspan's tenure in 2006, just to keep inflation contained via curbing the rate of economic expansion. It was not the first time the Fed raised interest rates for the same reason.

William Greider, in his book *Secrets of the Temple*, provides an historical account of the Federal Reserve Bank's actions during much of the last century.[6] Between 1933 and the mid-1970s, the central bank implemented government policies of setting caps on interest rates, which made it easier to borrow money at lower rates of interest, as well as provided a means of control over financing by the government. More attractive returns than those caps for bank deposits caused investors to withdraw funds for greener pastures. The net effect of that mass exodus was a tightening by lenders that essentially cut off new loans. It was a veritable "credit crunch" that frustrated banks and borrowers alike. It was an effective means of limiting lending by the central bank by causing a chain reaction via raising interest rates nearer and nearer to the ceilings in effect at the time.

The rescinding of the interest-rate caps took the brakes off the lending institutions, which naturally pushed rates to as high a level as they could without driving away borrowers. Within the new unrestrictive environment, the central bank could control lending only by pushing rates high enough to halt demand by borrowers (as opposed to when they could formerly produce the same results by halting supply by discouraging lenders). This affected the smaller businesses and less wealthy individuals the most. As drastic and callous as former Fed chairman Paul Volcker's regime was, causing prime lending rates to climb as high as 21 percent, it worked to put the brakes on inflation, albeit at the cost of a painful economic recession. However, the means of control—raising interest rates—was a double-edged sword, because too high a level would stifle the ensuing economic recovery. The central bank could not in the end effectively

6. Ibid., 659–660.

slow down debt expansion. The private sector and the government alike went further into debt.

Considering the skyrocketing budget under the current Republican administration of President George W. Bush at the time of this writing, there is evidence that more than one historical parallel is at work.

Money Isn't Free

The cost of money is dependent upon interest rates. The history of the United States is a history of debt financing. The British Crown prevented the minting of currency by the thirteen colonies as means of controlling them, and everything was transacted in notes instead. Taxes were often paid for in commodities. George Washington actually had to borrow money for the coach to take him to his inauguration, despite the fact that he was a fairly wealthy man with extensive land holdings and other assets—he did not have any cash liquidity. Today, there is not only one corporate debt rating service in this country, but three: Moody's, Fitch, and Standard & Poor's.

Interest rates have their own cycles of supply and demand that reach periodic peaks and troughs. Colonial-era rates were generally capped at 6 percent, based on British usury laws. Some did, however, exceed that limit, with Massachusetts setting a legal limit of 8 percent in 1661 and Pennsylvania seeing commercial rates as high as 10 percent from 1750 to 1800.

Interest rates have an inverse affect on bond prices. The roller-coaster ride of bond yields ranging from 2.5 percent to 8 percent in the nineteenth century is summarized by Sidney Homer.[7]

During a sixty-year period that started in 1798, government interest-rate yields saw greatly increased volatility over the prior era of New England municipal yields. The period from 1798 to 1810–1811 saw a decline in rates, although they increased slightly in 1805. The period around the War of 1812, from 1810–1811 to 1815–1816, was a time of rising yields, although still below the 1798 levels. That period was followed by pronounced yield declines to below 1798–1811 period levels, which lasted until 1825. The next period, which lasted until 1848, was one of gradual increases in municipal yields and skyrocketing yields on newly issued federal bonds. The following period, which lasted until

---

7. Sidney Homer and Richard Sylla, *A History of Interest Rates*, 4th ed. (John Wiley & Sons, 2005), p. 287.

1858, was one of a decline in federal yields, although little change in municipal yields. The next period, which lasted until 1865, was one of Civil War spikes in federal yields, yet still below 1798 and 1814–1815 levels. Municipal yields for the same period began to advance, but fell off sharply in 1863.

The post–Civil War period that lasted until 1873 was marked by declines in not only federal and municipal yields, but those of railroad bonds as well. That period was followed by a twenty-five-year bull market for government and corporate U.S. bonds with dramatically declining yields (due to the inverse relationship between bond prices and yields).

The twentieth century saw a bear bond market in bond yields from 1899 to 1920, as yields rose from a little over 3 percent to a peak of 5.5 percent. During the ensuing bull bond market from 1920 to 1946, the yields declined to 2.5 percent. In the next bear market from 1946 to 1981, the bond yields shot up to a record 14 percent. There was a bull bond market from 1981 to 2003.

In the twenty-first century, 2003 marked a change in the roughly twenty- to twenty-five-year cycle that had emerged since the beginning of the twentieth century. If the cycle has come full circle once again, and if the bull market ended in 2003, we should now be a few years into the next long-term bear bond market. Monitoring technical price levels within the context of the overall underlying economic cycles that drive the markets provides for a powerful melding of analytical approaches.

On the other hand, economic forces are not always rational in nature. As Alan Rohrbach,[8] president of Rohr International (a financial services consultancy), states in his article on Rohr International's website entitled "1970's Redux: Son of Stagflation":

> And while intellectually aggressive individuals may learn the lessons of history, whole cultures rarely do. As such, they are (as Georges Santayana has cautioned) "… doomed to repeat it …" Considering the most recent historic phase was the Dot.Com Boom Fantasyland (metaphor consistent with our long-held belief that the developed world's governments are running a Disneyland for Dummies), by comparison current circumstances appear dire indeed.[9]

---

8. Alan Rohrbach provided the foreword to this book.

9. http://www.rohrintl.com/pdf/TH050321.pdf; p. 2. This Web link takes you to the thirty-seven-page report called "Institutional Trend Insight, Special Market Highlight, Monday, March 21, 2005, 1970's Redux: Son of Stagflation."

More often than reason would entertain, it is the irrationality of people that can cause major price swings. Price may or may not reflect actual value. The problem is that when price is either much higher or lower than actual value, it is destined to eventually return to a realistic level. People can feed the fires of their delusions for only so long. Eventually, someone realizes that the emperor wears no clothes and pulls up stakes, which causes a chain reaction of investors yanking their funds from the market en masse that brings down the whole house of cards. It is the truly wise who can see through all of the mirages and swoop in to pick up shares at bargain-basement prices instead of at the inflated levels that the maddened crowds pay in their feeding frenzy.

The flow of money in our post-modern free market society has been in the direction of the most wealthy, as the trend of the rich getting richer while the poor get poorer continues through the ages. Despite the recent trickle-down phenomenon of increased investment in stocks by the American middle class (and now even the college crowd that is part of Jim Cramer's fan base), the stock market remains predominantly a rich person's game. Distribution of wealth in capitalistic societies is not merely uneven—it is obscenely skewed and lopsided.

Conclusion

A trader is basically a lone maverick out to retake possession of some chunk of that humongous pool of assets. In view of the competition, it behooves that maverick to be as well prepared as possible to play this high-paced and often brutal game. Just as an NFL quarterback would be a reckless fool to go onto the field lacking helmet and shoulder pads, a trader or investor who is uneducated with respect to the reality of risks and rewards is on a fool's errand. Technical analysis is not just about finding a buying or selling opportunity, it is also about determining the level of risk attached to any such opportunity.

This chapter shows how complex and potentially unreliable fundamental analysis has become since the era prior to the 1970s (which is the principal reason for it being supplanted by technical analysis as the primary approach to price forecasting), and how understanding the fundamentals of capital itself is essential for an informed view of capital markets. As undeniably valuable as the grasp of the factors of supply and demand is for a trader, without the aid of technical tools it is sorely inadequate for price-level projections and risk assessment in today's global marketplace.

Summary of Chapter 2

- Increasing complexity of global financial markets has made the fundamental approach to analysis extremely unwieldy as a stand-alone methodology without technical tools.

- Understanding the nature of capital itself and its underlying fundamentals of supply and demand is important for attaining insights into financial market fundamentals in general.

- Manipulation of underlying forces by the central bank and large commercial institutions often has an overriding influence on price trends that is more powerful in moving markets than supply-and-demand factors.

- Looking to technical levels is a must in the face of markets that are otherwise behaving irrationally with respect to the fundamentals.

CHAPTER 3

Chart Patterns: Landscape of the Market

Classical chart patterns are used by market technicians because of their statistically high reliability. Those patterns help forecast direction, and, with a little practice, they are not difficult to spot on price charts. Some patterns are used to determine price levels of established value. Others are used to spot trends, while some are used to assess the likely end to trends and some used to assess the likelihood of the continuation of a trend.

To describe classical patterns as the "landscape" of chart analysis is an accurate metaphor, for discerning such patterns is the most obvious manner in which people become aware of general trend and countertrend formation. "Landscape" also indicates the degree to which the terms and concepts used to describe the theory and practice of chart analysis are the foundation for the proper understanding of more refined indicators.

Whether simple indications of moving average support and resistance, or more complex evolutions of price trends to confirm potentials signaled by more esoteric indicators, the concepts of support and resistance, breakouts, and even signal failures are, for the most part, expressed in variations of the features and functions discussed in this chapter. It is therefore important to consider the review of the trend and pattern indications as a framework for the broad context of trend decisions that apply to other methods, as well as the specific structure and function of these particular projections in their own right. This chapter examines channels, support and resistance, trend lines, reversal patterns, gaps, and continuation and other patterns.

Channels

Market prices are never moving in a straight line for very long, as any person who has looked at price charts knows. What they do, in fact, is follow a trajectory over time (up, down, or sideways) within upper and lower bounds (which you can see clearly as typically parallel trend lines, if you draw them along the

FIGURE **3.1**

Channel Patterns

Source: eSignal

intermediary tops and bottoms that form). This is what produces the channel-
ing effect that shows up on charts: the markets bouncing back and forth rather
than moving in a single direction. Often the market will appear to be forming
some other pattern, such as a triangle, flag, or pennant (discussed later in this
chapter), only to eventually trade along those (usually) parallel boundaries that
were not formerly apparent.

   Figure 3.1 is a daily chart of gold futures. A commonly used tool called the
"Andrew's pitchfork" was used to draw channel lines on the chart. Note the price
meandering aimlessly in the downward sloping channel from June until October

that eventually bounces off the upper and lower parallel lines. The same is true of the later upward sloping channel from November through April. In both cases, prices bounce back and forth between support and resistance levels, forming recognizable channels.

Channels are part of many other formations. Support and resistance levels and trend lines are components of channel lower and upper boundaries, respectively. Technicians look to prices extending beyond channel boundaries as potential breakout signals. Prices touching channel boundaries are often used as places to buy (when they touch the lower boundary) or sell (when they touch the upper boundary). Channels also may be narrowing or widening formations rather than parallel ones.

Well-known trader and author John Murphy discusses some other uses of channels:[1]

- Weakening or shifting of a trend when the price fails to reach a channel upper or lower boundary is an early indication that breakout at the opposite boundary is imminent.
- Significant breaks beyond channel boundaries are used to adjust trend lines to make them steeper in the prevailing direction.
- Channels can be used to project the extent of short-term price swings after a breakout by using the channel boundaries to measure the extension—with the expectation that the length of extension should be equal to the channel width.

It is clear that channels are useful for a number of different purposes. Any technical analyst should be thoroughly acquainted with their identification on charts and their implications for price movement.

Support and Resistance

The hills and valleys that define the contour of lines plotted on price charts in the form of bars or candlesticks provide visual cues for technicians that allow them to identify support and resistance. Support is a price level that the marketplace has set as a rock-bottom level below which trades will not be able to occur as long as the level supports perceived value. Resistance is a price level that the

---

1. John J. Murphy, *Technical Analysis of the Futures Markets: A Comprehensive Guide to Trading Methods and Applications* (Prentice Hall, 1986), pp. 86–87.

marketplace has set as a ceiling above which trades will not be able to occur as long as the level remains a maximum of the outer limits of perceived value.

When the market is in a trading range, also known as a "congestion area," price will tend to remain above support and below resistance, although those levels might be tested multiple times before the price rejects them and proceeds to move in the opposite direction after they are tested and hold. When those levels fail, it is often a harbinger of future price action. The failure of a support level may be an omen of something as modest as an orderly extension of the break to the next incremental support or something as dramatic as an imminent market crash. The failure of a resistance level may be the beginning of a rally to new levels (which may be new historical highs or a breakout from a range within which price has been contained for a prolonged period of time).

Technical support and resistance are also important psychological levels, and the longer they have remained intact, the more important they are. When these levels are tested, traders nervously await the outcome: Will the level hold or will it fail? Will the market retreat and reverse from its current direction, or will it plunge right through? Many breakout systems rely on that outcome to generate buy or sell signals.

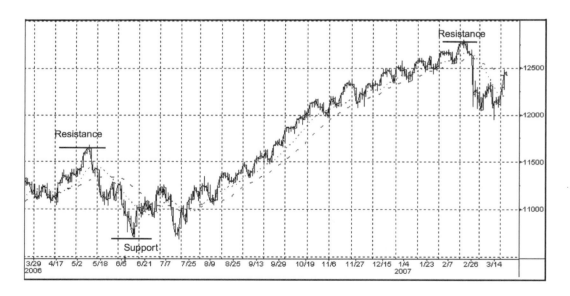

FIGURE 3.2

Support and Resistance Levels (Dow Jones Industrial Average)

Source: Bloomberg

Figure 3.2 shows major support and resistance levels for the Dow Jones Industrial Average on a daily candlestick chart. When the support level established in June 2005 was tested in July of that year, it held, and the market advanced to test the resistance level established in May of 2005. That resistance level was tested in September and held for a few days around the thirteenth of the month, but then the market rallied through the level to reach a historical high in February of 2007, setting a new resistance level.

The resistance levels marked on the chart resemble mountain peaks, whereas the support level marked resembles a crevasse. Support and resistance often are defined by such peaks and valleys with steep slopes and sharp peaks and trenches, due to the market quickly rejecting the level as an extreme that is too far away from perceived "mean" value.

In this example, the psychological reaction of investors created a ripple effect on stock prices across all sectors and companies with those sectors. Most stocks benefited as the market rebounded from resistance, but most of them also suffered as the market retreated from the resistance set at its historical high. Those are strictly technical phenomena, and the fundamental strength or weakness of individual, publicly held companies represented by the average was not the determining factor. Investors tend to give more weight to underlying economic factors than to sales figures and corporate balance sheets, reasoning that economic booms can whisk even weak companies along with them whereas economic recessions can help topple even the biggest industrial monoliths. Technical analysis gives traders the advantage of being able to make sense out of such price behavior, which is something that a fundamental view will not provide under such circumstances.

Intermediary Support and Resistance

Figure 3.3 shows intermediary support and resistance levels that are established and tested between the establishment and testing of major levels. The support level established on April 17, 2006, is tested in May 2006 and holds, but then fails in June. The same level is again established as support in August 2006. The resistance level established in April 2006 is tested in August 2006 and holds for a few days until it eventually fails. The resistance level established in July 2006 becomes a support level in August 2006.

This is a common phenomenon—old resistance becoming new support. Similarly, old support tends to become new resistance later on. It can be seen on the same chart as the support level established in January of 2007 that later

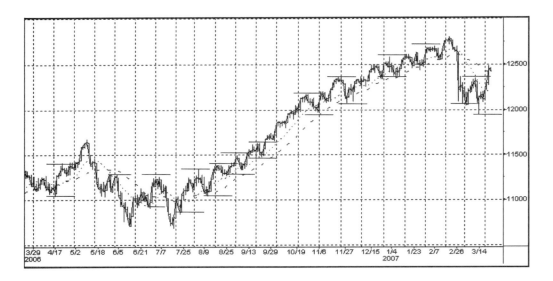

FIGURE 3.3

Intermediary Support and Resistance Levels (Dow Jones Industrial Average)

Source: Bloomberg

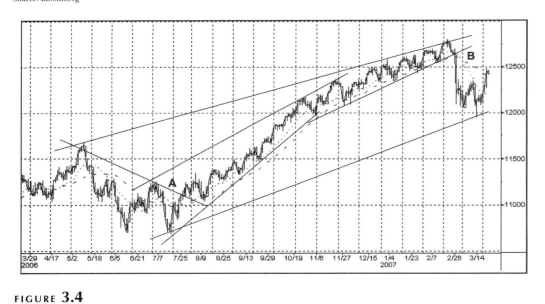

FIGURE 3.4

Trend Lines (Dow Jones Industrial Average)

Source: Bloomberg

became a resistance level in March 2007. The support level established at the end of November 2006 is tested a few months later and holds for several days until it is penetrated and a support level from early November is tested and holds. The intermediary levels of support and resistance are significant in the shorter term, whereas the major levels are significant for the longer term. It is all about context; short-term swings will be impacted by the former, the beginnings and endings of major trends will be impacted by the latter.

Trend Lines

Figure 3.4 shows trend lines drawn on a daily candlestick chart of the Dow. Lines are drawn along the tops of peaks or the bottoms of valleys with either an upward or downward slant, depending on the direction of the trend. Prices that respect a trend line are an indication of good potential for trend continuation, whereas prices that break a trend line indicate a potential reversal of trend.

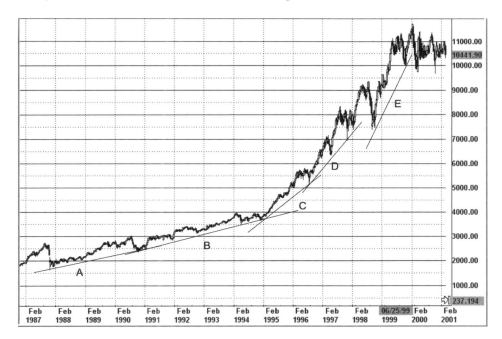

FIGURE **3.5**

Trend Lines and Breakouts

Source: eSignal

In July 2006, the bearish trend line was broken (A) and a long-term upward trend ensued, and then in February 2007, the bullish trend line was broken (B) and prices fell off sharply. Prices are likely to establish a support level when they meet a trend line drawn along daily lows, and they are likely to establish a resistance level when they meet a trend line drawn along daily highs.

In a classic breakout bull market, prices begin an upward trend from a level that has been sideways for a prolonged period of time, usually range-bound. The slope of the trend lines gradually gets steeper as the trend picks up steam. In **Figure 3.5**, the slope of the trend line is very gentle, but it gets gradually steeper and steeper (B, C, and D) until it is almost vertical (E). Once a trend is that strong, with a trend line of extremely steep upward slope, market technicians start to look for signs of either a correction or an all-out market crash in the form of a long-term bear market. The shift to a bracketed market beginning in August 1999 was the first indication of a weakening of the bull market.

Reversal Patterns

Chart formations that are used to forecast the probability of a shift in trend to a new trend in the opposite direction are referred to as reversal patterns. They can occur at the end of major or minor trends, or even at the end of very short-term intraday price swings. Technical analysts remain alert for those patterns and then look for confirmation of a reversal. If the pattern as a prognosticator of a shift in price direction fails, signs of substantial extension of the prior trend are monitored.

The "head and shoulders top" is an easily identified formation on a price chart. It literally jumps out at anyone who is familiar with its shape and is on the lookout for one, and with practice recognition comes easily. Although it is supposed to resemble the contours of a human head and shoulders, it is really more like a mountain peak flanked by two foothills.

A head and shoulders (H&S) top consists of a new high in an uptrend (the left shoulder) on heavy volume followed by a dip in prices along with a decline in volume, then followed by an ascent to a slightly higher high (the head) with high volume, a subsequent dip to back near the low of the first dip with declining volume, and an ascent to a slightly lower high than the peak at the head of the formation with lower volume than the prior two rallies and a dip below the neckline of the formation. The breakout below the right neckline should preferably

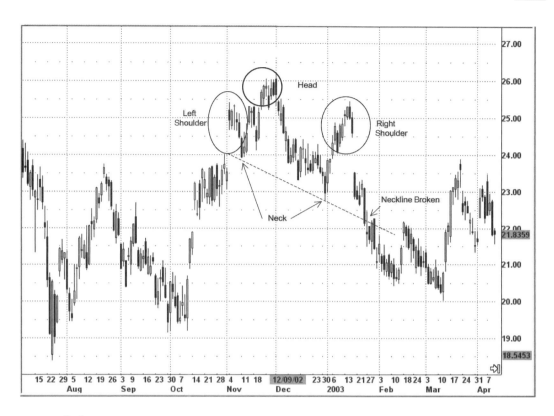

FIGURE **3.6**

Head and Shoulders Top

Source: eSignal

occur on a daily close. By drawing a line under the two valleys between the tall
mountain peak (head) and the left and right shoulders (flanking foothills), the
slant of the neckline can be more easily seen. It may have little or no slant, or it
may be slanted up to the right or down to the right.

A head and shoulders top is seen on the daily price chart for Microsoft stock
in **Figure 3.6**. The left and right shoulders in a head and shoulders pattern
are not always even; one shoulder may be at a higher or lower price level than
the other shoulder. The key (for obvious reasons—what makes it resemble a
human head and shoulders contour) is that both shoulders peak out at lower
levels than the head. The neckline in the chart in Figure 3.6 is tilted down to the
right. Necklines in head and shoulders patterns are not always even. Downward

penetration of the right-side neckline is confirmation that the pattern is fully formed and that a sell indication is imminent.

A head and shoulders bottom is simply a head and shoulders top flipped upside down, also known as the classic "inverse head and shoulders." A left shoulder forms in a down trend, followed by a modest rally prior to the extension to a new low to form the head at a lower price level, and finally another limited rally back near the previous reaction high followed by a dip that does not reach the previous low, forming the right shoulder. **Figure 3.7**, a daily chart for UnitedHealth Group stock, shows such a formation. In the case of this particular head and shoulders bottom, the right neckline is tested a few times over a period of several months after the formation is completed, and then the market eventually rallies further into January 2007.

Traders and authors Robert Edwards and John Magee describe confirmation signs for head and shoulders formations:[2]

- Lower volume at the top (or bottom in a reverse H&S) of the head than the volume at the top (or bottom in a reverse H&S) of the left shoulder. However, this occurs with only a third of such formations. Hence, it is not a conclusive confirmation sign.

- After the top (or bottom in a reverse H&S) of the head is formed, prices drop below the top of the left shoulder. Another inconclusive sign of confirmation.

- Declining volume as the right shoulder is forming and prices reach the top (or bottom in a reverse H&S) of the left shoulder. Not entirely conclusive.

- The breaking of the neckline after the formation of the right shoulder—this is the most conclusive sign. High probability of a reversal in trend direction to follow (about 80 percent), but not a certainty.

In addition to head and shoulders formations, there are other reversal patterns, such as double or triple tops/bottoms, rounded tops/bottoms, and island reversals. Double tops have the shape of the letter "M," and double bottoms have the shape of the letter "W." Triple tops have an additional peak, and triple bottoms have an additional trough, as the name implies. Rounded tops and bottoms are identified by the curved shape. Island reversals are identified by a series of bars that are separated from the prices before and after the series by gaps on

---

2. Robert D. Edwards and John Magee, *Technical Analysis of Stock Trends* (John Magee, 1966), pp. 54–55.

FIGURE 3.7

Head and Shoulders Bottom

Source: eSignal

the chart. Examples of these various other types of reversal patterns are shown in some of the charts that follow.

It is essential for any technical analyst to be familiar with the various types of reversal patterns that foreshadow major/minor tops and bottoms on price charts. Although they are not the equivalent of having a crystal ball, they nonetheless have a high probability of predicting a new price trend in the opposite direction.

Gaps

When the market opens higher than the previous day's high and does not trade back to the previous day's high, it leaves a gap on the price chart. When the market opens lower than the previous day's low and does not trade back to the previous day's low, it also leaves a gap on the chart. Gaps are particularly meaningful to a chartist. They are an indication that something is out of kilter, because prices traded to an extreme away from perceived value and then did not swiftly return to the price level of perceived value.

Depending on where in an existing trend a gap occurs, it will be one of three key types: breakaway, continuation, or exhaustion. A breakaway gap occurs at the beginning of a major trend. A continuation gap, as its name implies, occurs somewhere in the middle of a major trend (there may be more than one continuation gap in any given trend). An exhaustion gap occurs near the end of a major trend. A gap in the middle of a trend is invariably a mixed signal: it can

FIGURE **3.8**

Gaps, Pennant, and Double Top

Source: eSignal

portend either substantial longevity left in the major price trend or a counter-trend on the horizon.

The daily chart for Google stock in **Figure 3.8** has a few gaps. The breakaway gap in September 2006 is followed in mid-October by an upward trend that breaks through a resistance level that was established in early July 2006. The continuation gap near the end of October is confirmed by a continued rise in prices until the exhaustion gap in mid-November followed by a breakaway gap near the end of November as a downward trend begins. Gaps are a sign of either continuation of a trend or completion of a trend. On their own, they do not provide a conclusive sign of either continuation or reversal of trend. They need some type of further confirmation. For example, if you were to take a long position in anticipation of continued strength of a bullish trend after the appearance of a gap following a significant upswing, you would look for the sign of that same gap being an exhaustion gap instead. The sure sign that it is more likely an exhaustion gap would be the price dropping to fill in the gap. Another example would be the formation of an island reversal (examples of this pattern are shown later in this chapter) as confirmation of an exhaustion gap signaling the end of a trend.

Continuation and Other Patterns

Continuation patterns, as their name implies, are used to forecast a continuation of an existing trend. If one of them occurs during an uptrend, the continuation of the rally to higher levels is a high probability, and if one of them occurs during a downtrend, the continuation of the sell-off to lower levels is a high probability. Confirmation via a breakout in the direction of the prevailing trend is necessary to treat a continuation pattern as conclusive, especially because they can sometimes be reversal patterns.

Triangular formations can be continuation or reversal patterns, but are more typically continuation patterns. Pennants and wedges are particular types of triangle patterns. A pennant formation is one of the more common continuation patterns, which can occur during trends in either direction. Note the pennant formation in Figure 3.8 that begins in July 2006 and ends in September 2006. That pattern consists of a flagpole formed by a series of bars/candles in one direction and then a triangular channel that narrows at the end. The triangular formation is attributed to uncertainty as the bulls and bears assess their current positions and whether or not to double down or exit. Although a pennant is

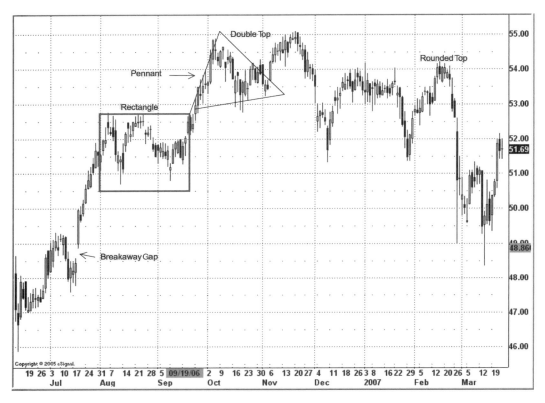

FIGURE **3.9**

Gap, Rectangle, Pennant, Double, and Rounded Tops

Source: eSignal

typically a continuation pattern, in this case it was a reversal pattern instead, and prices turned around and headed in the opposite direction.

The chart in Figure 3.8 also has a double top, an easily identifiable reversal pattern consisting of a formation that resembles the letter *M*.

Figure 3.9 is a daily price chart of Bank of America stock, which has both continuation and reversal patterns. A major uptrend is foreshadowed by a breakaway gap in mid-July 2006. The rectangle that forms in August and September is another type of continuation pattern. It is followed by a pennant formation (continuation pattern) and then a double top (reversal pattern) in October and November. In February 2007, there is a rounded top formation, another common reversal pattern. Rounded tops and bottoms are sometimes called "saucer

FIGURE **3.10**

Wedge Patterns

Source: eSignal

tops" and "saucer bottoms," due to their curved contours, as opposed to peaks and crevasses with sharp pointed contours. In general, rounded bottoms are more prevalent than rounded tops, as market prices tend to rise very gradually at first as opposed to the type of behavior that occurs with a downside correction after a major rally: a swift retreat from a new high.

Wedges, another category of continuation patterns, are incomplete triangles. When prices are defining a channel on the chart that is narrowing over time, either a wedge or a triangle is forming. Once the price breaks out to one side or the other (as continuation patterns, the expectation is that the price continues in the same direction that was under way when the formation began), and if the triangle is not completed, there is a wedge instead. **Figure 3.10**, a daily price

FIGURE **3.11**

Triangles and Diamonds

Source: eSignal

chart of JP Morgan stock, shows a breakaway gap in July 2006 followed by a major uptrend. The first wedge formation in August–September 2006 foreshadows a continuation of the trend as expected. The later wedge formation in January–February 2007 is followed by a reversal in trend. To attempt to anticipate the price direction with continuation patterns can be hazardous to your risk capital, especially if you are impatient and jump in too soon. It is much wiser to first see in which direction the price begins to break prior to putting on a position.

In **Figure 3.11** (a continuation of the chart in Figure 3.6), which is a daily price chart of UnitedHealth Group stock, there are three continuation patterns in a row after the formation of a head and shoulders bottom (shown in Figure 3.6) and the beginning of an uptrend. The triangle formed in

July–August 2006, the diamond (another type of continuation pattern, which is identified by its diamond shape) formed in September–October 2006, and the second triangle formed in November–December 2006 all indicate a prolonged period of uncertainty followed by a continuation of the upward price direction. The breakaway gap in January 2007 is confirmed by a steep decline over several days as the market corrects. That particular stock price did not make a steep breakout to the long side, but rather meandered on a gradual ascent over a period of eleven months.

Figure 3.12 is a daily price chart for Freeport-McMoRan Copper & Gold stock. The price continues its upward rise after the triangle formation in July–August 2006. The exhaustion gap in September 2006 is followed by a reversal

FIGURE **3.12**

Gaps and Reversals

Source: eSignal

pattern called an "island reversal," which consists of a few price bars followed by a breakaway gap, essentially creating a formation that is disconnected from the bars on either side of it (an island). A rounded top forms in November–December 2006. The breakaway gap in early December 2006 is followed by a sell-off, and after the continuation gap in early January 2007, the downward trend continues for a couple of days. Another exhaustion gap followed by an island reversal shows up at the end of February 2007 into early March of that year. Note how the price then reversed direction to sell off to the level of support established in early February. It was an excellent opportunity to trade on the short side of the market.

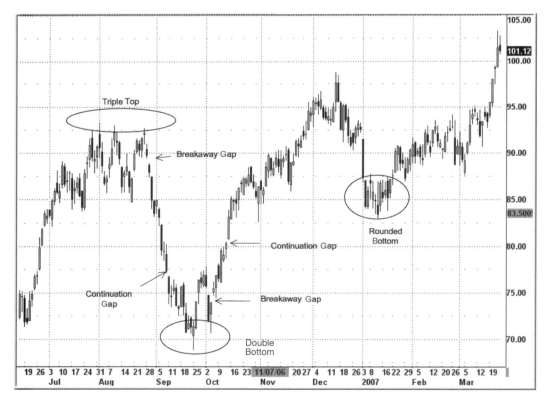

FIGURE **3.13**

Gaps, Tops, and Bottoms

Source: eSignal

Figure 3.13, which is a daily price chart of Marathon Oil stock, shows a triple top formation in July–August 2006, followed by a reversal in trend. Triple tops and bottoms are like double tops and bottoms with an additional test of the first high/low in the formation. This particular triple top had additional confirmation by a breakaway gap. Then, a continuation gap showed up when the

FIGURE **3.14**

Flag Pattern

Source: eSignal

downward trend was about two-thirds done. The double bottom formation in September–October 2006 is confirmed by a breakaway gap followed by a strong upward trend. After the sell-off in December 2006 into early January 2007, a rounded bottom forms and the market breaks through resistance in March 2007 in a steep ascent.

The flag pattern is shown on the daily price chart of the Dow in **Figure 3.14**. It is like a pennant, except the channel portion of the formation is parallel rather than narrowing. It is another continuation pattern. It has the same significance as other continuation patterns such as pennants, and needs some additional confirmation in the form of a breakout in the direction of the prevailing trend. If the price breaks out in the opposite direction, then it should be viewed as a likely reversal indication.

Fibonacci Retracements

Fibonacci ratios are a commonly used means of projecting the extent of a retracement of a price swing. Leonardo of Pisa, aka Fibonacci, a thirteenth-century Italian mathematician famous for introducing the Hindu-Arabic number system (with the zero) to Europe, also studied financial markets and devised a numerical set known today as the Fibonacci sequence. That particular set of numbers begins with zero and each member of the set is equal to the sum of the previous two members, which yields the following beginning to that infinite sequence: 0, 1, 1, 2, 3, 5, 8, 13, 21, 34, 55, 89, 144, 233, 377, 610, 987, 1,597, 2,584, 4,181, 6,765, 10,946, 17,711, 28,657, 46,368, 75,025, 121,393, 196,418, and so on. There are three ratios used for Fibonacci retracements. The first of those ratios is 61.8 percent, which is derived by dividing any number in the Fibonacci series (beginning with 8) by the number that follows it, for example, 8/13 (the decimal equivalent being 0.6153). The higher the number in the sequence, the closer the ratio becomes to 0.618, for example, 55/89, which has a decimal equivalent of 0.6179. The second ratio, which is 38.2 percent, is derived by dividing a number in that same series by the number found two positions to the right, for example, 55/144 (the decimal equivalent being 0.3819). The third ratio, which is 23.6 percent, is derived from dividing a number from that same series by the number found three positions to the right, for example, 8/34 (the decimal equivalent being 0.2352).

Constance Brown, in her book *All About Technical Analysis*, emphasizes the utility of Fibonacci retracements:

Professional traders use these ratios constantly on market data to identify support and resistance in any market and for any time horizon…. Anything with an expansion/ contraction or growth and decay cycle will support the application of Fibonacci ratios. This is a universal constant…. Fibonacci ratios will help you to identify and manage your risk/reward ratio in any market in which you decide to invest or trade.[3]

Figure 3.15 is a daily chart of Google with Moving Average Convergence Divergence (MACD) plotted underneath. The large rally from August through late November 2006 is measured, and the various Fibonacci ratios are plotted

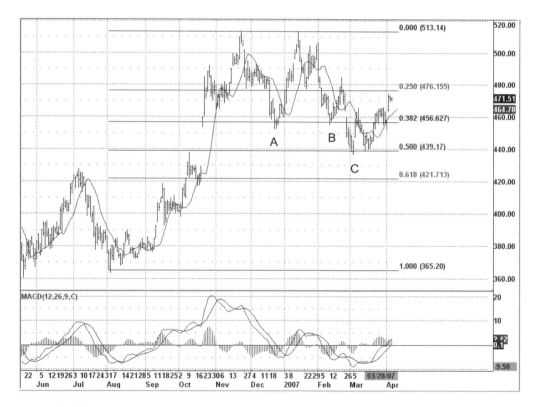

FIGURE **3.15**

Fibonacci Retracements and MACD

Source: eSignal

3. Constance Brown, *All About Technical Analysis* (McGraw-Hill, 2003), p. 88.

with horizontal lines. The 38.2 percent retracement level was tested in December (A) and a buy signal was generated on the MACD at the same time. The level was penetrated slightly and the market rallied back to its recent high. The next retracement again tested the 38.2 percent level (B) and bounced off it, then price was pushed down to the 50 percent retracement level in early March 2007 (C) and a buy signal was generated on the MACD as the market found support as expected and began a new rally. It is prudent to watch those ratios when assessing potential support and resistance in combination with other technical analysis tools.

Conclusion

Chart patterns are like road signs for the chartist. They do not describe future price action with 100 percent certainty; rather, they serve as warnings about what may lie ahead, kind of like a sign that you might find on a highway that reads "Caution. Watch for Icy Conditions on Bridge Ahead."

Nonconformance is an indication of a lower level of reliability. For example, head and shoulders patterns with very uneven necklines are not as strong an indicator as conforming patterns with level necklines. A slant in neckline against the expected direction of price (down being the expected direction at a top and up being the expected direction at a bottom) is a particularly bad omen.

As noted in the beginning of this chapter, various forms of support and resistance are the basic chart indications that are useful in their own right and assist in establishing the theoretical and practical implications of more sophisticated analyses. With no hierarchy of merit or use implied in the order in which they are noted, basic trading highs and lows, congestion support, and resistance, trend line, and channel projections, and the more extensive time and price perceptions intrinsic in patterns and gaps each have a role to play. In addition to their own utility, some will relate more closely to trend indications on market reactions from techniques such as moving average analysis. At other times, such as the extension of trends to the extreme boundaries of channels, the chart activity will relate to "overbought" or "oversold" indications on oscillators, or pending cycle high or low projections.

What is most important is that this landscape provides a basic language of the features and functions intrinsic to the more advanced methods as well. We have now established a basis for further discussion of those techniques, and their multidisciplinary application. It is hoped that this concise review of chart analysis will both be a valuable guide in its own right and encourage a more effective practical appreciation of the additional theories and techniques, as well as an enlightened approach to risk management.

Chapter 3 Summary

- Reversal patterns that herald the end of the prevailing trend and the start of a new trend in the opposite direction include head and shoulders tops/bottoms, double and triple tops/bottoms, rounded tops/bottoms and island reversals.

- Continuation patterns that indicate the probability of a significant extension to the current trend include pennants, flags, triangles, wedges, rectangles, and diamonds. When there is a failure of trend continuation, those same patterns become reversal patterns.

- Gaps often occur at the beginning, middle, or end of trends. Gaps at the beginning of a trend are called "breakaway gaps." Gaps in the middle of a trend are called "continuation gaps." Gaps at the end of a trend are called "exhaustion gaps."

- Fibonacci retracement levels, in addition to chart patterns, are useful in anticipating the extent of countertrends.

- Chart patterns need confirmation in the form of some price movement in the expected direction. In the case of head and shoulders patterns, the breaking of the neckline after the right shoulder is formed is the most significant confirmation signal.

- All the various classical chart patterns indicate the high probability of some significant price movement ahead, and for that reason they should not be ignored by the technical analyst.

CHAPTER 4

Alternative Charting Techniques

Because technical analysis leans heavily on price charts, it is important to be aware of the variety of techniques used to construct such graphical representations. To the technical analyst, charts provide much more information than a simple historical record of transactions over time. Price charts help an analyst spot key levels of support and resistance, price channels, and general strength of trends via trend lines that are superimposed upon the price bars. They are the basis of recognizable and repeatable patterns that portend the continuation or reversal of bearish or bullish trends with statistically significant reliability.

The most well-known type of price chart is the Open/High/Low/Close (OHLC) bar chart. There are, however, various other types of charts used by technical analysts. Japanese technical analysts, for example, have developed an Asian rendition of that old favorite, the candlestick chart. Point and figure charts treat the time element in an entirely different manner than OHLC bar or candlestick charts treat it, as is seen in detail in the section on them that follows. Market Profile charts shift the emphasis from price to volume and bear no resemblance whatsoever to those other types of charts.

Candlestick Charts

Japanese candlesticks contain the same information on each bar as the standard OHLC bars, but represented slightly differently from a graphical standpoint. The difference is that certain patterns jump out at the chartist, whereas with traditional bar charts these patterns may not be so easily identifiable. The Japanese analysts also have their own language of market patterns with some degree of overlap with Western analysis, although perhaps more poetic.

A candlestick has two components: a body, and upper and lower shadows. The body resembles a cylindrical candle in profile and the shadows resemble candlewicks. The range between the open and close for the time frame of the candle is the upper and lower boundaries of the candle's body. If the market closed higher for the candle, then a white (or other light color) body is typically plotted on the chart. Conversely, if the market closes lower for the candle, then a black (or other dark color) body is plotted. The range between the high of the candle's time period and the top of the candle body is plotted with a vertical line, and the range between the low of the candle's time period and the bottom of the candle's body is similarly plotted. As you may have already surmised, if the market closes at the same price it opened for the candle's time period, then the candle will have no vertical dimension to its body. If there is not a difference either between the top of the candle's body and the candle's high or between the bottom of the candle's body and the candle's low, then there will be no shadow plotted at that end of the candle.

There are special terms for the various candlestick formations. Gaps, for example, are referred to as rising or falling windows, depending on whether they occur during an upward or downward trend, respectively. The Western designation of the gaps visible on OHLC bar charts as either breakaway, continuation, or exhaustion gaps is more descriptive of what they represent with relationship to price trends.

Figure 4.1a shows a number of candlestick patterns for the front month of the light sweet crude oil futures contract. As the market formed a bottom at the end of August going into early September, the first reversal pattern that showed

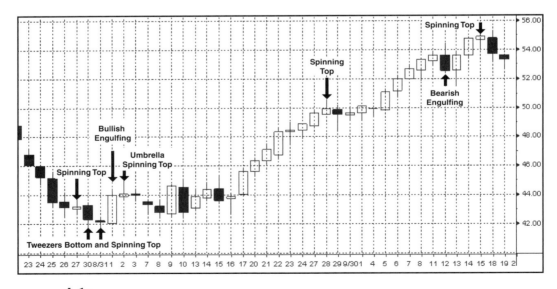

FIGURE **4.1a**

Candlestick Patterns on Crude Oil Futures

Source: Bloomberg

up was a spinning top. These are candles that have small real bodies. A subsequent spinning top showed up two days later in combination with a formation called a "tweezers" bottom. In a tweezers formation, the shadows line up either at the bottom or the top, depending on whether the market is in a downtrend (tweezers bottom) or uptrend (tweezers top). The third spinning top is of the variety known as an umbrella, due to its longer lower shadow that makes up the handle of the umbrella. The following candle is what is known as an engulfing bullish candle, due to its white body extending beyond the black body of the prior day's candle at the top and bottom. Then there are two spinning tops, and the market stalls for several sessions before continuing the new uptrend that is under way. In the final week of September, the market again stalls with a series of spinning-top candles before finding a top in mid-October with a bearish engulfing candle followed by another umbrella candle. Spinning tops, umbrellas, engulfing candles, tweezers, and windows are all patterns that tend to signal a reversal in trend.

Figure 4.1b, which is a continuation of the chart in Figure 4.1a, shows an umbrella spinning top that causes a temporary shift in trend to the upside until the market continues its descent. At the end of October is a bullish reversal

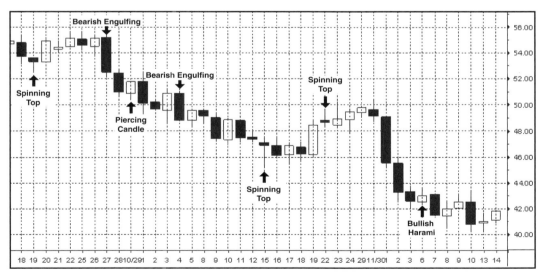

FIGURE 4.1b

Candlestick Patterns on Crude Oil Futures

Source: Bloomberg

signal known as a "piercing candle," wherein the body of the white candle pierces, ideally at least halfway, into the range of the black body of the prior day's candle. This is then followed by a bearish engulfing candle as the market shrugs off the reversal signal and continues its descent until mid-November when an umbrella spinning top marks the start of a new rally, the end of which is heralded by a spinning-top candle four days later.

The next bottom in mid-December, as seen in **Figure 4.1c**, is signaled by another reversal pattern known as a "bullish harami," in which a large-body black candle is followed by a white candle (in this case a spinning top) that has a range that fails to extend beyond the upper or lower boundary of the black candle. A bearish harami is just the opposite when found in an established uptrend. Several days later, a reversal candle known as a "doji morning star" occurs. Dojis are candles that have no real body, due to the opening and closing prices for the candle being the same. When a doji takes the shape of a cross, it is referred to as an evening star at the top of a rising trend when it gaps up on its opening price, or a morning star at the bottom of a decline when it gaps down on its opening price. In early January, a high wave candle occurs as

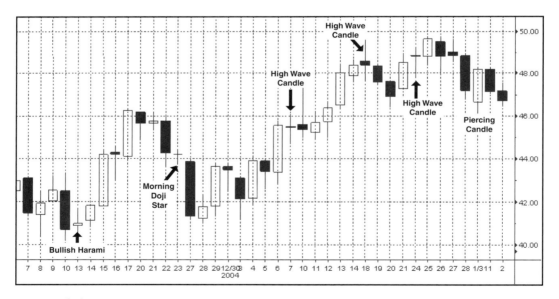

FIGURE 4.1c

Candlestick Patterns on Crude Oil Futures

Source: Bloomberg

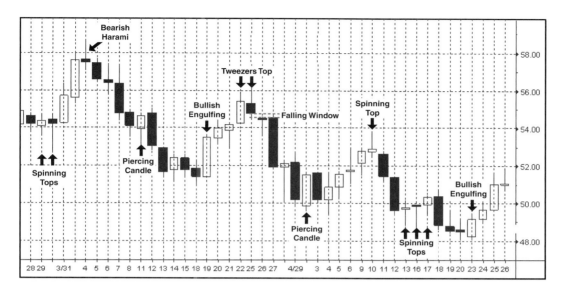

FIGURE **4.1d**

Candlestick Patterns on Crude Oil Futures

Source: Bloomberg

part of a bearish harami pattern. A high wave candle is a type of spinning top that has extremely long shadows at both top and bottom. The market stalls for three days, but does not reverse in this case. However, two high wave candles occur later in January as the market forms a double top. A piercing candle occurs at the end of January, but the market has not yet established a trend as it has started a sideways channel.

In **Figure 4.1d**, a bearish harami signals the reversal of an uptrend in early April. Five days later a piercing candle occurs, but it is a false buy signal. The actual reversal comes several days later with a bullish engulfing pattern. The market reverses again near the end of April after a tweezers top and a falling window. A bottom at the beginning of May is heralded by a piercing candle. Six days into the new rally, it fails as a spinning top occurs. Then a double bottom occurs along with a series of spinning tops and a bearish engulfing candle.

Figure 4.2a shows a chart of the 100-ounce gold futures contract at Chicago Board of Trade (CBOT). A series of rising and falling windows occurs in late October. A dark cloud cover candle occurs at the beginning of November and then there is another one five days later. The opposite of a piercing candle, dark

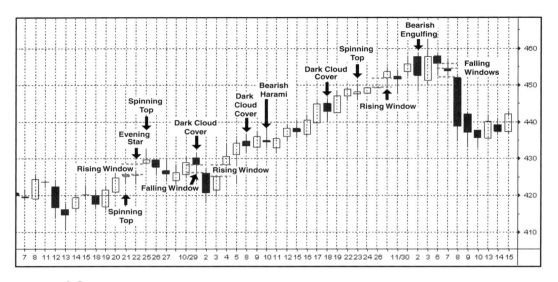

FIGURE **4.2a**

Candlestick Patterns on Gold Futures

Source: Bloomberg

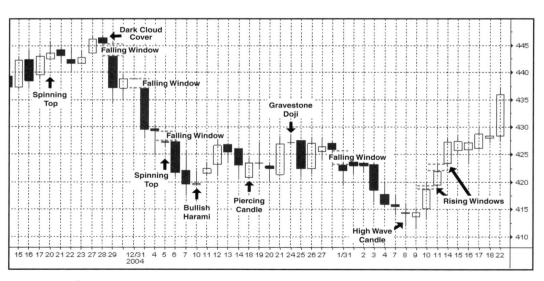

FIGURE **4.2b**

Candlestick Patterns on Gold Futures

Source: Bloomberg

cloud cover is when the body of the black candle pierces down into the body of the prior white candle. It signals a potential end to an uptrend. Then there is a bearish harami, but the market is still very strong in upward momentum and shrugs off those negative candles. The upward trend does not show signs of weakness until the next dark cloud cover and a subsequent spinning top several days later. A bearish engulfing pattern occurs at the actual top at the beginning of December, reinforced by a dark cloud cover and two falling windows in a row.

In **Figure 4.2b** there is another dark cloud cover and three more falling windows as the market sells off dramatically at year's end. In early to mid-January, two bullish reversal signals come with a piercing candle and a bullish harami, but the market does not find a bottom until early February with a high wave candle followed by two rising windows. Note the gravestone doji candle marked on the chart in late January. This is a type of doji that is considered to be a reversal signal when found in an uptrend and is identifiable by lack of a lower shadow.

The high wave candle at the end of February as seen in **Figure 4.2c** is part of a reversal pattern known as a "bearish counterattack," in which the bottom of the body of the black candle touches the top of the body of the prior white candle without piercing it. The first of two falling windows in later March are an

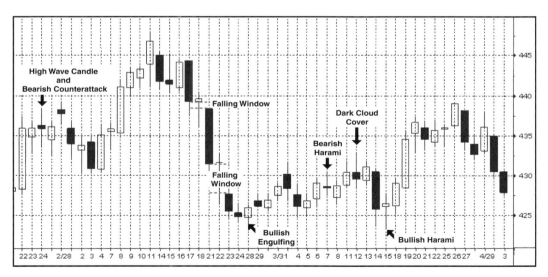

FIGURE **4.2c**

Candlestick Patterns on Gold Futures

Source: Bloomberg

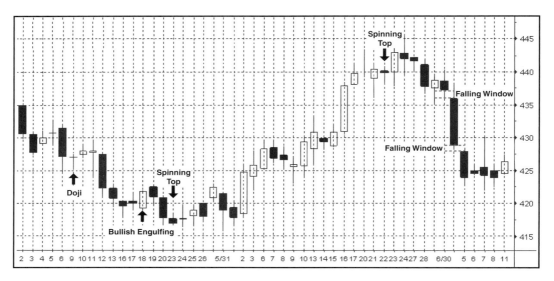

FIGURE **4.2d**

Candlestick Patterns on Gold Futures

Source: Bloomberg

indication that there is a reversal under way. The next bottom is signaled by a bullish engulfing candle in early April. There is also a bearish harami and dark cloud cover in early April, but the market has not yet established a direction as it trades sideways while developing a base from which to break out to the upside.

Figure 4.2d shows the formation of the next market bottom from late May to early June with a bullish engulfing candle, several spinning tops, and a rising window. Prices then top out in late June with several spinning tops and a couple of falling windows.

In **Figure 4.3a** the 10-year Treasury notes futures market declines following a bearish counterattack and two falling windows in late August to early September. The downtrend then reverses following a piercing candle. A dark cloud cover occurs several days later and the market forms a top with a bearish engulfing candle four days later. Then a new bottom forms in early October, heralded by a bullish harami and a spinning top. The series of white candles with large real bodies that occur in the uptrend form what is known as "three white soldiers." A new top forms in mid- to late October with two rising windows, a spinning top, and a falling window.

Continued weakness is indicated by the bearish engulfing candle in early November in **Figure 4.3b**. A minor rally comes after a couple of spinning

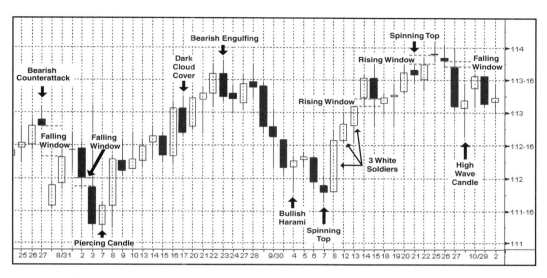

FIGURE **4.3a**

Candlestick Patterns on T-Notes Futures

Source: Bloomberg

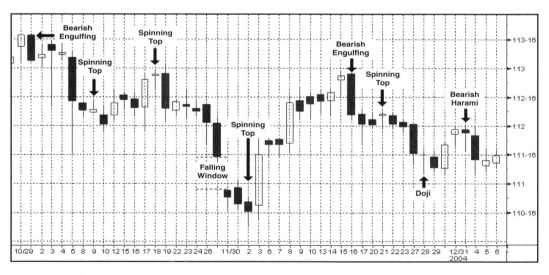

FIGURE **4.3b**

Candlestick Patterns on T-Notes Futures

Source: Bloomberg

tops in mid-November and is ended with a spinning top five days later. A falling window forms at the end of November, and then a bottom forms at the beginning of December with a spinning top. In mid-December, a top forms with a bearish engulfing candle. Then there is a minor rally late in the month signaled by a morning star doji. At the beginning of January, a bearish harami occurs and the market proceeds to sell off.

Several days later, a bullish counterattack shows up on the chart in **Figure 4.3c**, followed by a series of spinning tops and a high wave candle. After a very slight rise in prices, a dark cloud cover occurs followed by a series of spinning tops and a doji. At the end of January and then in early February, there are bullish engulfing candles, and the market finds a new high before selling off in mid-February. A few spinning tops occur near the end of February, but they are followed by a falling window indicating a continuation of the downtrend. Several spinning tops are followed by a slight rally at the beginning of March.

A small rally occurs in mid-March following a piercing candle, as seen in **Figure 4.3d**. A sell-off then follows a spinning top a few days later. A major

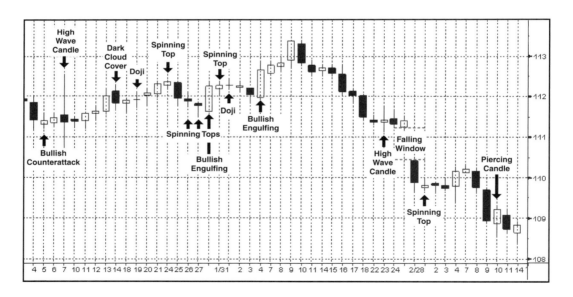

FIGURE **4.3c**

Candlestick Patterns on T-Notes Futures

Source: Bloomberg

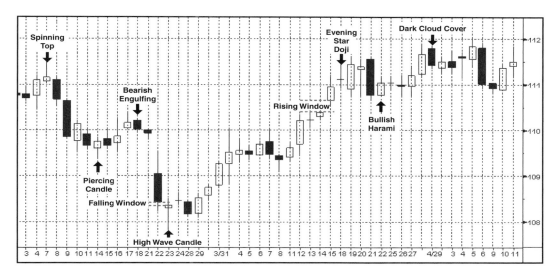

FIGURE 4.3d

Candlestick Patterns on T-Notes Futures

Source: Bloomberg

bottom then forms with a high wave candle followed by a doji after a falling window. An evening star doji (opposite of a morning star) occurs mid-April followed by a spinning top, but the following bullish harami indicates a continuation of the uptrend. The rally stalls following another evening star doji, and then at the end of April a dark cloud cover pattern emerges. A slight sell-off occurs, but the market still has much upward momentum, and the rise in prices continues.

The rally does not end even with a couple of spinning tops and a bearish harami showing up in mid-May, in **Figure 4.3e**. The market fails to find a top with the dark cloud cover in late May. There is no reversal of the uptrend at all until early June, with an evening star doji and dark cloud cover pattern. A triple top is completed following a bearish harami near the end of June. Finally, a bullish harami shows up on the chart at the beginning of July.

Figure 4.4a shows the CBOT mini-sized Dow futures contract forming an intermediary top with a bearish harami at the beginning of September, followed by a couple of spinning tops over several days. A piercing candle shows up, but because it is not at the bottom of a decline, it does not have any meaning as a

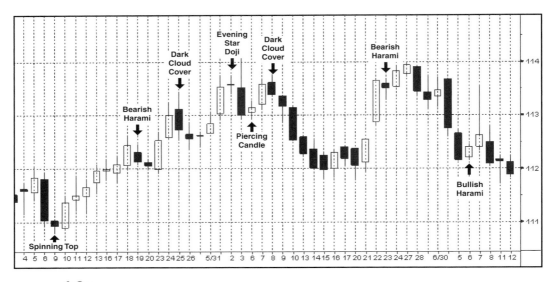

FIGURE **4.3e**

Candlestick Patterns on T-Notes Futures

Source: Bloomberg

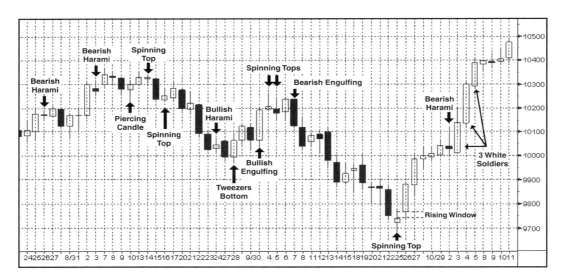

FIGURE **4.4a**

Candlestick Patterns on Mini-Sized Dow Futures

Source: Bloomberg

signal. An intermediary bottom then occurs at the end of September with a bullish harami followed by a tweezers bottom and then a bullish engulfing candle three days later. Two spinning tops and a bearish engulfing candle signal another reversal of trend as the market proceeds to continue its decline down a clearly defined channel. As the bottom of the channel is touched at the end of October, a spinning top followed by a rising window mark a major bottom as the market rallies very strongly into November with a three white soldiers pattern. A bearish harami is shrugged off as a potential reversal signal.

The market forms a sideways channel from late November into December as seen in **Figure 4.4b**. The market bounces within the channel with the appearance of a couple of long-legged dojis, which are dojis that have long shadows, as well as a high wave candle followed by a bearish engulfing candle. A rising window then portends the market's breaking out of its channel to the upside. It finds a top near the end of December with a spinning top followed by a bearish engulfing candle. It then continues its decline after a falling window shows up in mid-January.

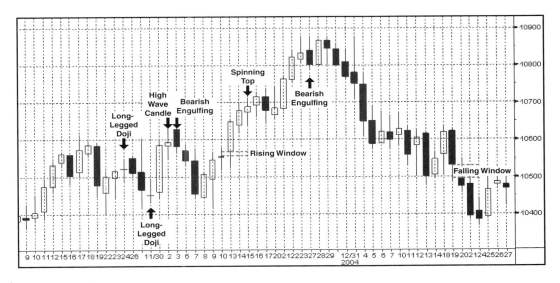

FIGURE 4.4b

Candlestick Patterns on Mini-Sized Dow Futures

Source: Bloomberg

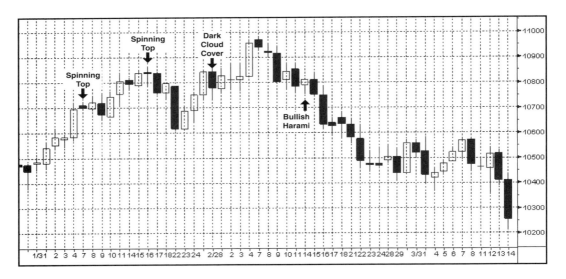

FIGURE **4.4c**

Candlestick Patterns on Mini-Sized Dow Futures

Source: Bloomberg

As shown in **Figure 4.4c**, a spinning top fails to forecast a top in early February, but another one signals a several-day slide later in the month. A dark cloud cover at the end of February also fails to forecast a top, since the top did not occur until five sessions later, after the market traded higher. A couple of spinning tops show up near the end of March, but the market merely trades sideways and fails to rally. The spinning tops in this case do not herald a reversal of the downward trend.

In **Figure 4.4d** you can see a bearish engulfing candle in early April that forecasts another big leg down in the established downtrend. A bearish pattern known as "three black crows," which is a series of black candles with long bodies, is marked on the chart. A spinning top then successfully signals a new rally, which takes off after a bullish engulfing candle at the tail end of April. A bearish harami then signals a decline, then the rally resumes with a bullish engulfing candle, which is the beginning of a three white soldiers pattern. A spinning top shows up mid-May, but the market fails to reverse direction, and it merely trades sideways in an extremely narrow range for a few weeks.

As seen in **Figure 4.4e**, a decline does not occur until mid-June with a bearish harami followed by two spinning tops. A new bottom forms beginning with

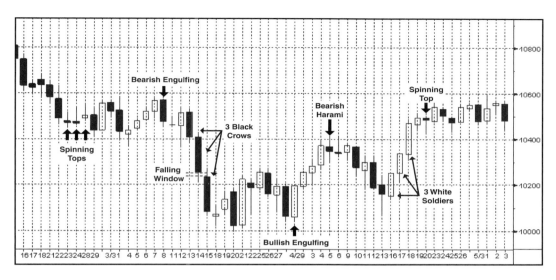

FIGURE **4.4d**

Candlestick Patterns on Mini-Sized Dow Futures

Source: Bloomberg

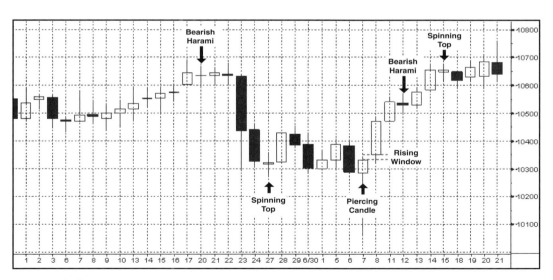

FIGURE **4.4e**

Candlestick Patterns on Mini-Sized Dow Futures

Source: Bloomberg

a spinning top and then is reinforced by a piercing candle followed by a rising window in early July. The market shrugs off a bearish harami and begins to stall with a spinning top several days into the rally.

Candlesticks and Intraday Charts

What about candlestick patterns on intraday charts with candles of shorter time frames? **Figure 4.5a** shows a fifteen-minute candlestick chart of the S&P 500 E-mini futures contract. The early morning upward momentum stalls, and it is followed by a decline with the appearance of a bearish harami (A) at 7:30 a.m. Following the formation of three black crows (B), a reversal occurs after a piercing candle (C) at 8:45 a.m. The market then declines after a dark cloud cover pattern (D) at 10:30 a.m. followed by a bearish engulfing candle (E) at 11:15 a.m. A reversal and new rally then follow one bullish harami (F) at 12:45 p.m. and then another one (G) at 1:15 p.m.

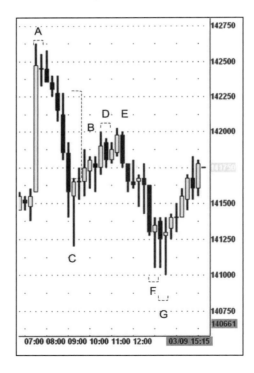

FIGURE 4.5a

Candlestick Patterns on S&P 500 E-Mini Futures

Source: eSignal

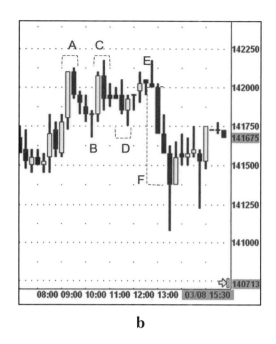

b

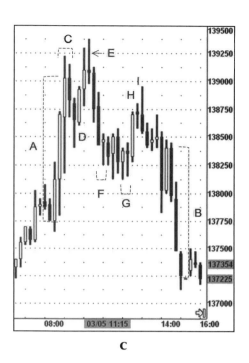

c

FIGURES **4.5b and 4.5c**

Candlestick Patterns on S&P 500 E-Mini Futures

Source: eSignal

Notice the following reversal patterns in **Figure 4.5b**: dark cloud cover (A) at 9:30 a.m., long-legged doji (B) at 10:00 a.m., dark cloud cover (C) at 10:30 a.m., bullish harami (D) at 11:45 a.m., hammer (E) (a type of doji with a lower shadow and no upper shadow, suggesting the shape of a mallet) at 12:15 p.m. Notice also the three black crows pattern (F) beginning at 12:30 p.m.

In **Figure 4.5c**, notice the three white soldiers pattern (A) at 8:00 a.m. and the three black crows pattern (B) at 2:00 p.m. Reversal patterns on the chart are dark cloud cover (C) at 9:00 a.m., bullish engulfing candle (D) at 9:30 a.m., long-legged doji (E) at 10:00 a.m., bullish haramis at 11:00 a.m. (F) and 12:15 p.m. (G), bullish engulfing candle (H) at 12:45 p.m., and doji (I) at 1:00 p.m.

Figure 4.5d shows five-minute candlestick patterns on the same futures contract: A dark cloud cover (A) as the rally fails just after 9:30 a.m., a bullish

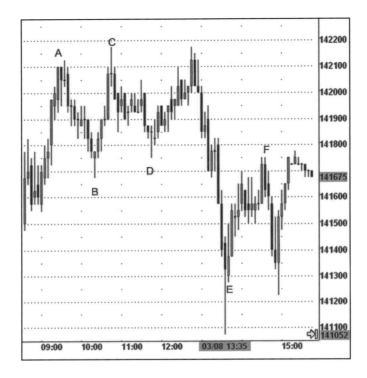

FIGURE **4.5d**

Candlestick Patterns on S&P 500 E-Mini Futures

Source: eSignal

counterattack/hammer combo (B) as the market forms a bottom shortly after 10:00 a.m., long-legged doji (C) as a top forms at 10:30 a.m., two consecutive long-legged dojis (D) at the bottom at 11:30 a.m., piercing candle (E) at the bottom at 1:40 p.m., and tweezers top (F) at 2:30 p.m.

In **Figure 4.5e**, another five-minute chart on the same contract, there is a dark cloud cover (A) at the top at 8:45 a.m., bullish engulfing candle (B) at the bottom at 8:55 a.m., high wave candle (C) at the top at 9:20 a.m., bullish engulfing candle (D) at 10:00 a.m., tweezers bottom (E) at 10:15 a.m., long-legged doji (F) at 11:00 a.m., piercing candle (G) at 12:15 p.m. (the market shrugs off the bearish pattern on its way up), and bullish engulfing candle at 2:25 p.m. (the market shrugs off the bullish pattern on its way down).

Candlestick patterns, as demonstrated by these charts, are not 100 percent accurate, but they do have a greater than chance probability of signaling market

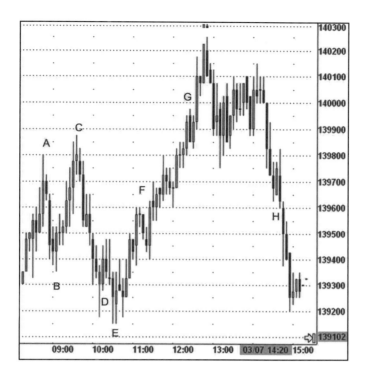

FIGURE **4.5e**

Candlestick Patterns on S&P 500 E-Mini Futures

Source: eSignal

reversals or trend continuation, just as the patterns discussed in Chapter 3 do. In combination with other technical analysis tools, they are an important weapon in a trader's arsenal. A word of caution regarding candlesticks: As with any tool, when the market fails to move in the anticipated direction that classic patterns otherwise indicate, it is best to cut your losses and wait for the next opportunity. In fact, it may be a signal to reverse your position and go with the direction of the trend.

Point and Figure Charts

Point and figure charts have been used for decades, and their principal advantage over OHLC bar and candlestick charts is their ability to filter out random noise. Support and resistance levels are identified in the same manner as they are on those other types of charts, as are trend lines. Time is not factored in for these charts, just changes in price. Price increases are plotted with the letter *X* and decreases are plotted with the letter *O*. A price change plot is determined by what is called the "box amount," which is a predetermined number of points. The reversal amount is a predetermined number of boxes, and it determines when the plot switches from *O*s to *X*s or vice versa. A column of *O*s or *X*s on the chart therefore is indeterminate with respect to time, which means it can vary considerably depending upon how long the price fluctuates before a reversal occurs. The charts here all have a reversal value of three boxes.

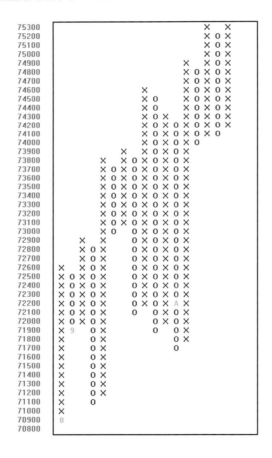

FIGURE **4.6a**

Point and Figure Chart of the E-Mini Russell 2000

Source: eSignal

```
81500                                          X O X O X
81400                                       X    X O X O X
81300                                       X O X O X O X
81200                                       2 O X O X O
81100                                       X O X O X
81000                                       X O X O X
80900                                       X O X O X
80800                                       X O X O X
80700                   X              X     X O   O X
80600          X      X O                X O X       O
80500          X O    X O      X         X O X
80400          X O    X O      X O       X O X
80300          X O X  X O      X O       X O X
80200    X    X O X O X O      X O       X O X
80100    X O X O X O X O       X O       X O X
80000    X O X O X O X O       X O       X O X
79900    X O X O X O X O       X O X     X
79800    X O X O X O X O        X O X    X O X O X
79700    X O X O X O X O X       X O X O X O X O X
79600    X O X O X O X O X O X O X O X O X O X O X
79500    X O X O X O X O X O X O X O X O X O X O X
79400    X O X O     O X O X O X O X O X O X O X O X
79300    X O       O X O X O X O X O X O X O X O X
79200    X        O X O X O X O X O X O X O X O X
79100 X   X       O  O X O X O X O X O X O X O X
79000 X O X        O X O X O X O X O X O X O X
78900 X O X        O X O X O X O X O X O X O X
78800 X O X        O X O X O X O X O X O X O X
78700 X O X        O X O X O X O X O X O X O X
78600 X O X        O X O X O X O X O X O X O X
78500 X O X        O X O X 1  O    X O X O X
78400 X O X        O X O    O X    X O X O X
78300 X O X        O X         O X O X O X O X
78200 X O X        O           O X O X O X O
78100 X O X                    O X O X O X
78000 X O X                    O X O X O X
77900 X O X                    O X O X O
77800 X O X                    O X O X
77700 X O X                    O X O
77600 X O X                    O X
77500 X O X                    O X
77400 X C                      O
77300 X
77200 X
77100 X
77000
```

FIGURE 4.6b

Point and Figure Chart of the E-Mini Russell 2000

Source: eSignal

Figure 4.6a shows a point and figure chart on the E-mini Russell 2000 stock index futures. Trend lines are drawn on the chart just as they would be for a candlestick format chart, and are used for the same purpose of projecting future levels of support and resistance.

Figure 4.6b is another point and figure chart for the same instrument in a different time frame. Note the wedge pattern forming, indicative of a potential reversal in the trend.

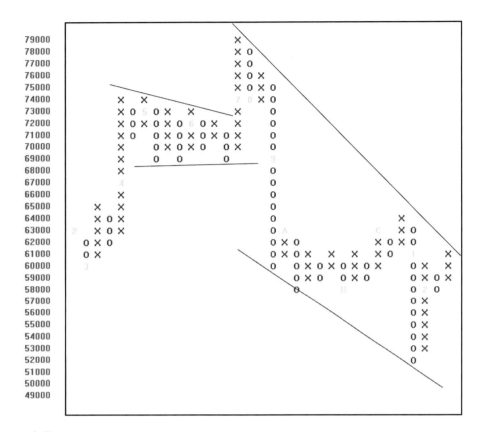

Source: eSignal

FIGURE 4.7

Point and Figure Chart of Mini Crude Oil Futures

The point and figure chart of the mini crude oil futures in **Figure 4.7** shows a flag pattern on the left, which is indicative of a reversal in trend, and a descending channel on the right half of the chart. The analyst would look either for the price to stay within the upper and lower boundaries of the channel or for a significant price swing in the direction of any breakout beyond those same boundaries.

Note the descending channel in the chart of the 10-year Treasury notes futures in **Figure 4.8**. Any breakout from the upper or lower boundaries of that formation would be the first indication of a significant price swing in the direction of the breakout.

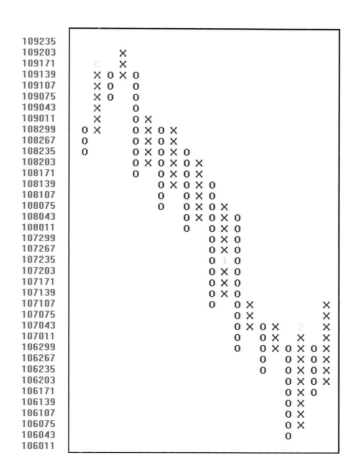

FIGURE **4.8**

Point and Figure Chart of T-Notes Futures

Source: eSignal

Volume and Technical Analysis

In addition to following price trends, monitoring volume is critical to a thorough analysis. If there is not enough volume, the market loses liquidity and wild short-term price swings can result. A spike in volume also can serve to nudge the market in one direction or another, depending on whether the large traders fueling the move are predominantly bears or bulls.

Market Profile Charts

Market Profile charts are tools for assessing volume at various price levels. Market Profile charts are the creation of J. Peter Steidlmayer in conjunction with the Chicago Board of Trade. They became extremely popular with CBOT floor traders back in the 1980s, and can be useful in conjunction with other types of analysis. The higher the volume at any given price, the more likely that the price level in question is a fair value as determined by the auction action itself, so the theory goes. What is most striking about Market Profile charts is that they reveal patterns that other types of charts do not, and mainly the classic bell curve from Statistics 101. Such curves represent the first, second, and third standard deviations of the overall volume distributed across the span of prices from one extreme of the curve to the other extreme. The area that represents the first

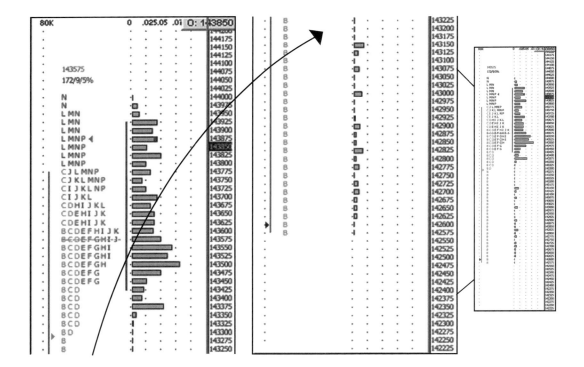

FIGURE **4.9**

Market Profile Chart

Source: eSignal

standard deviation, where 70 percent of the total volume is concentrated, is referred to as the "value area."

The construction of a Market Profile chart is fairly simple, as can be seen in **Figure 4.9**. The trading session is broken up into periods of equal length using letters of the alphabet to designate each period. Originally the periodic component was thirty minutes, but Market Profiles with longer or shorter periods have been used as well. The standard that has been arrived at over the years is to designate the half-hour period beginning at 9:00 a.m. eastern time with a capital *A*, followed by the next period beginning at 9:30 a.m. ET with a capital *B*, and so on. In constructing the chart, only one letter per period is drawn for each price during that period and always as far to the left as possible without overlapping letters from more than one period. The letter designation is referred to as a Time-Price Opportunity, or TPO. The first hour of trading is called the "initial balance area," which on the chart is marked by a vertical line on the left of the profile, covering the range of prices in the B and C TPO tracks, marking the half-hour brackets beginning at 9:30 a.m. ET (8:30 a.m. central time) and 9:00 a.m. ET (9:00 a.m. CT[1]), respectively. The value area on the chart is marked by the vertical line to the right of the profile. The charts depicted here, which are courtesy of eSignal, also contain a volume histogram for each price to the right of the profile, displayed as horizontal bars. Note the bell curve formation around the value area in Figure 4.9.

Both Steidlmayer and James F. Dalton (prominent authors of books about Market Profile) discuss markets as either trending in one direction or trading within a narrow range (bracketed). They claim that markets trend only 20 percent of the time and that the other 80 percent of the time they are bracketed. This is a case of the 80/20 principle in action. The idea was first stated by Italian economist Vilfredo Pareto in 1897. He studied the distribution of wealth in Europe and noticed that 80 percent of assets were concentrated in the hands of the wealthiest 20 percent of the population, and that it was the same proportions for as many centuries in the past for which he could obtain data. In parallel to that phenomenon, 80 percent of market prices are occurring in the periods that are bracketed, with the remaining 20 percent occurring during the periods of active price movement to either significantly

---

1. As I am based in the Chicago area, I will be referring to the time brackets in central time from this point on.

higher or lower levels. One does not even need to chart prices with Market Profiles to discern that pattern. (It is also obvious on bar or candlestick charts, as levels of support and resistance clearly delimit the channels wherein prices trade in sideways fashion for prolonged periods of time.)

Another manifestation of the 20 component of the 80/20 principle is in the typical price corrections of 20 percent that occur on a regular basis after a strong rally of market prices to new highs (either recent or historical). Also, a statistic often quoted is that, of all traders in speculative markets such as futures, only 20 percent of them turn a profit and the other 80 percent rack up net losses. Sometimes those markets are depicted as zero-sum games, which in theory is correct, but in actual practice is not entirely accurate, for it does not take into account the commercials whose cash positions are hedged by the use of forward contracts. Those market participants make up a significant percentage of trading volume and open interest.[2]

Traders have been known to devise strategies based on the 80/20 rule. For example, one could trade silver futures by selling short whenever a historical resistance level was tested and buying whenever a historical support level was tested. This could be an effective strategy for a period of many months extending into years as that particular contract failed to break out of its fairly narrow range. You can apply that concept to trading the value areas of either the daily Market Profile charts with thirty-minute TPO time frames or even with composite profiles of five trading sessions or longer using the same thirty-minute TPO time frames. It is simply a question of devising some strategy whereby one buys near the bottom extreme of the bell curve and sells near the top extreme of that curve. It typically takes at least three overlapping TPO tracks to begin forming the base of a bell curve on the left and then it either fills out as expected or fails as prices actually break out to the upside or downside. Sometimes the bell curve pattern fills in evenly from top to bottom, but more often it will tend to fill in the upper half of the curve first, then the bottom half or vice versa. One potential strategy might be to make a single trade from one extreme of the curve to the other. Another potential strategy is to look for multiple opportunities to trade the upper and lower extremes and exit at predetermined price objectives.

---

2. Open interest is the number of open positions as the total of all contracts on both the long and short side of the market.

Another aspect of market analysis that is made easier by utilizing Market Profile charts is tracking phases of price movement. This can be broken down as follows:

1 Series of prices in one direction
2 Trade to a price to stop the market
3 Develop around that stopping point
4 Move to efficiency (retracement)[3]

The formation of a bell curve with its value area is a visible cue that the four phases are playing out in a constant rhythm that repeats over and over again. The fourth phase is sometimes skipped as the market goes from the third phase to the first phase of a new cycle. Those phases are part of a vacillation between an inefficient market that is out of balance (trending) and an efficient market that is in balance (trading or bracketed).

Market Profile bell curve formations are not always cookie-cutter patterns that provide a money tree from which a trader can simply pluck ripe cash with little or no effort. Notice in Figure 4.9 that the base of a bell curve is established with three overlapping TPO tracks in the B, C, and D time frame TPOs from 8:30 a.m. CT to 10:00 a.m. CT, subsequent to the initial spike to the long side losing momentum. The upper extreme of the bell curve is extended to a higher price level in the L TPO period towards the tail end of the session and the market then fills out the bell curve at the upper end but fails to trade back near the lower end of the curve. That is a variation of the bell curve formation to expect from time to time. It is just one of many such variations on a central theme. Observing the Market Profiles as they form over several months or years, or in lieu of that, studying many historical Market Profile charts, is a necessary exercise to become knowledgeable about those variations of the formation of that most commonly occurring pattern.

The phenomenon of prices tending to trade back to the other side of a bell curve formation when one extreme of that formation is tested also can show up on a bar or candlestick chart. If you plot a short-term moving average (from three to eight bars for example) projected a few bars/candles ahead on an intraday chart such as a one-minute or five-minute bar or candle, whenever the price deviates from the plot of that projected moving average, there is a higher

---

3. J. Peter Steidlmayer and Steven B. Hawkins, *Steidlmayer on Markets, Trading with Market Profile*, 2nd ed. (John Wiley & Sons, 2002), p. 71.

probability of the price trading back towards the average. How many ticks that deviation is depends on the particular market one is analyzing. It might be five ticks for one market and fifteen ticks for another market. Whether the chart is of a Market Profile, bar, or candlestick type, the same information is being captured about where the market auction has found value, and trading volume will invariably accumulate in that range while in the period of a bracketed situation until price breaks out to a new level of value.

The flip side of the coin with Market Profile is to attempt to identify likely breakouts to get on the right side of a trending market rather than trade back and forth in a bracketed market. That is quite a bit trickier to accomplish effectively, however. Not only that, but it is more likely to yield a strategy with a lower percentage of winning trades and a higher percentage of losing trades, no matter how expert the trader becomes at identifying setups for breakouts to the long or short side indicated by volume at price analysis via Market Profile charts. To offset that weaker win/loss ratio, it would behoove the trader to seek to maximize profits and take as large a piece of a breakout move as is possible without exiting a position too early.

Figure 4.10a shows a Market Profile for the March 2007 S&P 500 E-mini futures on 12/13/2006. On that chart are levels to either sell short (F and G periods) or trade the long side (H and M periods) as the outer extremes of the base of the bell curve formation filled out with three overlapping TPO tracks. The top portion of the bell curve filled out first, then the lower portion after the range of the curve was extended lower by four ticks in the J period.

Figure 4.10b is of a profile for March 2007 S&P 500 E-mini futures on 12/12/2006. The bell curve is extremely lopsided, but it is a bell curve distribution of trading volume nonetheless. Into the G period the session was appearing to be a weak one with potential for a major sell-off, but the market managed to rally strongly later in the session to fill out the top of the curve. Note the slope of the curve at the lower extreme. With that type of pattern, which occurs fairly frequently, the length of the tail in the G period is a gauge of where each overlapping TPO track is going to find its low before trading towards the higher extreme of the bell curve formation. Hence, there should not be an expectation of getting long near the bottom of that buying tail. The formation of the buying tail is considered by Market Profile analysts to be an indication of strong buying activity entering the market to give the price action some upward momentum in the near term.

Figure 4.10c shows a downtrend day profile for 2/27/2007 on the S&P 500 E-mini futures. The market starts out bracketed in the first hour and a half (the

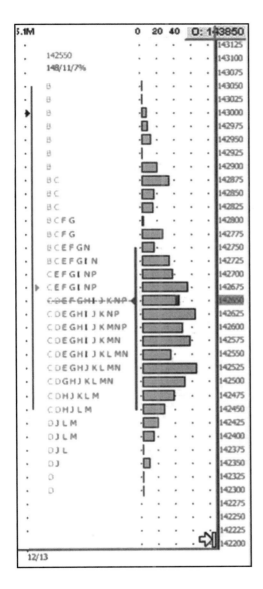

a

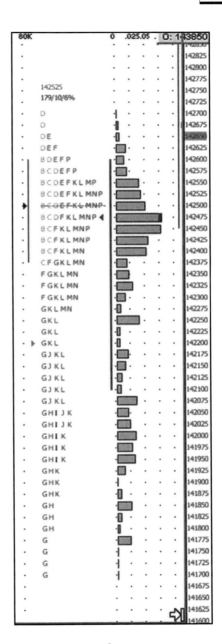

b

FIGURES **4.10a and 4.10b**

Market Profile of S&P 500 E-Mini Futures

Source: eSignal

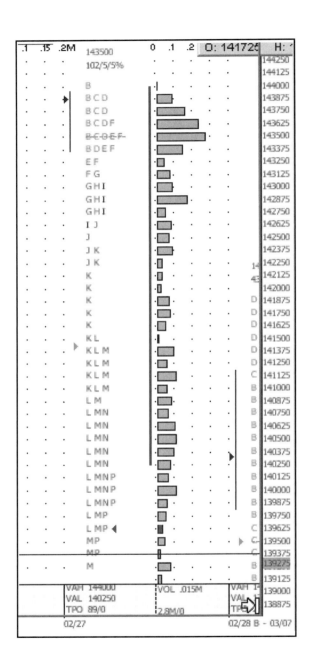

FIGURE 4.10c

Market Profile of S&P 500 E-Mini Futures

Source: eSignal

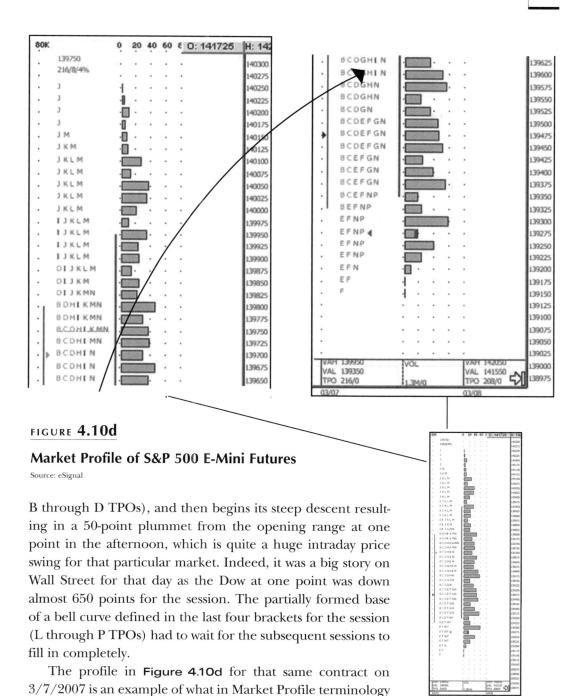

FIGURE **4.10d**

Market Profile of S&P 500 E-Mini Futures

Source: eSignal

B through D TPOs), and then begins its steep descent resulting in a 50-point plummet from the opening range at one point in the afternoon, which is quite a huge intraday price swing for that particular market. Indeed, it was a big story on Wall Street for that day as the Dow at one point was down almost 650 points for the session. The partially formed base of a bell curve defined in the last four brackets for the session (L through P TPOs) had to wait for the subsequent sessions to fill in completely.

The profile in **Figure 4.10d** for that same contract on 3/7/2007 is an example of what in Market Profile terminology

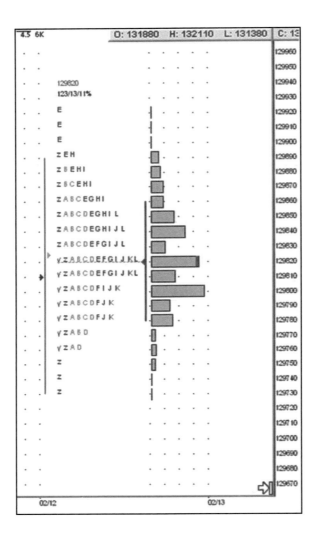

FIGURE 4.11a

Market Profile of Euro Currency Futures

Source: eSignal

is known as a neutral day, which is a bracketed or nontrending session characterized by range extensions in both directions. A range extension is a price move that has overlapping TPOs and extends beyond the initial balance area. The early range extension at the bottom of the profile occurs in the E and F TPOs. The later range extension at the top of the profile occurs during the I, J, and K TPOs.

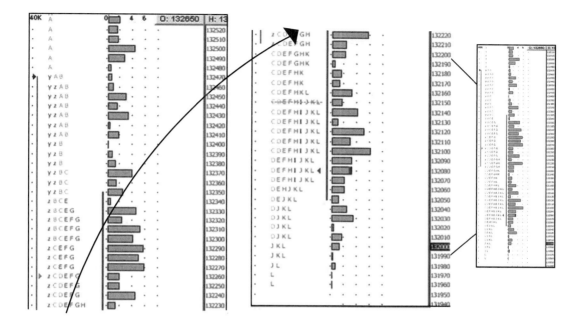

FIGURE **4.11b**

Market Profile of Euro Currency Futures

Source: eSignal

Neutral days indicate uncertainty as other time-frame buyers and sellers both enter the fray. Other time-frame participants are those that have a longer range strategy than the day time-frame players. Narrow brackets are defined by day time-frame traders and range extensions and trending prices are defined by other time-frame traders. Neutral days often forecast reversals in trend.

Another type of nontrend day is shown in the profile for euro currency futures on 2/12/2007 in **Figure 4.11a**. The bell curve forms without any range extensions beyond the initial balance area.

Another type of normal day called a "normal variation day" is shown in the profile in **Figure 4.11b** for the euro futures on 12/14/2006. There is a range extension at the bottom of the profile equal to the length of the initial balance area, and the market fills out a bell curve without continuing any downtrend for the session. Normal variation days occur much more often than normal days and are the most common type of pattern in Market Profile charts, with neutral days being the second most common.

An approach for predicting market breakouts is combining several sessions into a single profile chart. **Figure 4.12a** shows such a composite profile from 2/28/2007 to 3/7/2007 for the S&P 500 E-mini futures. A symmetrical large bell curve formation is fairly well established prior to the market trading to a higher level on 3/8/2007. Any trades at the upper or lower extremes of the bell curve on high volume serve as an early signal that a breakout to a new level of value is imminent. Any such trades on low volume indicate an opportunity to fade the extreme.[4]

As with daily profiles, bell curve formations are not always symmetrical and are often skewed to one extreme or the other. Any profile that forms a shape like the letter *p* during an upward price trend is a sign of increased short-covering activity, indicating low potential for follow-through on the upside. Any profile that forms a shape like the letter *b* during a downward price trend is a sign of increased long liquidation, indicating low potential for follow-through on the downside. The next few examples illustrate asymmetrical bell curve formations.

The composite profile in **Figure 4.12b** is for the same market from 2/13/2007 to 2/26/2007. A bell curve formation with a mature top portion and a partially mature bottom portion, or skewed to the top of the standard deviation, is clear on the chart.

A similar formation is visible in the composite profile for 10-year Treasury notes futures from 2/28/2007 to 3/8/2007 in **Figure 4.13**. The bell curve is not perfectly symmetrical, but is more so than the formation in Figure 4.12b.

The composite profile for euro currency futures from 2/14/2007 to 3/9/2007 in **Figure 4.14** shows a very wide and short bell curve skewed towards the bottom of the standard deviation. With any profile, whether single session or multisession, the wider the bell curve, the more balanced the market is between buying and selling activity. Elongated bell curve formations, on the other hand, occur during situations of imbalance, wherein one-sided auctions drive the price up or down as opposed to within a bracketed range. Market Profile asymmetrical bell curves may or may not fill out to become symmetrical formations; prices may migrate to new levels of perceived value without such a filling out occurring.

---

4. Fading the extreme means taking a short position near the upper boundary of the bell curve or taking a long position near the lower boundary.

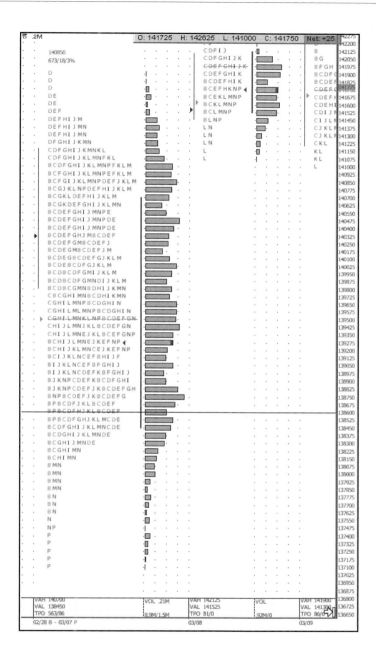

FIGURE **4.12a**

Multiday Market Profile of S&P 500 E-Mini Futures

Source: eSignal

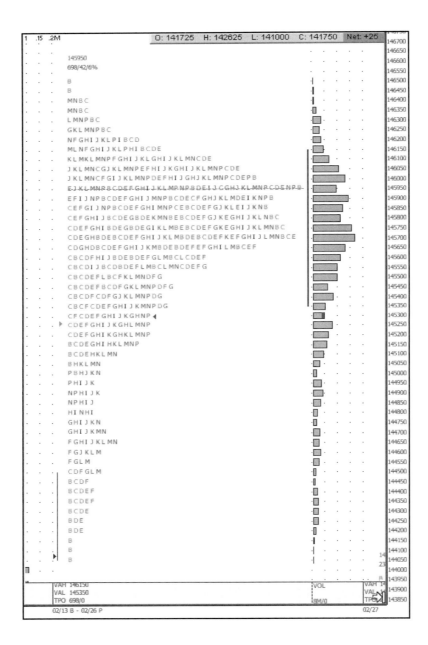

FIGURE **4.12b**

Multiday Market Profile of S&P 500 E-Mini Futures

Source: eSignal

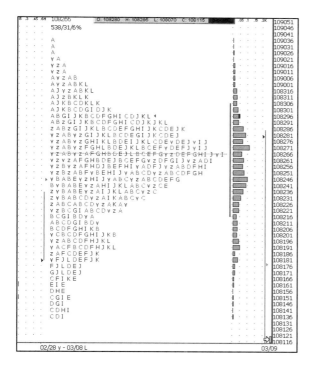

FIGURE **4.13**

**Multiday Market Profile
of T-Notes Futures**

Source: eSignal

FIGURE **4.14**

**Multiday Market
Profile of Euro
Currency Futures**

Source: eSignal

Market Profile Pitfalls

Market Profile chart expert James F. Dalton has raised key points regarding the misuse of profile charts by many traders, noting a common failure to realize that the distribution of prices around a bell curve is a natural progression, and that they also need to be put into context. Otherwise, the tendency will be to miss the forest for the trees—focusing on the charts and even seeing patterns that simply are not there.

Dalton also points out that adding volume at price to the mix often provides clues as to what impact large orders are likely to have in the near term, as well as what the repercussions are when there is no follow-through on price based on the expectations of those large traders. For the professional trader in particular, having fine-tuned volume tools that streaming data and sophisticated software provide is a boon of incalculable benefit. Popular widely used indicators, like moving averages and Bollinger bands, although valid as tools, fail to account for the volume level, because they are based solely on price. On their own, they will fail to alert the analyst to the clues that volume at price provides based on whether the prices were made on low or high volume.[5]

Traders who focus too narrowly on one piece of market-generated information without considering it in the overall context of the market are subject to seeing patterns that do not actually exist. For an analyst to avoid that pitfall, any candidate for a newly discovered pattern should be subjected to rigorous verification via statistical methods on an adequate sampling of price data before attempting to use that pattern to forecast trend continuation or reversal.

Market Profile Charts and the Liquidity Data Bank

A tool that was designed for use as an adjunct to Market Profile charts is the CBOT's Liquidity Data Bank (LDB). It is a useful report of total volume, calculation of the value area, dispersion of volume, percentage of volume by trader type, acceptance of value outside of the value area, high-volume concentrations, top 5 versus bottom 5 tick analysis, and trend tests. It breaks down trading volume by category of trader represented as Customer Type Indicators, or CTIs. The first category is CTI 1 and is local floor participation, which means professional traders in the pits at the exchange. CTI 2

---

5. James F. Dalton, Robert Bevan Dalton, and Eric T. Jones, *Markets in Profile, Profiting from the Auction Process* (John Wiley & Sons, 2007), pp. 106–110.

is commercial clearing members. CTI 3 is members filling orders through other members. CTI 4 is members filling orders for the public or any other type of outside customer.[6] As described on the Chicago Board of Trade product website: For each price, the total long and short volume of each CTI category is recorded, as well as the aggregate of all trades across those four categories. Those are produced in three formats: Detail, Summary, and 70% Value Area (the same as the first standard deviation of the bell curve of the Market Profile). The information is downloadable in various data formats and selectable by date range and product type by pit-traded or electronic market. Daily totals and totals for each fifteen-minute interval of the trading session are provided.

The monitoring of trends in total volume over time is a valuable tool for detecting trend exhaustion or imminent breakouts from bracketed price levels as volume declines. The value area, as discussed in the preceding section on Market Profile charts, is important for a number of reasons. Analyzing dispersion of volume provides footprints left by other time frame participants by comparing the volume above and below the price within the value area with the highest volume. Other time frame buyers leave their footprint in the form of higher volume below the highest volume price, and other time frame sellers leave their footprint in the form of higher volume above the highest volume price. Dispersion of volume shows hidden information about the market that is not clear from the Market Profile alone, which would only show uncertainty in a bracketed market. Day time frame participants, the locals in the pits, leave their footprint in the form of high CTI 1 percentages, whereas other time frame participants leave their footprints in the form of high CTI 2, CTI 3, and CTI 4 percentages. When other time frame participants are active, there is a higher probability of trending in price to occur. LDB reveals information about value outside of the value area that the Market Profile chart will not, for example when the commercials as CTI 2 become active and indicating the probability of price moving to a new level where value will be established. LDB pinpoints levels where price is likely to spend time as value is found via high-volume concentration. Comparing the sum of the 5 percent of total volume figures at the top of the range with the

6. James F. Dalton, Eric T. Jones, and Robert B. Dalton, *Mind Over Markets: Power Trading with Market Generated Information*, 2nd ed. (Traders Press, 1999), pp. 135–136.

5 percent of total volume figures at the bottom of the range (top 5 versus bottom 5) can often signal a bias to the long or short side. Trend potential is tested by LDB via averaging the highest 5 percent of volume figures (the lower the average, the higher the indication of a trend), or via summing the percentage of total volume figures in the opening range (the lower the sum, the higher potential for a trend to ensue).

Another variation of the standard OHLC bar or candlestick types of chart is the use of a logarithmic scale, which is based on a percentage change in price rather than fixed increments. Certain patterns that would otherwise be hidden from view are plainly visible when using such a scale.

The trader's toolbox should include a variety of charting techniques. Each type of chart provides certain clues to the potential future direction and the infancy or maturity of a trend that is under way. Without the assistance that those variegated graphic tools provide, one is trading with blinders on, and having tunnel vision is a consequence.

Conclusion

Using a variety of charting techniques can enhance technical analysis. Standard OHLC bar charts do not always tell the entire story. For one, they do not take volume into account, and not all prices are equal. Prices where heavier- or lighter-than-average volume occurs are significant reference points for the technical analyst. The amount of time spent at a price is also indicative of how close that particular price is to fair value as perceived by market participants. Trades at extremes from value will not remain at those levels for long, particularly when there is light volume. The market will tend to auction swiftly back to the area of accepted value. Standard OHLC bar charts also are not as effective in filtering out noise as are point and figure charts.

Summary of Chapter 4
- Open/High/Low/Close price charts are not the only type of chart used by technical analysis.
- Japanese candlestick charts have become increasingly popular in recent years, and essentially graph the same components on candles as OHLC charts graph on simple vertical bars. Candlestick patterns complement standard chart patterns as used on OHLC charts.

- Market Profile has an advantage over other types of price charts due to its ability to highlight levels of accepted value and price levels where heavier trading volume occurs.
- Liquidity Data Bank is a useful adjunct to Market Profile on account of the information the tool provides about the activity of larger traders.

CHAPTER 5

Indicator Soup: Not-So-Secret Recipes

Chart patterns are a form of visually oriented technical analysis. Technical indicators involve nonvisual numeric analyses of market data, which include price, volume, and open interest (depending on the indicator). The output of the analysis is then plotted on or adjacent to (usually below) a price chart. The most common and widely recognized indicator is the simple moving average of closing prices that is plotted on top of price bars as a continuous smoothed line.

In calculating an indicator, a series of data components is utilized in mathematical formulas based on algebraic equations and trigonometric or calculus-based functions or a branch of statistics known as time series analysis. Taking a set of the basic calculated components (also referred to as "data points") over a predefined period of time is the main thrust of indicator processing. For example, an average of x number of days' closing prices is assessed for x number of days and plotted accordingly. The average itself is not very useful as an indicator, but charting it over time as a moving average is quite useful for the purpose of technical analysis.

The most common method of identifying a trend for a stock is to see if the stock is above its 200-day moving average of daily closing prices for an uptrend or below its 200-day moving average for a downtrend. Obviously, given the extremely long period for the moving average, that type of analysis is meant to flag the most major of trends. It is essentially a filtering mechanism that eliminates noise from the price data.

Another popular approach that is more sensitive to short-term price swings is to combine a long-term moving average with one of shorter duration, such as an eighteen-day moving average and a nine-day moving average for a futures market. If the shorter-term average crosses above the longer-term average, it is supposed to forecast a continued uptrend. If the shorter-term average crosses below the longer-term average, it is supposed to forecast a continued decline in prices. That approach does not lag as much as the 200-day moving average analysis; however, it will not be nearly as effective as a noise filter. That is the trade-off.

Correctly predicting the point at which a trend has reached its logical conclusion is the other piece to the puzzle. A number of indicators are designed specifically for that purpose, and are supposed to sense when the market is either overbought or oversold. For example, an Elliott Wave analyst will look to the wave counts to see if a series of five or seven legs has occurred within an ongoing impulse wave. To find a place for bargain prices, that same analyst will be on the lookout for the completion of a corrective wave with its A-B-C legs. Someone who pays close attention to trend lines will watch for those that are so steep that they are close to 90 degrees in angle. Once such a line is broken, it is considered to be the omen of imminent reversal of trend. One problem with trend analysis is that once a trend is clearly under way as a major swing on a price chart, it is often getting close to exhaustion as momentum starts to wind down. In other words, new buyers are no longer rushing in on the way up or new sellers are no longer rushing in on the way down. What happens when there are more sellers than buyers? The market retreats from its new highs. What happens when there are more buyers than sellers? The market rebounds from its descent. For that reason, weathering the price swings involved is aptly characterized as a roller-coaster ride.

The Pitfalls of Indicators

One pitfall with indicators is that they can be followed too religiously, without consideration of other factors. If they are used in a vacuum during technical analysis—in other words, irrespective of the price action itself—then they could easily be taken out of context. Looking at an indicator by itself without setting it side by side with some type of price chart and the patterns therein is like trying to see the back of your head with a single handheld mirror. An indicator is merely a way of assessing something about the strength or weakness of a trend in prices that may not be easily apparent from a price chart alone. One indicator also should be balanced by other indicators that measure some other dimension of the price movement, to keep the analysis from being lopsided or too skewed to one set of variables. If an indicator generates a sell signal in the presence of the formation of a head and shoulders bottom, this should certainly give the analyst pause. Another approach to corroboration of indications is to apply indicators across multiple time frames instead of within a single one.

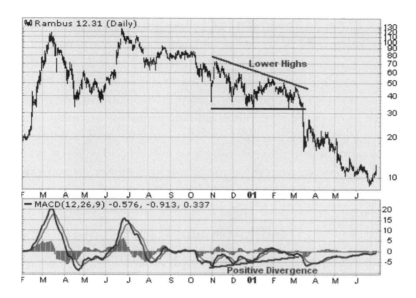

FIGURE **5.1**

MACD with Price/Indicator Divergence

Source: StockCharts.com

The importance of corroborating indicators is shown in **Figure 5.1**, which is a chart of Rambus stock with the Moving Average Convergence Divergence (MACD) indicator plotted underneath. A divergence between the price and the indicator occurred from late 2000 into 2001 with lower highs on the price chart and higher lows on the MACD line plot, which is bullish in outlook. The chart, on the other hand, also showed signs of major weakness with the wedge pattern that pointed to continuation of the established major downward trend. That is a clear contradiction between the two analyses, which should tell you to stand aside until an opportunity with a clear indication presents itself.

Use of indicators should not be mechanical. They need to be weighed in the context of everything else as part of your total analysis. Note that indicators usually do not have the same performance across all instruments or market circumstances. One of them may work well in a bracketed market on the S&P 500, but not so well with the same type of market conditions in wheat futures. Effective use of any indicator should involve careful study over large samplings of price data to see how it should fit into your trading strategies.

Appendix A at the back of this book contains a short list of the hundreds of indicators on the market today, along with some of the mathematical formulae used by them. Fortunately, traders do not have to calculate the indicators by hand, because any charting software package available is going to provide many of them either as part of the product or as third-party add-ins. Sorting through all of the indicators to see which ones actually provide some bang for the buck is what needs to be done, though, and that can take a considerable amount of time. Narrowing the number to be used to about half a dozen is a prudent approach, as opposed to attempting to use a large number, to make the task of analysis manageable rather than overwhelming.

Indicators and Price

Indicators are either leading or lagging, which means they occur either prior to some price move or after a price move is under way. Leading indicators generally involve a form of price momentum over a fixed look-back period, which is the number of periods used by the indicator's formula. For example, a ten-day Stochastic Oscillator would analyze the past ten days of price data exclusive of prior price data. Commodity Channel Index (CCI), percent range (%R, by Larry Williams), Relative Strength Index (RSI), momentum, and stochastics are a few examples of leading indicators.

Leading indicators probe the extent of momentum, a dimension of price action that is essentially the strength of a trend or the rate of change of price in one direction. Momentum, as breakouts on charts reveal with increasing slants to trend lines, will accelerate as a price swing picks up its pace. A good momentum oscillator, which is a common type of leading indicator, should sort out the difference between decline in momentum that is a precursor of a reversal in trend and decline in momentum that is part of a leveling of the rate of price increase to a median or norm. Momentum oscillators are like surfers who assess weather conditions to predict when some big waves for them to ride are due to roll into shore.

Being leading as opposed to lagging gives an indicator the advantage of getting a trader into and out of a price swing earlier, and perhaps at a better price level. With lagging indicators it is easy to get chopped up in bracketed markets due to the market's reversing direction just after entry on a trade—commonly known as being whipsawed.

A leading indicator, on the other hand, performs well in those markets. If used in a market that is trending, however, leading indicators usually only perform well with trades that are in the direction of the trend. Leading indicators are good at detecting oversold conditions in an uptrend and overbought conditions in a downtrend.

The downside of oscillators is potentially greater risk when a buy or sell indication gets a trader into the market prematurely and causes a stop-loss level to be hit. This can erode profits quickly. Using oscillators calls for caution to avoid getting caught in a trade.

One popular momentum indicator is the Relative Strength Index, or RSI. As mentioned previously, RSI is a leading indicator. It operates by comparing the average price change of the advancing periods with the average price change of the declining periods. It is plotted as a line on a grid with numeric values from 0 to 100 on the vertical axis. Higher values (above 70) indicate potentially oversold markets and lower values (under 30) indicate potentially overbought markets.

On the Google stock chart in **Figure 5.2**, RSI declined in July 2006 from a high of 75 until it reached a low of 25 near a major bottom. It touched 70 in early

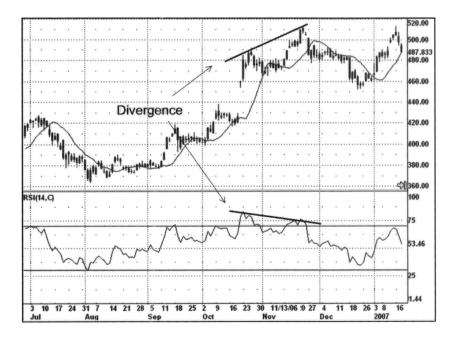

FIGURE 5.2

Relative Strength Index

Source: eSignal

September and the market temporarily paused without any significant decline, then the rally continued. The same thing repeated a month later and then RSI shot up over 80 as the price soared. The significant reversal followed by a short-term countertrend to the downside occurred in late November with divergence as the RSI had lower highs while the price had higher highs, which is a bearish indication.

Unlike RSI, moving averages and Moving Average Convergence Divergence (MACD) are commonly used lagging indicators that detect a trend once it already is under way. These types of indicators are an adjunct to chart patterns, which usually do not reveal any major trend until the move is well under way. Lagging indicators perform well when trend lines are relatively steep on the chart, but not in sideways or bracketed markets. Longer-term position strategies will favor lagging indicators, as opposed to short-term swing or scalping strategies that favor leading indicators. In nontrending markets, lagging indicators usually will result in being chopped up in the whipsaw price action characteristic of those conditions.

Figure 5.3 is a daily chart of the S&P 500 E-mini futures contract. MACD is plotted with lines and a histogram of vertical bars. Typical use of the indicator is to look for buy and sell indications when the lines cross (in this case, the darker line crossing above the lighter line for a buy and crossing under the lighter line for a sell). The sell indications on this chart occurred several times in the major uptrend, but they are against the trend. The buy indications were fewer, but much more useful for a trading strategy on account of the filtering out of many unprofitable trades. Note that sometimes a reversal of trend on the histogram at peaks and troughs can be indicated early on (more of a leading feature of the indicator) as the bars begin to shorten in a trough or peak. To use the indicator in this respect, it is better to wait for two consecutive shortened bars, as often a single one is a false signal.

Lagging indicators, because their main purpose is to detect a trend, can give a trader the ability to get into a position for the long term and potentially ride out a price swing for most of its duration. That is not a foregone conclusion on every signal, however. Trailing stops to protect locked-in profits need to be part of the strategy, as well, in order to avoid a whipsaw move that can turn an otherwise profitable trade into a break-even or losing one.

The luxury of being less active and having fewer instances of jumping in and out of the market over time makes these indicators attractive, but the trade-off is that as soon as a market heads into a bracketed range, the buy

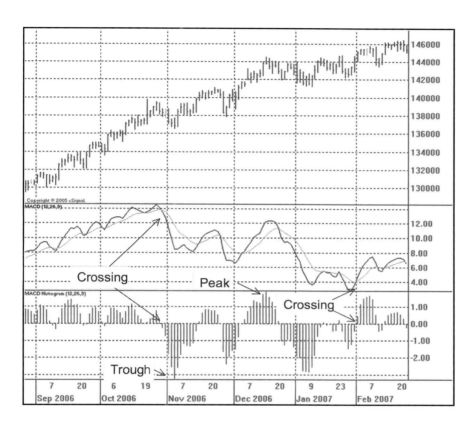

FIGURE 5.3

MACD

Source: eSignal

and sell signals become unreliable. Standard chart analysis needs to be part of the picture to assess when the indications should be heeded and when they should be disregarded. Because the lagging characteristic of trend-following indicators means that a move is usually well under way when a signal occurs, any trade is going to take a relatively small piece out of a price swing (maybe a third to half of the total move, optimistically), and often it is going to result in break-even trades when trends do not have enough length and breadth.

Implementing Indicators

As illustrated in the discussion on alternative charting methods in Chapter 4, markets trend only 20 percent of the time. The other 80 percent of the time they are range-bound. Thus, as a general rule, leading indicators should be utilized 80 percent of the time and lagging indicators should be utilized only 20 percent of the time, if you are to have a strategy that best suits prevailing market conditions.

Technical indicators require some measure of fine-tuning by optimizing their parameters. A shorter look-back time frame is going to generate signals earlier due to increased sensitivity that is attained, but it is at the expense of a higher frequency of false signals. Conversely, longer look-back time frames generate later signals, but with a higher level of reliability. Some happy medium is desirable, so setting a look-back period that is neither too short nor too long is the answer, but that requires some playing around with different parameters to see the results. Optimum win/loss and risk-reward ratios are dependent upon the fine-tuning process, if technical indicators are to be used effectively.

A common question with respect to all of the indicators on the market is: If those indicators are so effective at forecasting prices, as those who purvey them would like everyone to believe, then why are they even offering them to the public instead of keeping them for their own trading purposes? First of all, no indicator is the equivalent of a crystal ball that lets you see future price direction. Indicators are merely tools that give some indication of probable market behavior. It is up to the technical analyst to evaluate the utility of any indicator under varying market conditions. That means taking the time to study how the indicator performs over time in light of the trader's personal trading style.

A long-standing indicator for the stock market is the ratio of total shares that are increasing in price (advancing) to total shares that are falling in price (declining), which is commonly referred to as the "advance-decline line." Standard indexes such as the Dow, S&P 500, and Russell 2000 (which is an index of small-cap stocks) have a direct correlation with that ratio. More advances generally occur in an uptrend and more declines generally occur in a downtrend. Indexes are designed to take the "temperature" of the entire stock market via a snapshot of bellwether issues representative of all of the major sectors, usually weighted as part of an overall average. Analysts who watch the ratio of advances to declines keep an eye out for when they are out of kilter with those measures of price such as the indexes. That becomes obvious when plotting the stock price or index side by side with the advance-decline ratio and divergences show up in the form of higher highs on the price with lower highs on the ratio and conversely lower lows on the price and higher lows on the ratio. It can often serve to give you a heads-up on a reversal in the near future despite the otherwise strong slope to a trend on a price chart.

One indicator respected by many market technicians is the MACD. Even more useful with that indicator are divergences between peaks or valleys in the line plot or histogram bars and highs or lows on the bar chart. In other words, if the bar chart makes a higher high but the MACD makes a lower high, it is a sell indication, and if the bar chart makes a lower low but the MACD makes a higher low, it is a buy indication. The MACD for the five-minute chart of the contract in **Figure 5.4a** shows a divergence as the price makes a lower low, but

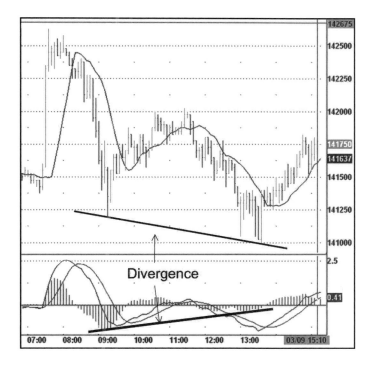

FIGURE 5.4a

MACD—Price/Indicator Divergence

Source: eSignal

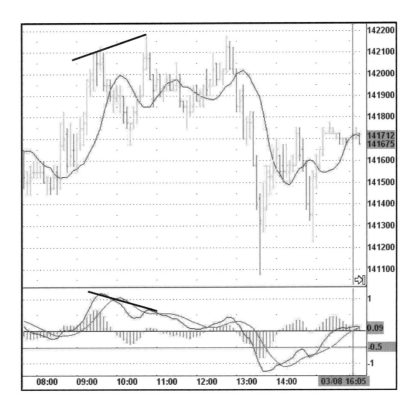

FIGURE **5.4b**

MACD—Price/Indicator Divergence

Source: eSignal

the histogram makes a higher low at 1:20 p.m., which correctly forecasts a rally at the end of the session.

A divergence occurs in the MACD plotted on the five-minute chart for that market in **Figure 5.4b** at 10:35 a.m. as the price makes a higher high and the MACD makes a lower high on both the line plot and the histogram bars. Resistance is tested just before 1:00 p.m. after the first decline, followed by a more dramatic 10-point sell off.

The chart in **Figure 5.5a** shows a crossing buy indication at 10:45 a.m. followed by a 10-point rally. The crossing sell indication at 12:50 p.m. correctly predicts a 7.5-point dip. Potential profit per contract, if both signals

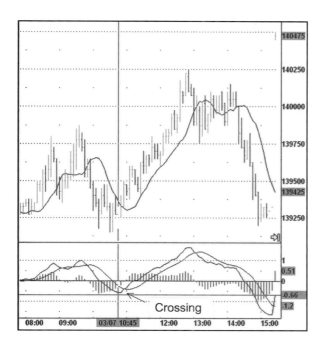

FIGURE **5.5a**

MACD—Crossing on Indicator

Source: eSignal

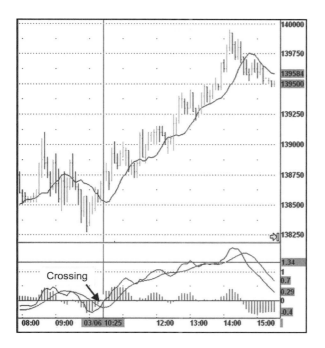

FIGURE **5.5b**

MACD—Crossing on Indicator

Source: eSignal

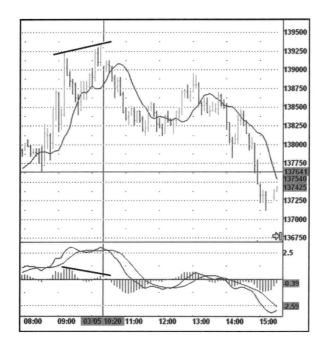

FIGURE **5.6a**

MACD—Price/Indicator Divergence

Source: eSignal

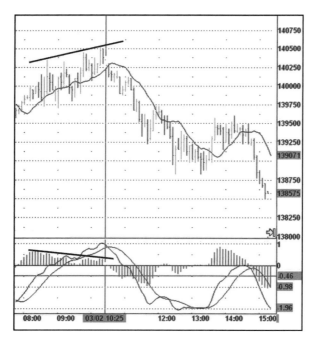

FIGURE **5.6b**

MACD—Price/Indicator Divergence

Source: eSignal

were traded, would have been near 17.5 points, which at $50 a point would mean $875.

The buy crossing indication for that market on the chart in **Figure 5.5b** correctly forecasts the bullish trend for the day; however, there are a number of false sell crossing signals as the market merely pauses without opportunity for significant profit on the short side, and the overall pattern is a narrow upward sloping channel.

An effective divergence sell indication is clear in the chart in **Figure 5.6a** as the price makes a higher high while the MACD line plot and histogram bars make a lower high at 10:20 a.m. The forecasted tip is 17.5 points.

A 7-point dip is correctly forecasted by the divergence on the chart in **Figure 5.6b** as the price makes a higher high and the MACD histogram bars make a lower high at 10:25 a.m., resulting in a total down move of 7 points, which translates into $350 per contract.

The Price Rate-of-Change (ROC) indicator as seen in the chart for S&P 500 E-mini futures in **Figure 5.7** displays the difference between the current price and the price a select number of time periods ago. The difference can be displayed

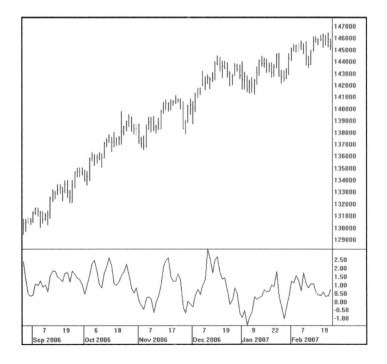

FIGURE 5.7

Rate-of-Change Indicator

Source: eSignal

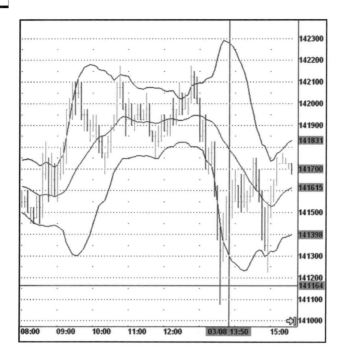

FIGURE 5.8a

Bollinger Bands

Source: eSignal

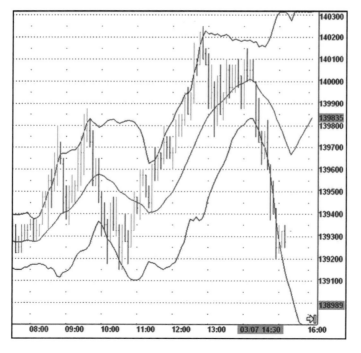

FIGURE 5.8b

Bollinger Bands

Source: eSignal

either in points or as a percentage. It is a centered oscillator that also fluctuates above and below the zero horizontal line. A ten-day ROC, which is the parameter used in the plot in Figure 5.7, measures the percentage price change over the last ten days, which means a higher value for a greater change in price. Increases in price result in positive readings on the indicator (above zero), whereas decreases in price result in negative readings (below zero). As a centered oscillator, ROC has shortcomings with respect to identifying overbought/oversold markets, in comparison with banded oscillators like RSI and fast and slow stochastics, so by combining it with those other indicators a better indication can be had.

Bollinger bands are a price envelope plotted around the price bars on a chart, based on a simple moving average as the base and standard deviation calculations for the width of the band. **Figure 5.8a** is a five-minute chart of the S&P 500 E-mini futures with Bollinger bands plotted. Note how the width between the upper and lower bands expands and contracts with volatility, being extremely narrow between 10:30 a.m. and 12:30 p.m. and then expanding dramatically down after 1:00 p.m. As the price extended beyond the bands with that downward spike, it would be ideal to see other signs of a bounce to confirm a buying opportunity.

Figure 5.8b is another five-minute chart of the S&P 500 futures with Bollinger bands plotted. As the price hugged the upper band on the rally into the noon hour, it penetrated the band twice, then failed to reach the upper band around 2 p.m., indicating signs of a change in sentiment and weakness of the rally. The market then sold off precipitously, retracing nearly the entire day's range.

Combining Indicators

Experienced traders use a combination of noncorrelated indicators to provide additional confirmation of a buy or sell indication on any single indicator. Combining too many indicators, however, is not a good idea (for example, twenty or thirty different ones). You would do better to choose a handful (preferably in the range of three to five) that are dissimilar. (Indicators that are similar will not serve to complement one another.) The next series of charts show some trade setups using such an approach, with a minimum of four separate indicator signals in tandem as the rule of thumb. The main indication is that the difference between the price and an eight-bar moving average plotted three bars ahead is more than a certain number of ticks (which value depends on the particular market). A moving average of the low and the high is plotted and the

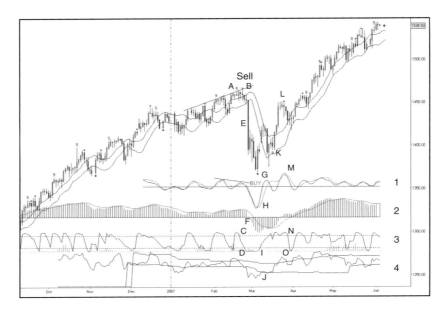

FIGURE **5.9**

Daily Chart with Multiple Indicators

Source: Wave59

difference between the high and the moving average of the low, and the low and the moving average of the high is calculated. **Figure 5.9** illustrates this indication on a daily chart of the E-mini S&P 500 futures.

The main indicator (as just mentioned) is the price reaching an extreme high (at least 10 full points) above an eight-bar moving average of the low projected three bars ahead (or reaching an extreme low below the same forward-projected moving average of the high). The third indicator from the top is a Lomb periodogram (3), which is a type of Fourier transform used to filter out noise in cycles. It is used widely in various disciplines, including the field of astronomy. The noise filter is the histogram at the bottom of the indicator. When the vertical bars become active by spiking higher, it means the signals provided by the line plot should be ignored. When the line crosses over the lower horizontal dotted line, it is a buy indication. Conversely, when the line crosses under the upper dotted line it is a sell indication. The numbers plotted along the candlestick bars constitute the proprietary 9-5 indicator invented by the creator of Wave59, Earik Beann. Although not visible in the shades of gray shown here, the 9 is either blue for buy indications or red for sell indications. The 5 is gold and is a reversal indication. The dots are part of Beann's exhaustion bars, with buy indications from those plotted below a bar and sell indications from those plotted above a bar.

The indicator at the top, just under the price candle bars, is Beann's Predict indicator (1), which uses a neural net to optimize the ultrasmooth momentum curve (or any other indicator on which you choose to run the Predict algorithm). The curve is plotted along with another plot that projects where the momentum will be a few bars ahead. It provides reversal signals when there is a crossover when the two lines plotted are at an extreme from the horizontal centerline.

The second indicator from the top is the MACD (2).

Finally, the indicator at the bottom is the adaptive zones (4), which are an optimized RSI that is sensitized to short-term volatility. The line plot crosses under the top horizontal line when the strength of a rally is waning and above the lower horizontal line when the strength of a decline is waning. With the exception of the main indicator, price/moving average divergence, and the 9-5 count, these are all lagging indicators. In other words, the market has already begun its reversal of direction by the time they are plotted on the screen.

The first signal marked on the chart in Figure 5.9 is a sell near the end of February 2007. A golden 5 (A) on the 9-5 count is conjoined with an exhaustion bars dot (B), a crossing on the Lomb periodogram (C), a crossing on the adaptive zones plot (D), and a price/indicator divergence on the Predict/ultrasmooth momentum curve (higher highs on the price and lower highs on the indicator). Note the rising channel formation on the chart. The price touches the top of the channel with the appearance of a couple of spinning top candles (just after the 5 over the prices). The breakout below the lower boundary of the channel is the final confirmation of the signal. The crossing of the MACD histogram below the centerline comes too late to be part of the setup for a trade.

A buy signal then occurs in early March 2007 with an extreme divergence of more than 65 full points between the price and moving average of the high. There is a buy indication on the exhaustion bars (G) (dot below the price candle), a crossing on the ultrasmooth momentum Predict indicator (H), and crossings on the Lomb periodogram (I) and adaptive zones (J). Lagging confirmation comes in mid-March after a pullback with a 9 on the 9-5 count (K) and a crossing above the centerline on the MACD indicator. The next sell indications near the end of March provide a level for exiting any long positions with a substantial profit: divergence between price and the moving average of the low of more than 50 full points, exhaustion bar [(L) dot over the price candle] and crossings on the Predict/ultrasmooth momentum indicator (M), Lomb periodogram (N), and adapative zones (O).

Indicators Across Multiple Time Frames

A powerful approach to using multiple indicators is to apply them across multiple time frames. **Figure 5.10** is a four-minute chart of the E-mini S&P 500 futures, and **Figure 5.11** is a one-minute chart of the same market for the same period. The indicators plotted are the same as those in the daily chart in Figure 5.9. Both time frames had sell indications just after 9:00 a.m. on June 1. On the one-minute chart there was a price/moving average differential (between the high and the moving average of the low) of more than fourteen ticks with divergence between price and two of the indicators: higher highs on the price (A) with lower highs on the Predict (B) and MACD (C). There was also a sell indication on the exhaustion bars [(D) dot over the candle] along with downward crossings of the upper horizontal line on the Lomb periodogram (E) and adaptive zones (F). On the

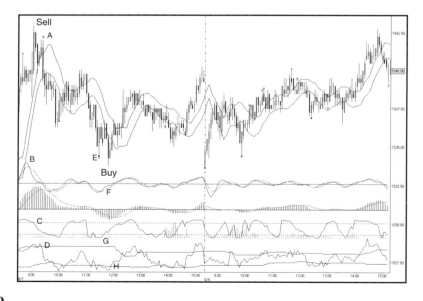

FIGURE 5.10

Four-Minute Chart with Multiple Indicators

Source: Wave59

four-minute chart, there was a sell indication on the 9-5 count [(A) a 9 above the candle] along with crossings on the Predict (B), Lomb periodogram (C), and adaptive zones (D).

A buy indication came in both time frames later in the session just before noon. On the one-minute chart there was a price/moving average differential (between the low and the moving average of the high). In addition, there was price/indicator divergence [lower lows on the price (G) and higher lows on the Predict (H) and MACD (I)], a buy indication on the 9-5 count (5 under the candle), and a crossing over the lower horizontal line on the Lomb periodogram (J). On the four-minute chart, there were buy indications on the exhaustion bars (E) and 9-5 count (E) and crossings on the Predict (F), Lomb periodogram (G), and adaptive zones (H).

Using the four-minute time frame indications to confirm signals on the one-minute time frame serves to reduce the number of trades while at the same time increasing the win/loss ratio. Fewer trades means less work for the trader, along with less stress overall. It is, therefore, advantageous to apply the set of chosen indicators to more than one time frame.

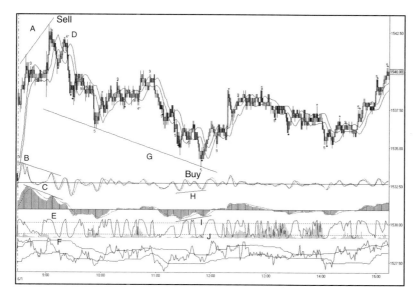

FIGURE 5.11

One-Minute Chart with Multiple Indicators

Source: Wave59

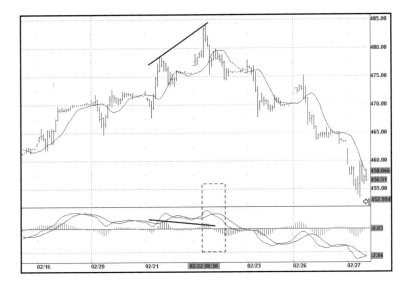

FIGURE **5.12**

Thirty-Minute Chart with MACD Indicator

Source: eSignal

An indicator in multiple time frames is considered to be a more reliable tool than one only in a single time frame. **Figure 5.12** is a chart of Google stock with the MACD indicator on a thirty-minute intraday chart. There is divergence between the price (higher highs) and the indicator histogram (lower highs) and a sell indication with the crossing of the lines.

Figure 5.13 is a daily chart on Google stock showing a similar pattern with the MACD in the longer-term time frame. This provides some additional confirmation that the pattern is valid as an indication.

Figure 5.14 is the same chart and MACD as a weekly chart, which uses an even longer-term time frame. The same pattern indicating a short bias is present, although the divergence between price and MACD is much less pronounced (yet still in evidence). Filtering trades through multiple time frames will have the net effect of increasing the reliability of an individual indicator. Using multiple noncorrelated indicators across multiple time frames should be the ultimate approach, in order to achieve the optimum reliability in a confluence of indicators from the trading toolbox.

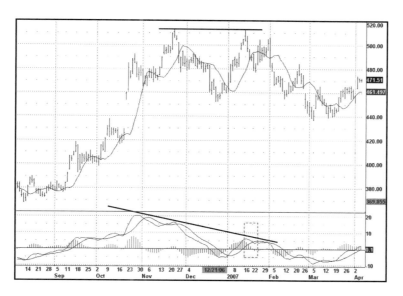

FIGURE **5.13**

Daily Chart with MACD

Source: eSignal

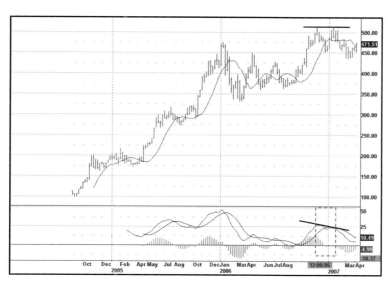

FIGURE **5.14**

Weekly Chart with MACD

Source: eSignal

Astrology as an Indicator

People have been using astrology in an attempt to predict future events for centuries. In the twentieth and twenty-first centuries, market analysts began using it to make trading decisions. There are various systems of astrology from various cultures around the globe. There is the Western system upon which daily horoscope columns in American newspapers are predicated. The Chinese have their own system, and there was another system developed in ancient India, called *jyotish*, which is Sanskrit for "eye of Veda." The Vedas are the ancient texts of the Hindu faith, and their various limbs, or Vedangas, included astrology and other disciplines such as medicine (Ayurveda). In the Vedic astrology system, planetary strengths are weighted for a natal chart (horoscope) based on their position in the sky. Earik Beann at Wave59 Technologies has charted those astrological calculations for a horoscope of the S&P 500 futures contract using the time it began trading as its "birthday" (**Figure 5.15**). Those are plotted beneath a daily price chart for the contract. The lightly shaded rectangles mark bullish indications and the dark rectangles mark bearish indications. Straight lines are plotted between the bullish and

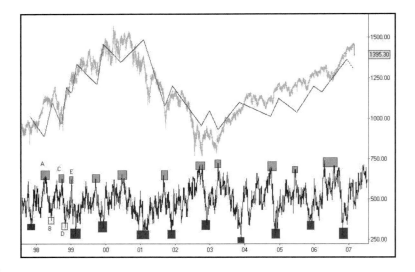

FIGURE **5.15**

Planetary Strength

Source: Wave59

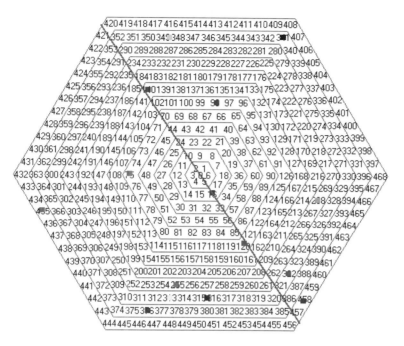

FIGURE **5.16**

Gann Hexagram

Source: Wave59

bearish indications, in order to see more easily the correlations between those indications and long-term price trends. Although it is not a timing mechanism of razor precision, it does appear to have tremendous value overall in predicting the occurrence of market tops and bottoms.

Another astrological feature of the Wave59 charting package is the Gann Hexagram, which is based on a chart W.D. Gann used with his Square of Nine number sequence in a six-sided layout. Earik Beann has plotted the longitudes of the Sun, Moon, and planets on the hexagram and connected alignments between them with lines. In **Figure 5.16**, there is an alignment of longitudes for the Sun and Mars on the hexagram. The dates of those alignments are useful as a timing mechanism for potential reversals in price trend.

Figure 5.17 is a daily chart of IBM stock with the Sun and Mars Gann Hexagram alignment dates marked with arrows. Market turning points occur

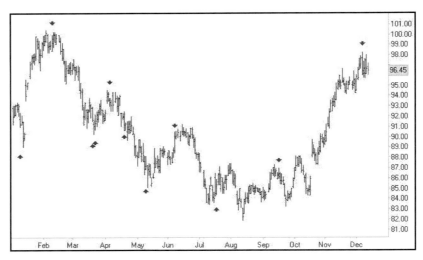

FIGURE **5.17**

Gann Hexagram Alignments of Sun and Mars: IBM Sun/Mars

Source: Wave59

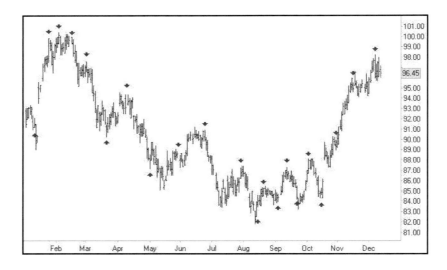

FIGURE **5.18**

Gann Hexagram Alignments of Venus and Mars: IBM Mars/Venus (Helio)

Source: Wave59

more often than not on or near those dates for that entire year. The trader would look to those turning points as opportunities to either get long in the case of the end to a downswing or to get short in the case of an end to an upswing.

Figure 5.18 is the same chart for IBM with the alignments of Venus and Mars on the Gann Hexagram, but this time with heliocentric positions utilized (planetary longitudes from the point of reference of the center of the Sun instead of an observer's position on the surface of Earth). Some of the same market turning points are pinpointed, along with a few others that are not found in the analysis in Figure 5.17. As with the preceding example, these are excellent opportunities for taking either long or short positions, depending on which direction is forecasted.

Conclusion

In preparing your personal recipe for indicator soup, it is wise to choose your ingredients carefully and ensure they complement one another. Just as putting too much of one spice will overpower the flavor of soup from the kitchen, using indicators that are closely correlated will result in an unbalanced analysis. A smaller number of indicators is preferable to an unwieldy large number, in order to provide a manageable approach to spotting buy and sell indications. Indicators should always be used in the context of market conditions and the overall chart patterns. They should be an adjunct to your technical and fundamental analysis, rather than your primary tools.

Summary of Chapter 5

- Using a single indicator is problematic, due to inherent weaknesses on account of varying market conditions. Any one indicator will perform better in a bracketed market while underperforming in a trending market (or vice versa).
- Certain indicators work best in trending markets, while other indicators work best in nontrending or bracketed markets.
- Selection of a set of indicators should be based on noncorrelated types and be of a manageable number (three to five should be adequate).
- Applying indicators across multiple time frames is advantageous for purposes of reducing the number of trades and increasing the win/loss ratio.

CHAPTER 6

The Market As a Wave Phenomenon

Waves are a subject of poets as well as physicists. In poetry, sounds of the surf and amber waves of grain speak to us of natural phenomena that ebb and flow with some rhythm that we find soothing or hypnotic. Scientists describe patterns in matter and energy, such as light or sound, in terms of their wavelike behavior.

To characterize market price activity as wavelike in nature is an analyst's means of applying the concept of waves to financial markets, which are a domain distinct from the subject matter of poets and scientists. The major difference is that it requires an abstraction from the physical auction of market transactions. Such abstractions come in the form of charts constructed by market technicians to record historical daily, weekly, monthly, and intraday prices. The advantage to charting prices and describing what those charts reveal as resembling either waves or some other familiar shapes is that it provides a tangible basis for recurring patterns that traders use to give them a probabilistic edge in their strategies.

To attempt to discern any patterns among raw price data, that is, transactions involving financial products changing hands in that peculiar type of auction found in those markets, would be virtually impossible for most people. That is because those transactions are just a series of number sets: quantity at price at time. Charting those transactions in a graphical representation is like connecting the dots to make them reveal some continuity as opposed to being a collection of disjointed events that otherwise have no relation to one another. It is price charts that render wave patterns visible. Such waves are not going to be readily apparent upon looking at the raw transactional data, which are a series of quantities and prices in chronological order. Charting makes the waves apparent.

The wave theories of Nikolai Kondratieff and Ralph Nelson Elliott inspired me to delve into research on cycles and prices. Elliott Wave has become a household word for many market technicians; however, it has remained a somewhat esoteric analysis technique. Unlike with mathematical models or indicators that leave no room for interpretation, the accurate counting of waves in their proper sequence relies entirely on the advanced skill of the analyst.

A wave is composed of a series of legs. Each leg of a wave is essentially a price trajectory in a single direction from point A (earlier in time) to point B (later in time). Complete waves are of two types: impulse[1] and corrective.[2] An impulse wave is always in the direction of the market's overall trend and a corrective wave, as its name indicates, is always counter to the trend. The impulse wave in an uptrend has five legs, consisting of a leg up (1), a leg down (2), a leg up (3), a leg down (4), and a final leg up (5). The corrective wave in an uptrend has three legs, consisting of a leg down (A), a leg up (B), and a final leg down (C). The impulse wave in a downtrend has five legs, consisting of a leg down (1), a leg up (2), a leg down (3), a leg up (4), and a final leg down (5). The corrective wave in a downtrend has three legs, consisting of a leg up (A), a leg down (B), and a final leg up (C). Michael Kahn[3] aptly describes the wave components (legs, or as he refers to them, waves) of the impulse plus corrective wave formation in an uptrend.

John Murphy's[4] description has a few more details than Kahn's, as well as some differences. Leg 1 is characterized by a shift in outlook from bearish to bullish at a market bottom or from bullish to bearish at a market top. This leg is typically the shortest of the five legs of a complete impulse wave. It may not be apparent as the beginning of a new wave as analysts are deceived into thinking it is a mere rebound from an extreme low or high price level.

Leg 2 is marked by its retracing of the price swing of Leg 1, which could be a percentage of that range or the entire range. The retracement is caused by either short covering near a top or long liquidation near a bottom. This leg often completes a head and shoulders top or bottom pattern as first half of the right shoulder.

Leg 3 is more often than not the longest of the five legs in the impulse wave with stocks, and must not be the shortest of the legs. Momentum picks up considerably during this leg. It serves to confirm the establishment of the new major or minor trend as something more significant than mere balancing within

1. A.J. Frost and Robert R. Prechter, *Elliott Wave Principle*, (New Classics Library, 1995), pp. 32–34.

2. Ibid, pp. 21–24.

3. Michael N. Kahn, *Technical Analysis Plain and Simple* (Financial Times Prentice Hall, 2006), pp. 267–268.

4. John J. Murphy, *Technical Analysis of the Futures Markets: A Comprehensive Guide to Trading Methods and Applications* (Prentice Hall, 1986), pp. 378–379.

a bracketed range. This leg is typically characterized by high volume and the appearance of gaps on the chart. Participants of many different time frames take positions and fuel the building momentum that serves to extend this leg.

As Leg 2 does with Leg 1, Leg 4 retraces part of the move of Leg 3, but must not reach as far as the range of Leg 1. Leg 4 is characterized by consolidation activity, including triangular patterns.

Leg 5 is usually the longest of the five legs with futures prices. It is characterized by divergences between oscillator-type indicators and prices, which serve to further confirm that the overall trend is reaching its logical conclusion prior to an imminent correction in the form of the following ABC corrective wave.

Leg A, the initial leg of a corrective wave, is typically characterized by its containment of five sub-legs in a mini-impulse wave formation, which serves to distinguish it from a mere pullback in the prevailing trend.

Leg B, which retraces all or a percentage of Leg A, is typically characterized

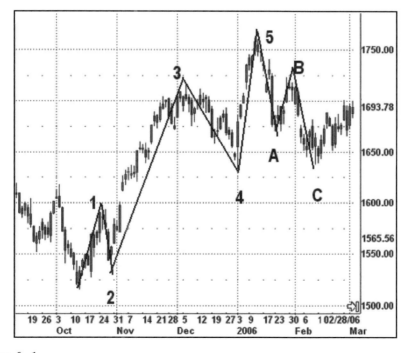

FIGURE 6.1

Elliott Wave on Daily Chart

Source: eSignal

by low volume. This leg may even extend beyond the extreme of Leg 5 of the prior impulse wave.

Leg C is characterized by penetration of levels of support and extends into the range of Leg 3 of the prior impulse wave. This leg often extends beyond the range of Leg A, and it may complete the right shoulder of a head and shoulders top or bottom formation.

An example of a complete impulse/corrective wave sequence is shown in **Figure 6.1**, which is a daily bar chart of the Nasdaq-100 Index for 2005–2006.

Waves are usually composed of smaller waves, and those smaller waves in turn are composed of even smaller waves all the way down to the smallest waves that

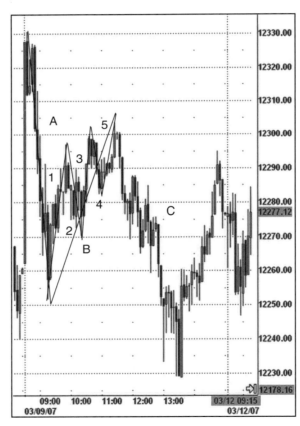

FIGURE **6.2**

Elliott Wave on Five-Minute Chart

Source: eSignal

can be found on intraday charts (for example, one-minute bar or candlestick charts). Elliott Wave patterns emerge on charts of various time frames. **Figure 6.2** is a five-minute chart of the Dow. A clear corrective wave has formed, with an A leg down, a B leg up, and a C leg down. The B leg up contains an impulse wave as marked with the numbers 1 to 5.

Figure 6.3 is a weekly chart of the Dow. A clear impulse wave pattern is discernable marked with numbers 1 to 5. Note that Legs 2 and 4 contain corrective A-B-C patterns.

Wave cycles in Elliott's scheme vary in length from the smallest subminuette, which is only a few hours long, to the Grand Supercycle of two centuries'

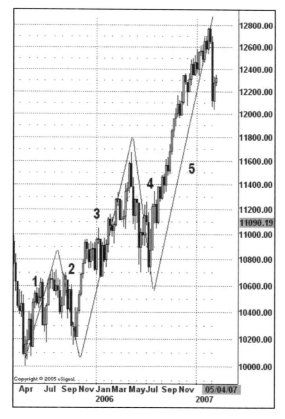

FIGURE **6.3**

Elliott Wave on Weekly Chart

Source: eSignal

duration. Murphy demonstrates how Elliott Waves are based upon Fibonacci's famous series:

> Each wave subdivides into waves of one lesser degree, which in turn can also be subdi-
> vided into waves of even lesser degree. It also follows then that each wave is itself part
> of the wave of the next higher degree.[5]

The first level of subdivision is done by taking the 1-2-3-4-5-A-B-C wave cycle and subdividing each of its legs as follows: Leg 1 as a 12345 subcycle, Leg 2 as an ABC subcycle, Leg 3 as a 12345 subcycle, Leg 4 as an ABC subcycle, Leg 5 as a 12345 subcycle, Leg A as a 12345 subcycle, Leg B as an ABC subcycle, and Leg C as a 12345 subcycle. Further subdividing each leg of the main cycle by drilling down from the cycle as a whole to its subparts and subdividing the smallest subparts further in the same schema generates a sequence of 1-2-3-5-8-13-21-34-55-89-144. Based on that means of subdividing waves according to the Fibonacci sequence, a correction must take place in three waves rather than five. There are other applications of Fibonacci to Elliott Wave theory. Murphy also discusses the Fibonacci retracement ratios that come into play with waves that retrace other waves in a cycle. Such ratios are utilized to effectively project the extent of a wave's legs.

A variation of the impulse wave that has a count to seven instead of to five can be seen in **Figure 6.4**, which is a monthly chart of the Dow. A corrective A-B-C wave follows.

The size of a wave's leg is measured by change in both price and time. A long leg could be caused either by a huge change in price over a short period of time or a slight change in price over a long period of time, or even by a drastic change in price over a long period of time. It is the length of the leg on the chart that matters as far as its relative size in relation to other legs. Measuring the length of wave legs is a key factor in the identification of Elliott Wave patterns. According to Elliott's theory, the third leg in a five-leg impulse wave cannot be the shortest leg of the wave. The application of that rule serves to filter out ambiguity with reference to the counting of wave components in many wave patterns. That is because often it is not clear at first glance whether a wave pattern is an impulsive or corrective wave cycle. If the third leg of a

---

5. Ibid., p. 375.

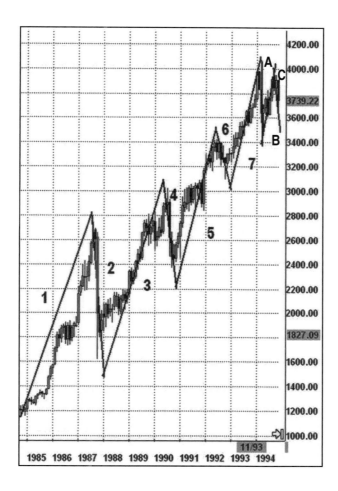

FIGURE 6.4

Elliott Wave on Monthly Chart

Source: eSignal

cycle is the shortest leg or the fourth leg extends into the range of the first leg, then it is a clear sign of being on the wrong track. Naturally, one problem with applying that rule is that it requires near completion of the entire cycle when the third leg is the shortest leg at the beginning of the fourth or fifth leg, because then you must wait to see if the fourth leg or even the final fifth leg proves to be the shortest leg of the cycle.

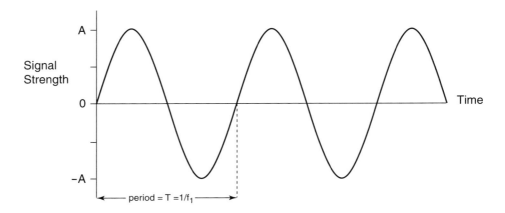

FIGURE **6.5**

Sine Wave

Elliott Wave analysis on intraday charts, as opposed to daily, weekly, or monthly charts, requires excluding inactive periods in twenty-four-hour electronic markets, because those will distort any patterns that are forming. In the case of U.S. financial markets, for example, the regular exchange hours should be used.

Sometimes wave patterns occur in nontrending sideways markets. Because there is no identifiable trend with such waves, they cannot be categorized as either impulsive or correctional. The market is simply bouncing back and forth within a narrow trading range. These periods are simply phases within a trend, and they may occur at the end of an impulse or corrective wave or in the middle of one of those patterns.

Markets exhibit another form of wave phenomena. Many classical chart patterns follow the contours of sine waves, which are used in many different branches of mathematics and science. A plot of a sine wave is shown in **Figure 6.5**. The amplitude is plotted vertically along the y-axis (marked as signal strength in the graphic) and time is plotted horizontally from left to right along the x-axis. The equation for the simplest form of a sine wave is:

$$y = A \sin(\omega t - \varphi)$$

which describes a wavelike function of time (t) with:

● peak deviation from center = A (also known as amplitude)
● angular frequency ω (radians per second)
● initial phase (t = 0) = −φ
    ■ φ is also referred to as a phase shift; for example, when the initial phase is negative, the entire waveform is shifted toward future time (that is, delayed). The amount of delay, in seconds, is φ/ ω.

This wave pattern occurs often in nature, including ocean waves, sound waves, and light waves.[6] The sine wave depicted in Figure 6.5 has a fixed amplitude, and markets that trade sideways without direction in a channel resemble such a pattern. When markets form triangle patterns on charts, they resemble sine waves where the amplitude decreases or increases. Other variations are sloping sine wave patterns of constant or varying amplitude such as flags, wedges, and pennants.

The daily chart of the Dow in **Figure 6.6** shows a sine wave pattern with decreasing amplitude that forms a triangle. If viewed as a wave pattern rather than a pattern that is bounded by a triangle, the fact that the amplitude of the wave is decreasing over time is an indication to the technical analyst that prices are continuing to consolidate into a range that is tightening. If the pattern occurs after an established trend has been under way, a breakout either in the opposite (or perhaps same) direction of the prevailing trend should be expected. Whether called a waveform or a triangle, the same market behavior of taking a pause in anticipation of the next swing one way or the other is in play.

Figure 6.7 is of a flag pattern on a daily chart of the Dow. The sine wave contours have constant amplitude, so the downward-slanting channel it follows is parallel between the upper and lower boundaries of its path. If the wave pattern is broken by prices extending beyond those boundaries, then the trader would look to trade in the direction of the breakout, especially if there is a concomitant surge in volume.

---

6. Also, a rough sinusoidal (inverse cosine) pattern can be seen in plotting average daily temperatures for each day of the year, although the graph may resemble an inverted cosine wave. In 1822, Joseph Fourier, a French mathematician, discovered that sinusoidal waves can be used as simple building blocks to "make up" and describe any periodic waveform. The process is named Fourier series, which is a useful analytical tool in signal processing theory.

FIGURE 6.6

Sine Wave Pattern in Triangle Pattern

Source: eSignal

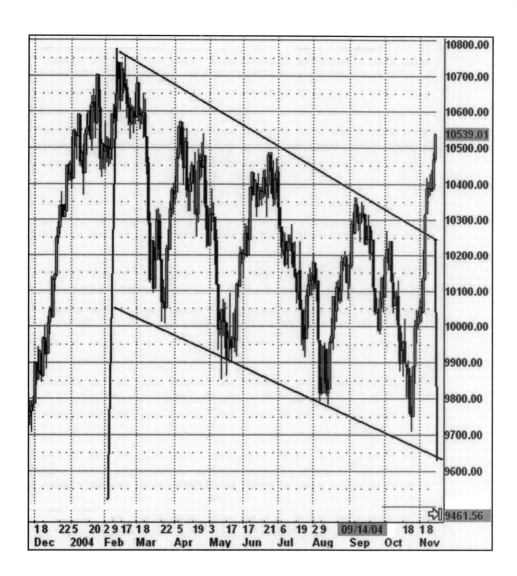

FIGURE **6.7**

Sine Wave in Flag Pattern

Source: eSignal

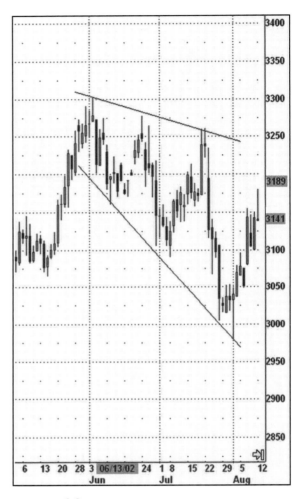

FIGURE **6.8**

Sine Wave in Pennant Pattern

Source: eSignal

FIGURE **6.9**

Sine Wave with Increasing Amplitude

Source: eSignal

A pennant formation is visible in the daily chart of the Dow in **Figure 6.8**. The sine wave has decreasing amplitude and follows an upward-slanting path. As discussed in Chapter 3, pennants are typically reversal patterns that signal the end to a price trend and the beginning of a countertrend.

A wedge pattern on the gold futures daily chart is visible in **Figure 6.9**. The sine wave has increasing amplitude and follows a downward-slanting path. The extremes of the price bracket are being extended, which is an indication of underlying market forces that are causing an increase in volatility. A potential breakout in one direction or the other is to be expected.

Conclusion

The markets are clearly not the same thing as standing air columns that propagate sound waves or large bodies of water that propagate surface crests and troughs. Nonetheless, they repeatedly display price swings that can be described as rhythmic and that cause the appearance of waves on price charts. There is a simple explanation for such phenomena: When prices reach extremes beyond perceived value, they inevitably retreat from those unsustainable levels to return to levels of accepted value. That price action and its four phases are discussed in detail in the section on Market Profile charts in Chapter 4. Technical analysts have effectively employed Elliott Wave theory to map out and project price trends of any duration, although mastery of the application of that theory is much more difficult than that of the techniques discussed in the previous three chapters.

Summary of Chapter 6
- An Elliott impulse wave has five subwaves or legs as the components of a minor or major trend.
- An Elliott corrective wave has three subwaves or legs as the components of a market correction of a major or minor trend.
- Elliott impulse and corrective waves contain smaller waves within each of their legs at shorter time frames and they are part of larger waves at longer time frames.
- Fibonacci sequences and ratios are used by many technical analysts in conjunction with Elliott Wave theory, particularly to project the extent of wave components.

CHAPTER 7

Leveraging Derivatives

Most average investors know little or nothing about derivatives markets, and thus are unequipped to use sophisticated strategies in trading. Buying and holding equities, bonds, and funds is what they generally do, and few even use stop-loss orders. They wait too long after a market slide to get out, and then half the time the market shoots right back up soon after they exit their positions. Even the majority of retail securities brokers are far from expert when it comes to derivatives. They are truly the domain of institutional and professional individual traders.

Many people shy away from markets they are unable to fathom out of fear of the great risks they perceive will bankrupt them in a heartbeat. They do not have a handle on sound risk-management principles in general and really should stick to fixed-rate instruments and money market accounts. They are taking enough risk on adjustable rate mortgages as it is. With a little study, though, most derivatives instruments can be understood by just about anyone.

Derivatives are used by investors large and small. When asked whether derivatives were materially changing in terms of their impact on the global and domestic market circa 1995, investing guru George Soros replied in the affirmative, although his own use of such instruments is very limited:

> They are. A lot of new and more esoteric instruments have been brought into existence. There has been a remarkable shift of the terrain as far as derivatives are concerned. It is an appropriate area for investigation. If, for example, you look at recently developed instruments that separate interest from principal, they are very interesting instruments.[1]

---

1. George Soros, *Soros on Soros, Staying Ahead of the Curve* (John Wiley & Sons, 1995), pp. 320–321.

Derivatives have their place in the portfolios of investors and traders who are comfortable with a high risk/high reward profile. The reason for the increased risk attendant with increased profit potential of a derivative over its underlying instrument is leverage rather than volatility. Derivatives are not any more volatile than the cash markets from which they are derived. In fact, they are usually much less volatile. For example, the premium of a stock option can never fluctuate as much as the stock price itself. Therefore, its volatility is never equal to the stock's volatility. Commodities never see the type of short-term price changes that equities often undergo on news that drastically affects perceived value of shares in any given publicly held company.

A futures contract, or forward contract, is a binding agreement to buy or sell a fixed amount and grade (if it is a physical commodity as opposed to a financial instrument such as a Treasury security) of a raw material or financial product with a fixed future delivery date. The futures exchange matches buyers and sellers in those markets, and a clearing entity that is a member broker of the exchange guarantees their transactions. In the United States, those markets were created in the nineteenth century to allow agricultural producers a means to protect themselves from events that could be catastrophic to their enterprise, such as wars, droughts, floods, and the like. In recent decades, futures products were created for precious and industrial metals, interest-rate instruments, stock indexes, and foreign currencies. The financial futures products, also known as intangibles, have supplanted the physical commodities as the flagship contracts with daily volume that is surpassed by only that of the NYSE and international foreign currency exchange markets. There are far more outstanding shares in equities and interest-rate securities than ounces of gold or silver in the world supply or bushels of grain sitting in silos and elevators, which would explain the popularity of intangibles. Another reason is that large financial institutions use these products on a regular basis.

A futures contract is also referred to as a "lot" or "car." The term "car" originates from the contract sizes that were a function of how much of a raw commodity would fit into a standard-size railroad boxcar, which is five thousand bushels of grain (the amounts vary for other commodities). Virtually no futures traders actually make or take delivery of the underlying commodity or instrument. The objective of making the trade is to either hedge against the risk of dealing in the cash market or to speculate with the goal of making a profit on price changes over time (provided the trader is clever enough to beat the odds against him as a small speculator).

Futures are highly leveraged markets. The margin required to trade them is typically 2 percent to 5 percent of the market value of the underlying cash instrument. If 100 percent margin were required, it would be extremely difficult to realize an appreciable rate of return on trades. On the other hand, the inherent risk would be greatly diminished. The element of high risk simply goes with the territory when it comes to leverage. If you want the potential for great short-term profit, you must be willing to assume great risk. For that reason, it is recommended that only risk capital be used for trading in derivatives. Risk capital means that losing the entire amount will not cause financial ruin for the trader. They will not lose their house nor will they be forced to file for bankruptcy if they lose their risk capital. Unfortunately, that message does not always sink in, and many a trader does find himself in dire straits when he ends up on the wrong side of a big market swing.

The mechanics of futures trading are slightly different from those of the stock market. As in stock trading, there are market and limit orders in futures, although stock traders typically do not use market orders (at least not if they know what they are doing). Instead, they will favor limit orders to avoid getting filled at an undesirable price. Futures traders, on the other hand, frequently use market orders. That is a consequence of the increased leverage. What would be a small price fluctuation over a short period of time in the cash market becomes quite a big move on a futures contract. Not getting filled on a limit order when the trader needs to either get into or out of a position as soon as possible is simply not acceptable. If the operator of a grain elevator can sell five thousand bushels of corn for two cents higher per bushel than the price at which he has purchased it, it means a profit of $100, which means a 2 percent rate of return. If a speculator profits from the same price increase on one corn contract with a margin requirement of $200, it means a 50 percent increase in trading capital. If some government report causes a four-cent-per-bushel drop in the market price of corn as a result of higher-than-expected crop yields from a recent harvest, the grain elevator operator takes a small loss. On the other hand, a futures speculator who is long has his margin on hand completely wiped out, and if the market drops further from there, he will receive a margin call from his brokerage firm to wire more money to deposit in his account to hold his long market position.

Leverage is a double-edged sword. It can make you suddenly rich or suddenly impoverished (if you recklessly stick your neck out too far). In futures you take either a long or short position. This means that if you buy first in anticipation of a price increase and then sell later, liquidating the position, you're playing the long side of the market. If you sell first in anticipation of a price decrease and then buy later, liquidating the position by "covering the short" or "buying back," you're playing the short side of the market. The only thing that matters is whether you successfully buy at a lower price than your selling price, not the chronological order in which the buying and selling are done.

To understand how that works, it helps to take time out of the equation, and that is functionally how it works when placing orders (whether it be electronically by computer or through a broker over the phone); one buys x contracts at a specific price or "at the market," or one sells y contracts at a specific price or "at the market." If the order opens a position upon being filled, it results in a long position if it is a buy order or a short position if it is a sell order. If the order closes an open position, then one is what is known as "flat," meaning having no position. Day traders always want to be flat at the close of a trading session. Because of their very short-term time frame and risk-management profile, holding a position overnight is precluded on account of the inordinate level of risk.

To place a futures order, four components are necessary: 1) the quantity; 2) the delivery month; 3) the instrument; and 4) the order type. For example, for a limit order on December wheat, an order might be "buying 10 Christmas 07 wheat at 4.20 and a quarter." "Christmas" is market slang for December delivery. Grain contracts are traded in minimum price increments of a quarter of a cent, which translates into $12.50 per five-thousand-bushel contract for each tick (minimum price increment). So the hypothetical limit order is for four dollars and twenty and a quarter cents per bushel. If the market is trading at the limit price or lower, then the order should be filled. Otherwise it will be considered to be unable, which means it is not capable of being filled at that time. The order can also be entered as "GTC," or good until cancelled, which means that it remains an open order until it can be filled or until the contract ends after its final delivery phase.

A sell stop order on the S&P 500 E-mini futures might be: "Selling 5 June 08 eminis at 1425.50 on a stop." As long as the market is trading at 1425.50 or higher the order is a "working" order, otherwise it is immediately rejected. Sell stop orders must be at a price at or below where the market is trading. If they happen to be right at the current market price, they will be filled at that price immediately, otherwise they will be filled as soon as they can be at whatever the price may be at the time of being filled (for that reason, stop orders are often filled at a slightly different price from the price on the order). Stop orders can be combined with limit orders in what are known as stop-limit orders, which effectively ensures that the order can be filled only at the price on the order or a better price. Better means at a lower price for a buy stop order or a higher price for a sell stop order.

Because not all orders are for the same size (quantity of contracts), and buy and sell orders have to be matched to generate a trade, multiple-lot futures orders often end up as split fills. For example, a 10 lot may have five contracts filled at one price, three contracts filled at another price, and two contracts filled at a third price. For big-volume traders that need to execute very large orders, this poses a logistics problem. They often need to split up their trades into several smaller orders that can be spaced apart in time over several hours or even days to get them filled at desirable price levels. Also, extremely large orders can easily move prices up in the case of a buy or down in the case of a sell, which could have a negative impact on a large trader placing such an order. Market liquidity can drop off quickly in extreme market conditions, known as "fast markets," which results in prices moving swiftly through many levels in one direction or maybe even in both directions in a very short period of time. This can be a problem for a trader using stop orders to limit losses on an open position. For that reason, experienced traders stand aside before scheduled reports, because the numbers in those reports can cause a reaction resulting in fast market conditions. For example, stock index and currency futures tend to experience price extremes when the minutes of regular meetings of the Federal Reserve Bank are announced, because changes in interest rates are critical to foreign exchange markets and share prices of publicly traded corporations.

Another important factor to take into consideration with futures markets is the jacked up transaction costs. No matter what the commission may be for buying and selling a contract (the "round turn" rate), that fee is multiplied by the number of contracts traded. If an active trader trades a thousand contracts in a year, then the costs will be the round turn rate times a thousand. Commissions are generally higher per trade than they are for discount commission rates on equities trades, on account of the combination of brokerage, exchange, National Futures Association (NFA), and electronic platform fees, which add up. As with anything else, volume commands a discount and the more contracts traded the lower the commission a trader is able to negotiate with his brokerage firm. Note that many retail futures brokers are not clearing members of exchanges, so they need to charge higher commissions as a markup of the costs they incur to clear the trades through a Futures Commission Merchant (FCM), which is an entity that clears trades as an exchange member. Dealing directly with a clearing member of the exchanges can very well mean a substantial savings in transaction costs, but, generally speaking, brokers who cater to smaller traders are going to charge more than those who confine themselves to large institutional and hedge clients. The ultimate means of getting the per trade costs down is to buy or rent a seat on a futures exchange. Members enjoy much lower fees than the general public, and they will be able to clear trades on the exchange without having to deal with a retail middleman. Purchasing or leasing a seat will be out of reach for many individual traders due to high purchase prices and monthly lease rates. Those not so well heeled may want to consider trading out of a trading arcade that can get them reduced commissions and fees and even provide them with additional trading capital.

Forex Market = High Leverage

Forex is by far the most heavily traded market in the world today, with its daily volume dwarfing all other markets by comparison. Originally, trading in currency pairs was open only to banks, but it was opened to the public in 1998. Forex contracts, known as lots, are for the "spot" (cash) market, although there are equivalent futures contracts also traded for most major world currencies including the euro, Swiss franc, Canadian dollar, Australian dollar, and Japanese yen. The main pairs are those against the U.S. dollar, but other combinations, known as exotics, such as euro/yen or yen/Australian dollar also are traded. Leverage in Forex markets is even greater than the leverage in futures: 100 to 1 for full-size contracts and 200 to 1 for the mini contracts.

Despite the minimum price tick being a hundredth of a cent on Forex contracts (which is the same as for futures), the very high leverage more than makes up for it. Forex dealers normally do not charge any commissions. The cost is built into each trade with the PIP (percentage in point) spread, which means the difference in the quoted price and what the trader will get on a filled order. If there is a two PIP spread, then the trader has to sacrifice two ticks or $25 at $12.50 a PIP. The PIP spread varies among Forex dealers, but many offer one PIP spreads to customers.

Forex always has been an entirely electronic market, so the trader will be expected to have a trading computer with a high-speed Internet connection at his disposal to trade through a Forex dealer. Many securities firms and futures brokerage houses have a Forex desk available to their customers. Setting up a

Forex account requires specific agreements and risk disclosure statements to be signed (that is the case with futures and options as well).

Options Markets = More Leverage with Better Control of Risk

There are options markets for stocks, futures, Forex, and swaps (the swapping of one instrument for another—options on them are known as "swaptions"). A call option is the option to purchase 100 shares (or one contract). A put option is the option to sell 100 shares (or one contract). The market against which an option can be exercised is called its "underlying" instrument.

For example, exercising a call option on a stock results in the purchase of 100 shares. Options (except for European-style options, the discussion of which is not within the scope of this book) have an expiration date and a strike price. They must be exercised before the expiration date. The strike price is the price at which they will be bought or sold at the settlement date. If the strike price of a call option on a stock is lower than the current market price of shares of the stock, then the option is said to be "in-the-money." If the strike price of the call is higher than the current share price, then it is an "out-of-the-money" option. Options that have a strike price equal to the current share price are called "at-the-money" options. The purchase price of an option is called its "premium." Premium has two components: Intrinsic value, which is a function of how much the option is in-the-money, and time value, which is a function of how much time is left before the expiration date.

One advantage options have over their underlying instruments is increased control over risk. That is because the most capital that is risked on an options trade is the premium paid for the option. In the case of futures, that makes a huge difference, considering that the downside risk on a futures trade is virtually unlimited. That luxury comes with a price, however. Options are wasting assets due to their time value constantly eroding.

Although one needs a margin account in which to trade options, the loss of money on long option trades never results in a margin call. That is because the premium paid for the option is debited from the trading account upon entering the trade, and that is all the capital that is needed to hold the position. Selling options short, or underwriting them, is a different story. The money received upon selling a put or call is immediately credited to the trading account, but huge risks remain. For that reason many individual traders are restricted in the types of options trades they are allowed to make in their margin accounts. If the investor's amount of risk capital and level of sophistication are inadequate, the brokerage house may not approve trading of any options at all for that investor.

Derivatives and Leverage

Derivatives markets provide much greater flexibility with respect to speculative strategies and hedging of risk. On the other hand, they carry a much greater level of responsibility on the part of a trader to guard against catastrophic losses. Too many traders jump into the fray without an adequate education in the nature of those markets. The allure of potentially high short-term rates of return can be extremely captivating. But there is a reason account forms for derivatives markets are loaded with scary clauses and paragraphs referencing the risks and stipulating that the brokerage house in no way guarantees profits from trades. Government agencies determined many years ago that such steps were necessary to adequately inform and protect the public. Only the most sophisticated traders armed with full knowledge of what they are embarking upon should even consider getting involved directly in derivatives trading. All others should probably just seek out suitable funds managed by professional traders, such as ETFs, into which to sink a portion of their risk capital. Futures, for example, can enhance the performance of a portfolio as a result of participation in a noncorrelated arena, but that is dependent upon levelheaded and conservative strategies that will not cause losses that outweigh profits from equities and other securities on the cash side of the ledger.

Gary Gorton and Geert Rouwenhorst[2] looked at commodity futures monthly returns over the period between July 1959 and March 2004 and concluded that there was clearly a negative correlation between equities/bonds and commodity futures. In this heralded, ground-breaking study, they were able to attribute that to inflation, which is positive for commodities although negative for stocks, as well as to differing performance over the business cycle.

Gorton and Rouwenhorst point out that correctly timing futures trades is critical, due to potential unforeseen changes in the underlying spot price prior to the delivery dates of the futures contracts, and this couldn't be more true.

---

2. Gary Gorton and K. Geert Rouwenhorst, *Facts and Fantasies About Commodity Futures* (NBER Working Papers 10595, National Bureau of Economic Research, 2004).

Speculators in futures markets will expect a discount on the future price against delivery in order to provide the liquidity for the commercials that are hedging in those markets to manage the risk of spot prices that impact their normal business operations. Gorton and Rouwenhorst refer to this as a "risk premium" paid by the commercial hedgers for the luxury of locking in a spot delivery price for the underlying instrument. Hence, for the speculative trader, it is the change in the futures price that determines profit or loss rather than changes in the cash price. The other difference is that commercial hedgers are fully collateralized on account of their cash position, whereas the speculative trader is highly leveraged with a tiny fraction of collateral in the form of margin capital invested in any open positions.

In **Figure 7.1**, the graph shows that futures outperformed the spot market as tracked by Gorton and Rouwenhorst over the forty-five-year period they analyzed.[3] The increased performance of futures is quite dramatic. It is also apparent that the futures benefited from increased volatility in spot prices.

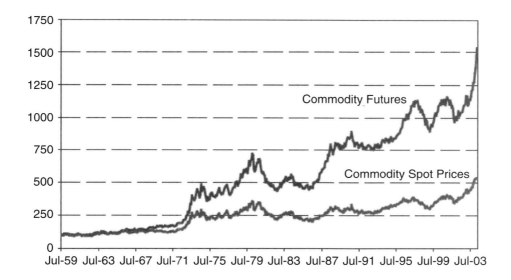

FIGURE **7.1**

Futures Compared to Cash

Source: © Gorton, Gary and Rouwenhorst, K. Geert

---

3. Ibid., p. 9.

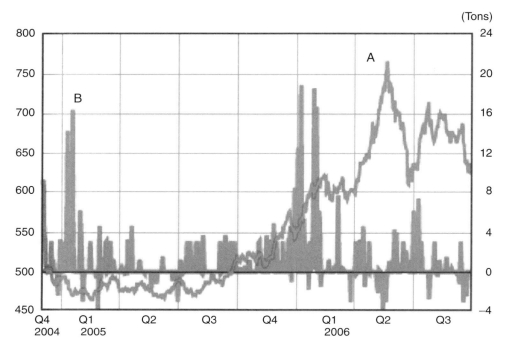

A   Gold price, USD per ounce (left-hand scale)
B   Daily change of gold ETF outstanding amounts (right-hand scale)

FIGURE 7.2

Gold and Gold ETF Prices

Source: © www.exchangetradedgold.com, Bloomberg

Like Phillippe Mongars and Christophe Marchal-Dombrat, Gorton and Rouwenhorst illustrate their case with investors in gold ETFs (exchange traded funds) who sometimes increase their holdings in those funds even while the price of gold is falling. As shown in **Figure 7.2**, that occurred in May 2006.[4] Gorton and Rouwenhorst stress that investor excesses cause price swings independent of the fundamentals of supply and demand.

4. Phillippe Mongars and Christophe Marchal-Dombrat, "Commodities: An Asset Class in Their Own Right?" Banque de France *Financial Stability Review* No. 9 (December 2006): p. 7.

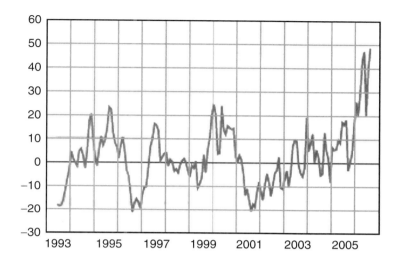

FIGURE 7.3

Annualized Returns on Futures and Cash Markets

Source: Merrill Lynch

The analysis by Mongars and Marchal-Dombrat of returns on futures versus spot prices from 1993 to 2006 shows variable results for most of that time frame until the last two years of that period, as shown in **Figure 7.3**.[5]

Rates of return, adjusted for inflation, of commodities futures are comparable to those of the stock market over the period tracked by Gorton and Rouwenhorst, although periods of inflation are more favorable to the futures prices, as shown in **Figure 7.4**, which graphs futures returns against stocks and bonds.[6] Both futures and stocks have higher volatility than bonds for that time frame.

Gorton and Rouwenhorst observed with respect to inclusion of futures in a portfolio that they effectively provide diversification due to negative correlation with the S&P 500 and long-term bonds. That diversification is enhanced by longer-term positions.

5. Ibid., p. 7.
6. Ibid., p. 11.

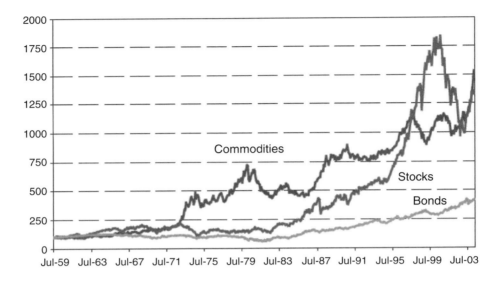

FIGURE 7.4

Performance of Stocks, Bonds, and Commodities

Source: © Gorton, Gary and Rouwenhorst, K. Geert

They found that during the periods when stocks had below-average rates of return futures had above-average rates of return. Gorton and Rouwenhorst note that:

> Commodities have historically provided a better hedge against inflation than stocks and bonds, which are negatively impacted by price increases. That is because of their direct link with the components of inflation and because they rise and fall with unexpected deviations from components of inflation due to the fact that futures prices include information about foreseeable trends in commodity prices.[7]

There are negative correlations between commodities and equities with respect to business cycles. Commodities perform well in the early stages of recessions when stocks are suffering, and they fall off at the later stages of recessions when stocks begin to take off.

---

7. Ibid., p. 17.

Negative correlation between futures and other asset classes is important for the use of them in hedging overall risk and balancing a portfolio as features of diversification. A portfolio that includes exposure to derivatives like futures and Forex spot currency pairs is therefore more balanced than a portfolio that includes only equities and bonds. Trading directly in futures and options on futures is one approach. Investing in the ETFs that trade in those instruments is another, indirect approach.

Conclusion

It is important to consider the nature of various asset classes as candidates for a trading portfolio. Derivatives have one advantage over stocks and bonds despite lower inherent price volatility, and that is leverage. Futures in particular serve to balance a portfolio due to their negative correlation with other markets. This is more than just theory, as the prominent and respected studies cited in this chapter demonstrate.

Summary of Chapter 7

- The high leverage of derivatives provides the opportunity for greater profits, but that comes with the price of elevated risk.
- Derivatives are not for the casual trader, and they require a much higher level of sophistication than other types of investments.
- Derivatives when added to a portfolio of stocks and bonds can enhance performance and provide further diversification as a hedge against downside risk.

CHAPTER 8

Finessing the Risk Factor with Spreads

Investing in any market carries with it a certain amount of risk. Granted, there is not much risk in buying and holding securities issued by the U.S. government, such as 90-day Treasury bills, 2-, 5-, or 10-year Treasury notes, or 30-year Treasury bonds (also known as the long bond), but it is still within the realm of possibility for the federal government to experience a financial crisis and default on those instruments, even if historically that has never happened. Savings accounts and certificates of deposits in banks are also virtually risk-free places to park one's capital, provided they do not exceed the maximum insured by FDIC of $100,000.

If investors or traders crave greater rates of return than those types of instruments offer, they must venture into riskier arenas such as equities and derivatives, unless they are satisfied with the principal residence that they purchased with a down payment and a mortgage as their sole investment. One way to spread risk is to let a fund manager do the work, in which case it is just a matter of creating a portfolio of various funds that invest in stocks, bonds, and money markets, something that the typical 401(k) plan offered by the typical employer provides via a benefits vendor.

George Kopp at Worldwide Associates, LLC, in Chicago, who is a futures trader and former market maker at the Chicago Board Options Exchange, has generously provided some of his insights on the use of two of the more commonly used options strategies: credit and debit spreads. A debit spread is a spread that involves the purchase of options that generates a debit in your trading account when you put on the position. There are a variety of strategies one can use in order to profit from these spreads, but always remember that your risk is the amount you pay for the spread. Your profit is limited to the amount you paid less the difference between the strike prices. For instance, on April 9, 2007, General Motors (GM) stock is trading at $32 a share and you have a bullish bias. The June 32.5 calls are trading at 1.9 and the June 37.5 calls are trading at 0.35. The difference between the two option prices is 1.55 (1.90 – 0.35 = 1.55), so the amount one is willing to risk is $155 per spread. The difference in strike prices is $5 (37.5 − 32.5 = 5), so if at June expiration GM is trading at 37.5 or higher, the spread is worth $5. Your investment of $155 is then worth $500. In terms of risk/reward, you need to consider whether you are willing to risk $155 to make $345. Keep in mind that the most you can make is $345 in this situation. So, 5 (the difference in the strike prices) less 1.55 (the amount you are willing to risk) equals 3.45.

With a credit spread, there is a net credit generated in your trading account from selling options. For example, on April 9, 2007, Google (GOOG) is above $470 a share and we are bearish on the stock. The April 450 calls are trading at 27 and the April 460 calls are trading at 20. Expiration is on Friday, April 21, with ten trading days left minus the $7 credit received. If we were to sell the spread at 7 (27 − 20 = 7), our risk would be $3, which is the difference in the strike prices (460 − 450 = 10). In order for us to make the maximum amount of profit, GOOG would have to go to 450 or lower between now and April expiration.

Some people sell credit spreads in both the calls and puts in the stock indexes. They sell out-of-the-money (OTM) spreads. This can lead to nice rewards, but it takes on a lot of risk. From the summer of 2006 through the first two months of 2007, the stock indexes enjoyed a nice orderly climb upward, and the volatility indexes, VIX and VXO (also known as the "fear" indexes), went to multiyear lows. Traders looking for credit spreads are hard-pressed to find risk/reward spreads when the volatility of the market is low. During this period, the market never even had a 2 percent correction, which would have caused volatility to jump. The market's first 2 percent correction in more than nine hundred days occurred on February 27, 2007—a trader who sold credit put spreads prior to that would have seen them explode, if not to at-the-money (ATM), to maybe in-the-money (ITM).

The Greeks

Before delving further into spreads (covered and naked spreads are discussed later), it's important to understand "the Greeks" and what they mean for trading positions.

The Greek letter delta represents the relationship between the rate of change of the option premium (price) and the rate of change of the price of the underlying instrument, stated as a simple ratio. For example, in the case of an at-the-money option, the premium typically changes approximately 50 percent as much as the price of the underlying, which equates to a delta value of 0.5. If shares of Microsoft rise or fall by $10, then the price of at-the-money puts and calls on the stock will rise or fall (depending on which direction the underlying shares trade and whether it's a put or a call) about $5 per contract. As the option trades more in-the-money, the delta for it approaches 1.0, and conversely as the option trades more out-of-the-money, the delta approaches 0. The delta never reaches 1.0, nor does it ever reach 0.

Based on delta, a single option contract will never completely hedge an underlying position. To be completely hedged would require purchasing and selling two at-the-money option contracts. However, the advantage to having a delta that is always less than 1.0 is that a cushion on the downside is accomplished without entirely neutralizing the upside potential for the underlying instrument. The other advantage to delta being variable, based on how far in- or out-of-the-money an option is, is that it allows the trader to utilize a wide variety of strategies that involve combinations of puts and calls at various strike prices.

Another component to option pricing is the erosion in time value, represented by the Greek letter theta. The premium of an option is the combination of its intrinsic value, that is, how much the option is in-the-money, and the value that is added to that based on how far away from expiration the option is at the time of its being traded. The time value consequently decreases going forward, and the rate of that decrease is theta. Theta accelerates to a great degree in the last few weeks before expiration. The consequence of that acceleration in the erosion of time value is that any long option position must be either liquidated or rolled over to an expiration date further out in time prior to reaching the last few weeks before its expiration. Otherwise, there is too much loss on the position to justify holding it that long. A short option position, on the other hand, benefits from the accelerated erosion in time value, because the more the premium declines, the higher the profit realized. The bottom line when it comes to theta is that the downside risk on long option positions is increased the longer they are held and especially as theta accelerates as the option nears expiration.

There is a whole slew of options strategies for hedging risk on a position, but the key to understanding their underpinnings is the Greeks, the letters of the Greek alphabet that stand for the various factors that influence option pricing. It stands to reason that Greek letters should be used, as they are commonplace in mathematics and statistics as symbols to represent abstract concepts.

Spreading the Risk Around

Option spreads help spread the risk around by either the covering of an options position by a position in the underlying market or by combining multiple puts and/or calls as naked (uncovered) spreads. They serve to keep the trader from being trapped in an unmanageable or unfavorable trade.

Covered Call

The point of spreading a position is to give oneself a cushion on the downside. The simplest such strategy with equities is the covered call. This involves selling a call option (a contract to sell 100 shares at a specified strike price to the purchaser of the option upon settlement at the expiration date of the option) against shares of a particular company in one's portfolio. The beauty of this particular strategy is that it not only offsets a decrease in value of the shares when the price drops as the opportunity to buy back the call at a lower premium arises, it also puts instant money in one's trading account.

There is a third feature that also makes selling covered calls an attractive strategy: erosion in time value. Every option is priced based on two components, intrinsic value and time value, which is referred to as the premium paid for it. The intrinsic value is based on how much the option is in-the-money, which refers to the difference between the strike price of the option and the current market price of the underlying instrument (in this case, the shares of stock). In the case where the strike price is lower than the current market price, if the option were exercised by the person who purchased it, the purchaser would be delivered shares at a discount, meaning built-in profit on paper. The time value is calculated based on how far out in the future the option will expire. The longer the time to expiration, the greater the chance there is for the underlying stock price to increase and thereby increase the value of the option as it trades more and more in-the-money. That is the risk traders who purchase a naked call (meaning they do not already own shares of the stock or have a short position in the stock with their brokerage firm) assume—that the time value of the option decreases daily and at an accelerating rate as the option nears expiration. For the seller of that call option, who is referred to as the underwriter or writer of premium, that erosion in time value works in his favor. That is because the more the premium for the option decreases, the cheaper it is to buy it back in the event the person who sold it wants to offset his position, effectively liquidating at a profit.

The reality is that stocks usually do not move in price by a significant amount in the short term. A seller of covered calls chooses options that are only thirty to forty-five days away from expiration and that are slightly out-of-the-money. One reason for not selling calls that are in-the-money is that they are more likely to be exercised, because they have a greater chance of still being in-the-money at expiration. That results in the turnover in the cash position as those shares are delivered to the buyer of the call option. What usually happens (probably about 80 percent of the time) is that the stock price does not fluctuate by very much, and the profits from selling the covered calls net the trader a healthy rate of return on his investment on an annualized basis, because he can turn around and sell more covered calls against his long cash position as soon as the ones he already has on the books have expired unexercised. Combine the profits from selling covered calls with dividend income, and it tends to be a very lucrative strategy, as long as stock prices do not take a nosedive in the near term.

Hypothetical covered call trade:
- Google stock is trading at $500 per share on June 22, 2008, and the portfolio is long 100 shares.
- One July 2008 505 call is sold for $500.
- If the stock is still trading at or near $500 and has not traded through the $505 strike price at the July expiration, the net profit is $500 on the option.

Covered Put

There is also a strategy for hedging a short position, which is the covered put. It works just like the covered call, except it is a long option position against a short position in the underlying instrument. The strategy involves selling a put (which is the option to deliver 100 shares of stock to the purchaser at the specified stock price and expiration date of the option) against a short position in the cash market. Being short a put means that the purchaser of the put has the obligation to deliver 100 shares of the stock at the specified strike price upon its being exercised. If the price of the stock rises, the loss to the trader who is short the stock (short selling is with the expectation that prices are going to fall, yielding the opportunity to buy back the shares of stock that were sold short at a profit as the position is offset) is partially offset by the decrease in premium of the put that the trader sold (intrinsic and time value both decreasing over time) that allows the trader to buy back the put at a lower price, netting a profit on the option.

Hypothetical covered put trade:

- Google stock is trading at $500 per share on June 22, 2008, and the portfolio is short 100 shares.
- One July 2008 495 put is sold for $500.
- If the stock is still trading at or near $500 and has not traded through the $495 strike price at the July expiration, the net profit is $500 on the option.

Naked Positions

Trading options without spreading is what's known as having a naked position. One can be long a call, long a put, short a call, or short a put. If one has a bullish outlook, one would be long a call or short a put. Because a put is the option to sell the underlying, then selling (writing) a put is essentially a long position, as opposed to buying the put in order to have a short position. Conversely, if one has a bearish outlook, one would be long a put or short a call. Because a call is the option to buy the underlying, selling (writing) a call is obviously a short position, as opposed to buying the call in order to have a long position.

There are various other options spread strategies commonly used in the markets in addition to covered calls and covered puts, and they are discussed in the section that follows. Keep in mind that lower strike prices are favorable to long call positions and short put positions, whereas higher strike prices are favorable to long put and short call positions. The idea is to buy low and sell high, so the option to buy at a lower strike price (call) or sell at a higher strike price (put) means being more in-the-money than out-of-the-money. Option premiums will be higher the more in-the-money the option is, and they will be lower the more out-of-the-money the option is. Purchasing an option results in a debit from the trading account, whereas writing an option results in a credit to the trading account. Trading options spreads has more flexibility than simply trading stocks, futures, or Forex contracts, or naked puts and calls, because it allows for strategies that can be profitable when markets fail to trend or when they have the potential to break out in either direction, as opposed to those other nonspread strategies that are entirely dependent on a substantial enough price swing in a single direction.

Strategies Involving Spreads

Synthetic Call

A synthetic call involves spreading a long stock position (shares owned) with the purchase of at-the-money or slightly out-of-the-money puts. That means the strike price of the puts should be equal to or slightly lower than the current stock price. Because of the erosion of time value on purchased options, there should be an adequate time until expiration on the puts, and they should not be held into the last month before expiration when the rate of erosion of time value (theta) accelerates (it erodes at such a high rate that it will wipe out any profits). If there is a loss on the stock on a decline in prices, it is limited to the difference between the loss on the stock and the increase in the price of the put. As long as the price of the stock increases more than the cost of the purchased option, the potential on the upside is unlimited. A naked call may have a similar risk profile, however, it is a wasting asset on account of loss in time value, and it does not pay dividends like a stock. Unlike the covered call strategy, which results in a net credit in the trading account from selling an option, there is a net debit from the purchase of the option at the outset of putting on the spread.

Hypothetical synthetic call trade:
- Shares of Google stock are trading for $500.15 on May 1, 2008, and the portfolio is short 100 shares.
- Buy one July 2008 500 put (at-the-money) selecting the strike price closest to the stock price.

Synthetic Put

A synthetic put, the opposite of a synthetic call, involves selling shares of the stock short and buying an at-the-money call. Although the position is bearish in outlook, it manages the downside risk of a rise in stock prices on account of the increase in value of the call offsetting to some degree a loss on the short stock position. Because the amount received for selling the stock short is greater than the cost of the option, there is a net credit in the trading account when initiating the spread position. Due to the negative impact of erosion in time value, the option should not be held into the last month before expiration. Profit potential on a decline in stock prices is unlimited as long as the difference in price on the stock from where it was sold short is greater than the cost of the put. This strategy has an obvious advantage over a naked short stock position or naked long put: capping of the downside risk via the long leg of the spread.

Hypothetical synthetic put trade:
- Shares of Google stock are trading for $500.15 on May 1, 2008, and the portfolio is long 100 shares.
- Buy one July 2008 500 put (at-the-money).

Straddle

A straddle is a simplistic strategy that has an advantage over a naked position of either the underlying instrument or puts or calls. Unlike those naked positions that have unlimited downside risk, straddles have limited downside risk. This is accomplished by buying both puts and calls with identical strike prices (ideally, at-the-money) and expiration dates (three months left to expiration is best, because this is a very short-term strategy). The maximum potential loss is the net premiums paid for the options. The other major advantage over being long or short shares (contracts) of the underlying is that there is profit potential on breakouts of the underlying's price in either direction, whereas with naked positions there is upside potential only if the price direction is correctly forecasted. For that reason, straddles are called a "direction-neutral" strategy. Not only must the stock have a substantial swing up or down, but it also must be a big enough move to overcome the erosion in time value of the long options. Bear in mind also that due to delta, the increase in option premiums is always less than the amount of change in price of the underlying. Keeping a straddle open into the last month before expiration is hazardous on account of the theta (rate of erosion of time value), which spikes as the option nears expiration. One other unique feature of a straddle is that it can be profitable on both long and short sides of the market. For example, if the stock price rallies and then has a correction, it is possible to sell the purchased call at a profit, and then make an additional profit on the purchased put after the correction. This type of trade is better suited to a market that has been trading in a narrow range and thus is primed for a breakout, as opposed to a market that currently has a strong trend under way.

Hypothetical straddle trade:
- Shares of Google stock are trading for $500.15 on April 1, 2008.
- Buy one July 2008 500 put (at-the-money).
- Buy one July 2008 500 call (at-the-money).

Short Straddle

A short straddle, which involves selling at-the-money puts and calls at the same strike price with a month or less left to expiration, has the advantage over the straddle of long options of not being negatively impacted by erosion in time value. In fact, the higher the theta, the more it works in favor of the position. On the flip side, the exposure to risk in either direction is unlimited. The short straddle's glaring flaw is that the market must stay in a narrow trading range in order to make modest profits and avoid the potential for huge short-term losses caused by events that precipitate major breakout moves in either direction. That is hardly an ideal risk/reward ratio, to say the least.

Hypothetical short straddle trade:
- Shares of Google stock are trading for $500.15 on June 15, 2008.
- Sell one July 2008 500 put (at-the-money).
- Sell one July 2008 500 call (at-the-money).

Strangle

The strangle is much like a straddle. Instead of purchasing at-the-money puts and calls, the strategy involves purchasing out-of-the-money puts and calls with the same expiration date (preferably three months out). So, instead of buying options with a strike price the same as the underlying's price, the calls should have a higher strike price and the puts should have a lower strike price than that of the underlying instrument. Both the long and short legs of the spread carry limited risk (the price paid for the options) with attendant unlimited upside potential. As with the straddle, erosion in time value has a negative impact on the position, and the same rule regarding exiting the trade before the last month prior to expiration similarly applies. The main advantage strangles have over straddles is the lower cost: the cheaper price paid for out-of-the-money options compared with at-the-money options. On the flip side, the delta is lower on out-of-the-money options than it is on at-the-money options, which means to obtain the same level of profitability on a strangle position as on a straddle position, a bigger price swing in one direction is needed.

Hypothetical strangle trade:
- Shares of Google stock are trading for $500.15 on April 15, 2008.
- Buy one July 2008 495 put (out-of-the-money).
- Buy one July 2008 505 call (out-of-the-money).

Short Strangle

A short strangle involves writing out-of-the-money puts and calls with a month left until expiration. The puts should have a lower strike price than the calls. This widening of strike prices improves the odds of making a profit over the long strangle. The trade is direction neutral, so a lack of volatility is favorable to the position—net profit is from the premium received for the options sold, in other words the net credit. It does not have a good risk-management profile, because there is unlimited risk in the event of a breakout of the underlying's price in either direction. Erosion in time value is a plus, because the options' positions are both short.

Hypothetical short strangle trade:
- Shares of Google stock are trading for $500.15 on June 15, 2008.
- Sell one July 2008 495 put (out-of-the-money).
- Sell one July 2008 505 call (out-of-the-money).

Strip

A strip is a bearish strategy built on the straddle. Puts and calls with three months left to expiration are purchased at-the-money as with the straddle, but twice as many puts as calls are bought. That means there is more profit potential on a decline in stock prices and increased risk over the straddle on a rise in stock prices. Also, a bigger swing of stock prices on the upside is required to make a profit than is the case for a straddle, because there are twice as many puts as calls, and the profit from the long leg of the position must be greater than the loss from the short leg.

Hypothetical strip trade:
- Shares of Google stock are trading for $500.15 on April 15, 2008.
- Buy two July 2008 500 puts (at-the-money).
- Buy one July 2008 500 call (at-the-money).

Strap

The strap is the bullish mirror image of the strip. The number of at-the-money calls should be twice the number of at-the-money puts in the position. The profit potential on the long side is increased over the straddle it is built upon, whereas the risk on the short leg of the position is increased over a simple straddle. To make a profit, a bigger swing in stock prices on the downside than for a direction-neutral straddle will be required.

Hypothetical strap trade:
- Shares of Google stock are trading for $500.15 on April 15, 2008.
- Buy one July 2008 500 put (at-the-money).
- Buy two July 2008 500 calls (at-the-money).

Guts

The guts is slightly different from its cousin the strangle. Instead of buying at-the-money options, in-the-money puts and calls are purchased with (ideally) three months left until expiration. For the same reason as with other strategies that involve long options, that is, erosion in time value, the position should not be held into the last month before expiration. The downside risk on the spread is limited to the cost of the options, whereas the upside potential is unlimited with dramatic breakouts in either direction. The net profit from an increase in option premium on either the calls on a breakout to the long side or the puts on a breakout to the short side will be that gain in option premium minus the erosion in time value minus the cost of the option on the losing leg of the spread.

Hypothetical guts trade:
- Shares of Google stock are trading for $500.15 on April 15, 2008.
- Buy one July 2008 495 call (in-the-money).
- Buy one July 2008 505 put (in-the-money).

Collar

A collar is basically an enhanced covered call: in addition to selling calls against shares of stock owned, puts also are purchased. The additional short leg of the spread, the long put position, limits the downside risk drastically, because the money lost on the stock price in a bear market is offset to a great extent by the increase in premium on the purchased put. The premium received from the sale of the call is a mitigating factor, and it is key to maximizing profitability on the strategy, which is cautiously bullish. It is meant to be a longer-term strategy as opposed to the short-term simple covered call. The put may be eighteen months or more out to expiration, whereas the covered call is going to be, ideally, a month away from expiration. The flip side of the strategy is that it limits the upside potential via the exercise of the calls when the stock trades through their strike price. Collars are meant for traders who wish to participate in equities without assuming the amount of risk that simply holding them in one's portfolio carries with it. The only effective way to manage that risk on shares alone is stop-loss orders when the market drops by a predetermined percentage, but that serves only to cut losses rather than to minimize them over a fixed period of time—the losses will still be incurred with no insurance from carrying options positions as a hedge. Spreading is often superior to going naked when it comes to the roller-coaster ride of playing the volatile financial markets.

Hypothetical collar trade:
● Shares of Google stock are trading for $500.15 on November 30, 2007.
● Buy 100 shares of stock.
● Buy one July 2009 505 put (in-the-money).
● Sell one December 2007 510 call (out-of-the-money).

Bull Call Spread

A bull call spread is a combination of calls involving buying a call that is at-the-money or slightly out-of-the-money and writing a call that is out-of-the-money. Both options should have the same expirations and they should have a lot of time value left—at least six months to expiration. In the event the trader's forecast of a rise in prices over the long term is correct, the long call will increase in value more than the short call decreases in value because of its higher delta. The erosion of time value on the long call is counteracted by the negative impact of that same erosion on the short call premium—in other words, the more the option price falls on a short position, the better. In addition to that benefit, the money received for the short call offsets the money paid for the long call. The downside risk of a drop in price of the underlying is hedged, because the premium of the short option will increase as the premium of the long option decreases. To profit from this strategy requires that the price of the underlying reach the strike price of the short call, which is higher than the strike price of the long call. Failing that, the trade is going to be either at breakeven or with a net loss. The net loss will be mitigated in comparison to being long a naked call, but, on the flip side, the profit potential is capped by the spreading of the long call against the short call.

Hypothetical bull call spread trade:
- Shares of Google stock are trading for $502.50 on November 30, 2007.
- Buy one July 2008 505 call (slightly out-of-the-money).
- Sell one July 2008 515 call (out-of-the-money).

Bear Call Spread

The bear call spread is similar to the bull call spread, except that it is designed with the aim of profiting from a decline in prices of the underlying over a long period of time. The short leg of the spread involves writing a slightly out-of-the-money call with a month left until expiration. The long leg involves buying a call that is even more out-of-the-money, that is, with a higher strike price, than the option sold short. Because the premium on the option sold is higher (it is closer to being in-the-money) than the option bought, money is credited to the trader's account when the spread trade is put on (executed). As with the bull call spread, the expiration dates need to be the same for both calls. A correct forecast of falling underlying prices means that the premium of both options drops and they expire worthless. The credit from the difference between the prices that is pocketed at the outset is the profit realized. The difference between that same net credit and the amount of money lost in premium on rising underlying prices determines whether the trade remains profitable or becomes one that is breakeven or, if the underlying price rises too much, a losing trade. To avoid a loss, the trader can liquidate the position when it reaches breakeven, although if the market then retreats, the trader is shaken out prematurely on an otherwise profitable position over the long term. It is really a judgment call, and depends on one's ability to see the bigger picture and what is likely to occur down the road. That is always the crux of trading: Being able to weather the noisy short-term fluctuations that should be disregarded in favor of the underlying long-term momentum in one direction.

Hypothetical bear call spread trade:
- Shares of Google stock are trading for $502.50 on June 13, 2008.
- Buy one July 2008 510 call (out-of-the-money).
- Sell one July 2008 505 call (slightly out-of-the-money).

Bear Put Spread

A bear put spread involves buying a put that is either at-the-money or slightly out-of-the-money and selling one that is more out-of-the-money (which means at lower strike price), both having the same expiration, with six months or more left until expiry. As its name implies, the strategy aims to profit from a decline in underlying prices. A debit is incurred in the trading account upon putting on the spread trade due to the higher premium on the put that is sold (it is in-the-money as opposed to the purchased put). As with the bull call spread, erosion in time value on the bearish position is counteracted by the short put's equal erosion (a drop in option price is desirable when one is short). Also, the money received for the written put offsets the price paid for the other leg of the spread. Think of this trade as the mirror image of the bull call spread. The underlying price must fall to either break even or make it profitable. If that does not occur, then there will be a net loss. The maximum loss on this strategy does not compare with the loss that would be incurred for buying a naked put and being wrong, but, on the flip side, the upside potential is limited due to the hedge leg (purchase of the put at the higher strike price) in comparison with the upside for the underlying, which has no cap.

Hypothetical bear put spread trade:
- Shares of Google stock are trading for $512.50 on November 29, 2007.
- Buy one July 2008 505 put (out-of-the-money).
- Sell one July 2008 510 put (slightly out-of-the-money).

Bull Put Spread

The bull put spread is designed with the aim of profiting from rising prices of the underlying. A naked put accomplishes that goal, but with this strategy one sells a put that is slightly out-of-the-money with a month left until expiration while buying one that is further out-of-the-money (at a lower strike price than the purchased put) with the same expiration. Money is credited to the trading account, because the price of the option sold is higher than the price of the option bought (one receives more money than one spends to put on the spread position). Ultimately, one sees a profit when the forecast of rising underlying prices is correct and the options expire worthless, resulting in a realization of the difference in price between the two. If prices fall instead, there is either less profit realized (the difference between the prices of the two options minus what is lost in premium), breakeven, or a net loss is incurred.

Hypothetical bull put spread trade:
- Shares of Google stock are trading for $707.50 on June 11, 2008.
- Buy one July 2008 700 put (deeper out-of-the-money).
- Sell one July 2008 705 put (out-of-the-money).

Calendar Call

A calendar call is basically a covered call with a long call on the long leg of the spread in place of owning shares (contracts) of the underlying instrument. In other words, instead of selling a call against 100 shares of stock, the trader writes a call while simultaneously buying one at the same strike price, which should be at-the-money or slightly out-of-the-money.

The long call, in order to emulate a stock position, should be far away from expiration when starting out the strategy. The written call will then be a month away from expiration. As long as the stock price does not spike higher, another call should be written upon expiration of the one currently written. That serves to generate a revenue stream from the written calls. If everything works according to plan, the net amount from selling calls will be more than the amount paid for the long-term call (the long leg of the spread). The downside risk comes from the event of the stock trading through the strike price prior to expiration of the first written call. There will be a net loss, because the delta for the long leg is only 0.5, and the amount to offset the short leg upon being exercised (having to buy back shares to deliver them at the strike price, which is now lower than the current share price) will end up costing double what is earned on the increase in premium on the long call. The amount received for the written call is inevitably going to be less than that difference, although it will mitigate it to some extent.

Hypothetical calendar call trade:
● Shares of Google stock are trading for $705.10 on June 3, 2008.
● Buy one February 2009 705 call (at-the-money).
● Sell one July 2008 705 call (at-the-money).

Calendar Put

A calendar put involves a calendar spread of purchasing an at-the-money or slightly out-of-the-money put a long time away from expiration while writing a put at the same price and a month away from expiration. As with the calendar call, if the stock is trading at the options' strike price when the short put expires, the premium received for the short leg of the spread is realized as profit and one can continue to write puts each month with the same objective. A rapid fall in the stock's price has the same consequence a rapid rise in price has for a calendar call: a net loss.

Hypothetical calendar put trade:
- Shares of Google stock are trading for $705.10 on June 3, 2008.
- Buy one February 2010 705 put (at-the-money).
- Sell one July 2008 705 put (at-the-money).

Bull Call Ladder

The bull call ladder is slightly more complicated than the bull call spread. In addition to buying calls near-the-money and selling calls out-of-the-money, it involves selling more calls further out-of-the-money. Because the short leg of the spread is strengthened by writing the additional calls, the downside risk is unlimited. Therefore, the expiration of all options in the position should be near-term. Also, the outlook is neutral rather than bullish as it is with bull call spreads. Profitability is maximized in the event that the stock price reaches the lower strike price of the written calls. If the price trades above the higher strike price of the written calls, it is a losing proposition to the degree that it penetrates that level—hence the unlimited risk profile of the spread. On the flip side, if the stock falls below the strike price of the long leg of the spread, then the loss in premium on the purchased calls will be greater than the premium received for the written calls, which results in a net loss, although it is additionally mitigated by selling the extra calls that are more out-of-the-money. This particular strategy best suits markets that have little short-term volatility and with only a slight increase rather than a dramatic breakout to the long side.

Hypothetical bull call ladder trade:
- Shares of Google stock are trading for $700.10 on June 3, 2008.
- Buy one July 2008 700 call (at-the-money).
- Sell one July 2008 705 call (out-of-the-money).
- Sell one July 2008 710 call (out-of-the-money).

Bear Call Ladder

The bear call ladder is like a bear call spread with a strengthened long leg. It involves selling slightly out-of-the-money calls and buying in-the-money calls, then buying additional calls further in-the-money. That means the strike price of the slightly in-the-money calls is lower than that of the written calls, and the strike price of the calls that are deeper in-the-money is even lower. So, there are three levels of strike prices, just as with the bull call ladder. It is bullish rather than neutral in outlook, because the additional long calls provide unlimited profit potential on the long side in the event of a dramatic breakout in that direction. The strategy works better as a longer-term trade, on account of the erosion in time value of the long leg of the spread. Losses are incurred when the stock price fails to trade either below the strike price of the short leg of the spread or above the lower strike price of the long leg of the spread. Its risk profile makes it a more conservative strategy than a bull call ladder.

Hypothetical bear call ladder trade:
● Shares of Google stock are trading for $705.10 on April 10, 2008.
● Buy one July 2008 695 call (in-the-money).
● Buy one July 2008 700 call (in-the-money).
● Sell one July 2008 710 call (out-of-the-money).

Bear Put Ladder

With a bear put ladder, in addition to buying near-the-money puts while selling slightly out-of-the-money puts, one sells more puts at an even lower strike price (more out-of-the-money). Like its cousin the bull call ladder, it is neutral in direction outlook as opposed to the bear put spread that it is built upon, which is a bearish strategy. Hence, its maximum profit potential is realized when the stock fails to break out in either direction and ideally trades somewhere in the territory of the range between the strike price of the long put leg of the spread and the higher strike price of the written puts in the short leg of the spread. Losses will be incurred in the event of a breakout to the long side that goes above the strike price of the long leg of the spread, which are somewhat mitigated by the amount of premium received from selling calls at the two different strike prices (the ones that are further out-of-the-money will obviously be priced lower than those at the higher strike price). Unlimited losses are possible in the event of a breakout to the short side that falls below the lower strike price of the written puts on the short leg of the spread.

Hypothetical bear put ladder trade:
● Shares of Google stock are trading for $707.10 on June 13, 2008.
● Sell one July 2008 695 put (out-of-the-money).
● Sell one July 2008 700 put (out-of-the-money).
● Buy one July 2008 710 put (near-the-money).

Bull Put Ladder

The bull put ladder is another bearish strategy involving the sale of slightly out-of-the-money puts while purchasing slightly in-the-money puts and additional puts that are more in-the-money (with an even higher strike price), all with the same expiration, which should be longer term. This strategy has unlimited profit potential in the event of a breakout to the downside below the lower strike price of the puts on the long leg of the spread. Net losses are incurred when the stock price trades between the strike price of the puts on the short leg of the spread and the higher strike price of the puts on the long leg of the spread.

Hypothetical bull put ladder trade:
- Shares of Google stock are trading for $707.10 on April 13, 2008.
- Buy one July 2008 720 put (in-the-money).
- Buy one July 2008 715 put (in-the-money).
- Sell one July 2008 710 put (slightly in-the-money).

Diagonal Call

A diagonal call is a bullish spread strategy that combines purchasing a deep in-the-money call with a long time left until expiration with writing a call that is either at-the-money or slightly in-the-money with a month left until expiration. The risk of the otherwise naked long call is hedged (covered) by selling the call option against the long-term position to create the short leg of the spread. The high purchase cost of the deep in-the-money call option is offset to a great degree, albeit not entirely, by the premium received for the written call. It has a distinct advantage over the calendar call strategy in that it won't result in a net loss on a dramatic price swing on the stock to the long side. In the event the stock trades through the strike price of the call on the short leg of the spread, resulting in being exercised, one can bow out gracefully by liquidating the long call with the object of purchasing the stock to deliver to the party that has exercised the call option one has written. An advantage to writing the call option is that it erodes faster in time value than the erosion of time value on the long option position, which works in the trader's favor from an income standpoint. As long as the stock fails to trade through the strike price of the written call, more calls can be written from one month to the next, essentially providing a revenue stream on the spread from the sale of the options. As long as the net profit from selling calls is greater than any loss in premium from the long call in the event that the bullish forecast is wrong, and it loses value through a combination of an erosion in time value and (if applicable) a drop in intrinsic value due to a drop in the stock price, the spread trade will remain profitable.

   Hypothetical diagonal call trade:
● Shares of Google stock are trading for $706.10 on September 21, 2007.
● Buy one July 2008 680 call (deep in-the-money).
● Sell one October 2007 710 call (out-of-the-money).

Diagonal Put

A diagonal put involves hedging a long deep out-of-the-money put that has a long time left until expiration with a short in-the-money put with a month left until expiration. Like its cousin strategy the diagonal call, it is also a bullish spread. It has advantages over the calendar put spread. It has a reduced cost on the long leg, which is an out-of-the-money put and therefore one with lower premium than the near-the-money put that is part of the calendar put. A sharp breakout on the long side causes a net loss with a calendar put, but that is not the case with a diagonal put. Erosion of time value has a negative impact on the long leg of the spread, and in the event the stock does not trade through the strike price of the short put, the position on the long leg of the spread will remain intact unless liquidated. In that case, the strategy of realizing net credits from continuing to write more puts will offset the loss in time value of the long put, and if it is more than that amount, will also keep the trade profitable.

   Hypothetical diagonal put trade:
● Shares of Google stock are trading for $706.10 on September 21, 2007.
● Buy one April 2008 put (deep out-of-the-money).
● Sell one October 2007 710 put (in-the-money).

Long Call Butterfly

A long call butterfly spread consists of the purchase of one in-the-money call, the sale of two at-the-money calls, and the purchase of one out-of-the-money call, all of them having a month left until expiration. It is a direction-neutral trade, and carries a low cost of the options while having an excellent risk/reward ratio. The risk is contained in the two long legs of the spread. The greatest profitability is achieved in the absence of volatility, in other words, when the stock is trading at the strike price of calls on the short leg of the spread at expiration. In that event, the difference between the strike prices of the calls on the short leg of the spread and calls on the long legs of the spread is greater than the net debit (cost of the purchase of the options minus the premium received for the options written, which is inherently very low). Risk is limited to net debit on the options prices.

Hypothetical long call butterfly trade:
- Shares of Google stock are trading for $705 on June 15, 2008.
- Buy one July 2008 700 call (in-the-money).
- Sell two July 2008 705 calls (at-the-money).
- Buy one July 2008 710 call (out-of-the-money).

Long Call Condor

The long call condor is a slightly more elaborate strategy than the long call butterfly in that the options on the short leg of the spread have different strike prices. The strategy therefore consists of buying one in-the-money call, selling one in-the-money call with a higher strike price, selling one out-of-the-money call (with a higher strike price) and buying one out-of-the-money call with a higher strike price. So, the lowest strike price is on the long in-the-money call, the next highest strike price is on the short in-the-money call, the second-highest strike price is on the short out-of-the-money call, and the highest strike price is on the long out-of-the-money call. As with the long call butterfly, the expirations on the options should all be a month away. Its risk/reward profile is similar to the butterfly call, that is, a low-cost trade with good profit potential and limited risk due to the long legs of the spread at the outer strike prices.

Hypothetical long call condor trade:
- Shares of Google stock are trading for $702.77 on June 15, 2008.
- Buy one July 2008 695 call (in-the-money).
- Sell one July 2008 700 call (slightly in-the-money).
- Sell one July 2008 705 call (slightly out-of-the-money).
- Buy one July 2008 710 call (out-of-the-money).

Long Put Butterfly

This strategy involves buying an out-of-the-money put, selling two at-the-money puts, and buying one in-the-money put. It is a direction-neutral strategy, so a lack of volatility is necessary for maximum profit on the trade. Risk is contained through the long legs of the spread at the outer strike prices, resulting in a good risk/reward ratio and giving the strategy an advantage over the short straddle upon which it is built. At the outset, there is a net debit in the trading account due to higher cost of the puts purchased versus the premium received for the puts sold. Profit is realized via the difference in strike prices on the short leg of the spread.

Hypothetical long put butterfly trade:
- Shares of Google stock are trading for $700 on June 15, 2008.
- Buy one July 2008 695 put (out-of-the-money).
- Sell two July 2008 700 puts (at-the-money).
- Buy one July 2008 705 put (in-the-money).

Long Put Condor

This strategy is basically a long call condor except with puts instead. It involves buying one lower strike price out-of-the-money put, selling one lower middle strike price out-of-the-money put, selling one higher middle strike price in-the-money put, and buying one higher strike price in-the-money put, all with expirations one month out or less (erosion in time value is a plus for the short leg of the spread). It is direction neutral, which means profit is maximized when the stock is trading in a narrow range at expiration as opposed to breaking out in either direction. Because the risk is contained by the long legs of the spread at the outer strike prices, the strategy has a favorable risk/reward ratio.

Hypothetical long put condor trade:
- Shares of Google stock are trading for $702.77 on June 15, 2008.
- Buy one July 2008 695 put (out-of-the-money).
- Sell one July 2008 700 put (out-of-the-money).
- Sell one July 2008 705 put (in-the-money).
- Buy one July 2008 710 put (in-the-money).

Short Call Butterfly

This strategy involves selling one in-the-money call, buying two at-the-money calls, and selling one out-of-the-money call, with identical expiration dates three or more months away from expiration. A breakout in either direction maximizes potential profit with this type of spread. There is a net credit generated from the short legs of the spread, because the premium received for those options is greater than the cost of the purchased options on the long leg of the spread. If the stock fails to make a significant move, there will be a net loss delineated by the difference in strike prices of the long leg, which will be more than the net credit of the short legs of the spread. Because a move up or down is desirable, the trade is direction neutral.

Hypothetical short call butterfly trade:
- Shares of Google stock are trading for $300 on April 15, 2008.
- Sell one July 2008 295 call (in-the-money).
- Buy two July 2008 300 calls (at-the-money).
- Sell one July 2008 305 call (out-of-the-money).

Short Call Condor

Similar to its cousin the long call condor, this direction-neutral strategy involves buying one in-the-money call, selling one deeper in-the-money call, buying one out-of-the-money call, and selling one deeper out-of-the-money call. All options should have at least three months left until expiration. A breakout in either direction on the stock price is profitable, and there is a net credit generated by the premium received for the written calls on the short leg of the spread, which is greater than the initial cost of the purchased options on the long leg of the spread. Its risk profile is not very good, though, with a huge amount of downside risk and not much upside potential.

Hypothetical short call condor trade:
- Shares of Google stock are trading for $302.75 on April 15, 2008.
- Sell one July 2008 295 call (in-the-money).
- Buy one July 2008 300 call (in-the-money).
- Buy one July 2008 305 call (out-of-the-money).
- Sell one July 2008 310 call (out-of-the-money).

Short Put Butterfly

This strategy involves selling one out-of-the-money put, buying two at-the-money puts at one strike price for both, and selling one in-the-money put, all with identical expirations at least three months out. Like similar winged spreads, it is direction neutral, and similarly it has a bad risk/reward profile with low profit potential combined with high risk. Breakouts in either direction on the stock price are profitable. A net credit is generated by the premium received for the written options on the short legs of the spread, which is greater than the initial cost of purchasing the options on the long leg of the spread. Profit is maximized when the stock price breaks out beyond one of the outer strike prices of the short legs of the spread.

Hypothetical short put butterfly trade:
- Shares of Google stock are trading for $700 on April 15, 2008.
- Sell one July 2008 695 put (out-of-the-money).
- Buy two July 2008 700 puts (at-the-money).
- Sell one July 2008 705 put (in-the-money).

Short Put Condor

This strategy, which is direction neutral like its cousin strategy the short call condor (being profitable on breakouts of the stock price in either direction), involves buying one out-of-the-money put, selling one deeper out-of-the-money put, buying one in-the-money put, and selling one deeper in-the-money put, all of which should have at least three months out to expiration and identical expiration dates. A net credit is generated initially by the higher premium received for the options on the short legs of the spread than the cost of the options purchased on the long legs of the spread. The risk/reward profile is not very good, with high risk combined with small profit potential.

Hypothetical short put condor trade:
- Shares of Google stock are trading for $702.88 on April 15, 2008.
- Sell one July 2008 695 put (out-of-the-money).
- Buy one July 2008 700 put (out-of-the-money).
- Buy one July 2008 705 put (in-the-money).
- Sell one July 2008 710 put (in-the-money).

Long Iron Butterfly

This strategy is actually a composite of two simpler strategies, the bull put spread with the bear call spread as its wings. It involves buying one out-of-the-money put, selling one at-the-money put, selling one at-the-money call, and buying one out-of-the-money call, all with identical expirations one month or less out. It is direction neutral, and profits are realized in the absence of volatility, in other words, when there is no breakout of the stock price in either direction. A net credit is generated by the sale of the options on the short legs of the spread, which are higher priced than the options purchased on the long legs of the spread. The four legs are not necessarily entered at the same time. The bear call spread may be added to an already open bull put spread position when the stock price trades to the upper boundary of an established range (retreating from a resistance level that is tested and holds). The risk/reward profile is excellent, with maximum profit achieved when the stock trades at the middle strike price at expiration.

Hypothetical long iron butterfly trade:
- Shares of Google stock are trading for $700 on June 15, 2008.
- Buy one July 2008 695 put (out-of-the-money).
- Sell one July 2008 700 put (at-the-money).
- Sell one July 2008 700 call (at-the-money).
- Buy one July 2008 705 call (out-of-the-money).

Long Iron Condor

Another direction-neutral strategy, the long iron condor involves selling one out-of-the-money put, buying one deeper out-of-the-money put, selling one out-of-the-money call, and buying one deeper out-of-the-money call, all with identical expirations ideally with a month or less left until expiration. It is essentially a composite of two simpler strategies: the bull put spread and the bear call spread. The position generally is put on completely at the outset, or the bear call spread may be added to an existing bull put spread position upon the stock price retreating from an established resistance level. There is a net credit at the initiation of the spread due to the premium received for the options on the short legs of the position being greater than the cost of the purchased options on the long legs of the position. Profit is maximized in the event of the stock price trading between the two middle strike prices at expiration of the options.

Hypothetical long iron condor trade:
- Shares of Google stock are trading for $702.50 on June 15, 2008.
- Buy one July 2008 695 put (deeper out-of-the-money).
- Sell one July 2008 700 put (out-of-the-money).
- Sell one July 2008 705 call (out-of-the-money).
- Buy one July 2008 710 call (deeper out-of-the-money).

Short Iron Butterfly

This direction-neutral strategy is like its cousin strategy the long iron butterfly. It involves selling one out-of-the-money put, buying one at-the-money put, buying one at-the-money call, and selling one out-of-the-money call all with identical expirations at least three months out. It is essentially a composite spread of a bear put spread combined with a bull call spread. A net debit is generated at the outset by the cost of call options on the long legs of the spread costing more than the premium received for the put options on the short legs of the spread. The risk/reward profile is not very good on account of the extremely limited upside potential, which is dependent upon a strong breakout in either direction by the stock.

Hypothetical short iron butterfly trade:
● Shares of Google stock are trading for $702.67 on April 15, 2008.
● Sell one July 2008 695 put (out-of-the-money).
● Buy one July 2008 700 put (at-the-money).
● Buy one July 2008 700 call (at-the-money).
● Sell one July 2008 705 call (out-of-the-money).

Short Iron Condor

This direction-neutral strategy is similar to its cousin the long iron condor, and involves buying one out-of-the-money put, selling one deeper out-of-the-money put, buying one out-of-the-money call, and selling one deeper out-of-the-money call, all with identical expirations at least three months out. Profit is realized via a large breakout move in either direction by the stock. A net debit is generated by the cost of the purchased call on the long legs of the spread being greater than the premium received for the puts on the short legs of the spread. It is a composite position built upon a bear put spread and a bull call spread. The risk/reward profile is poor on account of the limited profit potential and inordinate risk in the event the stock stays in a narrow range.

Hypothetical short iron condor trade:
● Shares of Google stock are trading for $702.50 on June 15, 2008.
● Sell one September 2008 695 put (deeper out-of-the-money).
● Buy one September 2008 700 put (out-of-the-money).
● Buy one September 2008 705 call (out-of-the-money).
● Sell one September 2008 710 call (deeper out-of-the-money).

Modified Call Butterfly

A modified call butterfly involves buying one in-the-money call, selling two at-the-money calls, and buying one out-of-the-money call, all with equal expirations one month or less out. This strategy is essentially a variation of a long call butter-fly. It differs from that one in the spacing of strike prices. Instead of being equally spaced, the lower and middle strike prices are spaced further apart than the higher and middle strike prices. It is bullish in outlook, but is potentially profit-able if there is either low volatility or a breakout to the long side of the stock price—in other words, as long as the stock price does not decline appreciably. Profits are maximized in the event that the stock price is trading near the middle strike price at expiration. A net debit is generated at the outset on account of the cost of the options on the long legs of the spread being more than the premium received for the written options on the short leg of the spread. The risk/reward profile is quite good, with very limited downside risk and decent upside potential.

Hypothetical modified call butterfly trade:
- Shares of Google stock are trading for $100 on June 15, 2008.
- Buy one July 2008 90 call (in-the-money).
- Sell two July 2008 100 calls (at-the-money).
- Buy one July 2008 105 call (out-of-the-money).
(Note that the 90 call is deeper in-the-money than the 105 call is out-of-the-money.)

Modified Put Butterfly
A modified put butterfly involves buying one out-of-the-money put, selling two at-the-money puts, and buying one in-the-money put, all with the same expiration one month out or less. A variation of the long put butterfly, instead of having equally spaced strike prices, the modified put butterfly has lower and middle strike prices spaced further apart than the higher and middle strike prices. It is bullish in outlook, although profits are maximized, if there is no volatility and the stock trades near the middle strike price at expiration. The risk/reward ratio is favorable, with low risk and decent upside potential. A net credit is generated at the outset, because the amount received for writing the at-the-money puts on the short leg of the spread is higher than the cost of the puts on the long legs of the spread.

Hypothetical modified put butterfly trade:
- Shares of Google stock are trading for $100 on June 15, 2008.
- Buy one July 2008 90 put (out-of-the-money).

- Sell two July 2008 100 puts (at-the-money).
- Buy one July 2008 105 put (in-the-money).

(Note that the 90 put is deeper out-of-the-money than the 105 put is in-the-money.)

Call Ratio Backspread

This strategy involves more purchased calls than written calls. Either buying two at-the-money call and selling one in-the-money calls, or buying three at-the-money calls and selling two in-the-money calls is involved. So, the ratio of purchased to written calls is either 2:1 or 3:2. The in-the-money options should be one or two strike prices higher than the at-the-money options, and all of the options should have the same expiration six months or more out. Although the strategy has a bullish bias with unlimited profit potential on the long side with a breakout of the stock price in that direction, some profit potential also is available on a breakout to the downside. The maximum risk, which is low, is in the event of no movement of the stock price in either direction. To effectively use this strategy, it should be with a net credit or at no cost. In other words, the premium received for the written calls on the short leg of the spread should be greater or equal to the cost of the purchased calls on the long leg of the spread.

Hypothetical call ratio backspread trade:
- Shares of Google stock are trading for $100 on June 15, 2008.
- Sell two December 2008 100 calls (at-the-money).
- Buy three December 2008 110 calls (in-the-money).

Put Ratio Backspread

With a put ratio backspread, the ratio of purchased to written puts has to be either 2:1 or 3:2. So it involves either buying two out-of-the-money puts while selling one at-the-money put, or buying three out-of-the-money puts while selling two at-the-money puts, all with the same expiration six months or more out (because this is a medium- to long-term strategy). This strategy is a mirror image of the call ratio backspread, with an extremely bearish bias involving unlimited profit potential on a breakout of the stock price to the short side, limited profit potential on a breakout of the stock price to the long side, and low risk of loss in the event the stock price fails to move. To be effective, this strategy should have either no cost or a net credit at the outset. So, the premium received for written options on the short leg of the spread should be equal to or greater than the price paid for the options on the long leg of the spread.

Hypothetical put ratio backspread trade:
- Shares of Google stock are trading for $100 on June 15, 2008.
- Sell two December 2008 100 calls (at-the-money).
- Buy three December 2008 110 calls (out-of-the-money).

Long Box

This direction-neutral strategy is built on a combination of the long and short synthetic future strategies. When the two are put together with the long synthetic future at a lower strike price, they offset each other. It involves selling an out-of-the-money put and buying an in-the-money call, both at the same lower strike price, along with buying one in-the-money put and selling one out-of-the-money call, both at the same higher strike price. Expirations, which are the same for all legs of the spread, should be ideally three months out. Many professional floor traders have used the strategy. There is usually a net debit at the outset, due to the cost of the long options being greater than the premium received for the short options. The position should be unraveled piecemeal on upward and downward price swings rather than all at once.

Hypothetical long box trade:
- Shares of Google stock are trading for $505 on June 3, 2008.
- Sell ten August 2008 500 puts (out-of-the-money).
- Buy ten August 2008 500 calls (in-the-money).
- Buy ten August 2008 510 puts (in-the-money).
- Sell ten August 2008 510 calls (out-of-the-money).

Substituting single stock futures for puts or calls can be done with any of the above strategies. Although they are not as liquid as the futures contracts on the major stock indexes, many of them have enough trading volume to be viable. The futures prices typically are going to be as volatile as the stock prices, and may even be more volatile. Although there is not the problem of erosion of time value with the futures, they will level off to the cash price as they approach the delivery date. If there is backwardation—the abnormal situation when the front months are being higher priced than the back months—that actually can be advantageous with long positions as prices will rise rather than fall to the cash price level. Substituting futures for the underlying stock with strategies like covered calls or puts and collars is another alternative to consider.

Hedging risk also can be accomplished without the use of options. That is done in a variety of ways. First, with equities the strategy is to diversify across a common sector or the entire market including all sectors. Owning shares in several different companies in the same industry effectively spreads the risk to some degree. Although it is still keeping all one's eggs in a single basket, it is a bigger and more diversified basket than owning shares in just a single company within that industry. Obviously, a balanced portfolio will not have an effective degree of diversification without including investment in as large a variety of sectors as possible. Studies have further shown that portfolios that include derivatives such as futures in addition to stocks and bonds outperform portfolios that do not.

In the derivatives markets that involve forward contracts, such as futures, there are a couple of different spread strategies utilizing just the underlying instruments. The first type is spreading a position across two different markets that are closely correlated. For example, having a long corn position simultaneous with a short oats position, or buying crude oil and selling heating oil. Typically, the signal to leg into a spread comes when the two correlated markets diverge from each other all of a sudden. They will be moving in tandem, and then one of them moves in the opposite direction from the other one. That tells the spread trader that the two markets will likely snap back into alignment with each other. This adds a dimension to a spread position beyond merely hedging risk: if the forecast is correct, then there is an opportunity to profit on both sides of the spread as the two markets reverse course and return to their normal state of moving in tandem. Both legs of a spread are not always entered simultaneously, nor are they always exited simultaneously. It really just depends on what is most advantageous based on what the market is doing at the time. Also, the spread position may be a reaction to market conditions affecting a nonspread position, or the conversion of the spread to a nonspread position may be a reaction to market conditions that affect the spread. For example, if some profit already is locked in on a nonspread position and volatility spikes, a trader may leg into a spread to protect the position from going from profitable to unprofitable.

The impact of volatility is, for the most part, tempered by spreading one futures contract against another. Without spreading, the massive leverage can result in catastrophic consequences with even a small percentage change unfavorable to a futures position. There is not an invariable cushion, however. If there is a huge breakout in price to the long side, the nearby futures (front months) will tend to shoot up much faster than delivery months further out, and in the case of a steep decline in prices, the delivery months further out (back months) will tend to drop more quickly in price than the months that are nearer to delivery. Additionally, spreads are not invariably less risky than nonspread positions—they could result in even more losses in the event both legs of the spread are unprofitable, in essence compounding the loss.

Spreads are not like ATM machines that spew out cash automatically. Using them effectively requires mastering analysis and good timing. Physical commodities have carrying charges for insurance and storage, which increase the price for contracts with delivery months further out. Backwardation can be fatal to a seasonal spread that is predicated on the normal pricing situation. Global events and overblown news stories can kick prices into high gear at a moment's notice, and what may have been going well for weeks or months might turn on a dime and wreak havoc on even the best engineered and executed spread position. It behooves any trader contemplating the use of spreads to not be lulled by the promise of profits with minimal risk. Leverage is also higher, with exchange margins on spreads being much lower than for nonspread trades.

Understanding market forces that affect prices is invaluable in effectively planning spreads. Large institutions and commercial players in the market will do their best to force down prices prior to making large purchases, and the same juggernauts have a vested interest in driving up prices prior to selling. They want to pick things up at a bargain and unload them at a premium, as any clever businessperson would. Manipulation of interest rates by the Federal Reserve Bank is a powerful factor, particularly with respect to stock prices, which tend to react negatively to rising rates. Commitments of Traders reports, which the Commodity Futures Trading Commission releases every Friday with statistics from the prior Tuesday (a three-day lag), contain total long and short positions of those large traders (it is a legal requirement to report any position that is over the size threshold of a reportable position). Analyzing how those positions are trending over time can give some clues as to what kind of pressure they are exerting on prices—loading up on long positions to bolster prices or doubling down on short positions to depress prices.

Correlated Spread Market

Intermarket spreads in foreign currencies would be across any of the following pairs, either as futures contracts or paired with the U.S. dollar in the Forex market: euro currency, Swiss franc, Japanese yen, British pound, Canadian dollar, and Australian dollar. What makes these good spreading vehicles is the fact that the strength or weakness of the U.S. dollar internationally will tend to cause all of their values to rise and fall in tandem.

Intermarket spreads in stock index futures are primarily across two among the following: Dow Jones Industrial Average, S&P 500 Index, and Russell 2000 (small caps), and, to a lesser extent, the Nasdaq (which is not as closely correlated as the other three are to each other).

Intermarket spreads in interest-rate futures are primarily across pairs among the various U.S. Treasury instruments: The 30-year Treasury bonds, the 10-year Treasury notes, and the 5-year Treasury notes. U.S. Treasury bills spread across the Eurodollars (also known as the TED spread) used to be extremely popular until the contract on T-bills was discontinued. The spread of 30-year T-bonds against 10-year T-notes is much more correlated than it was in the past due to the rise in volume of the notes as the volume of the bonds fell off when the Treasury stopped issuing those instruments for a period until bringing them back fairly recently.

Intermarket spreads in energy futures are typically executed across pairs of the following: light sweet crude oil, Brent crude oil, heating oil, unleaded gasoline, and natural gas. Because they are all petroleum or petroleum-related products, their common market fundamentals cause their prices to move generally in tandem.

Grain intermarket spreads are typically across pairs among any one of the following groups of correlated futures markets: 1) soybeans, soybean oil, and soybean meal; 2) corn, CBOT wheat, soybeans, and CBOT oats; and 3) Chicago wheat, Kansas City wheat, Minneapolis wheat, and Winnipeg wheat.

Intermarket spreads in precious metals futures are typically across silver and gold. The bulk of the volume in those markets used to be at the New York Commodities Exchange (Comex), but now there is competitive volume in electronic contracts on those metals at CBOT.

Intermarket spreads in soft futures markets are typically across any two markets among cocoa, coffee, cotton, and orange juice. In the livestock futures markets, intermarket spreads are typically across live cattle and feeder cattle.

Weintraub, Fiske, and Turner have described some seasonal spreads in *Trading Winter Spreads*.[1]

May Corn/March Corn

This is a bullish strategy based on a widening in carrying charges due to storage after the October harvest, as well as potential for a seasonal increase in demand and problems with transportation over the winter. The optimum time to put on a position is the first week of January. The optimum time to liquidate any position is prior to the first notice day in March.

December Corn/July Corn

This spread uses the December contract for the new crop and the July contract for the old crop. It is based on an outlook of either a substantial premium to the July side due to demand and acreage yield uncertainty or a narrow premium to the December side. The deferred month is therefore favored with less upside pressure on the nearby contract upon resolution of that uncertainty. The optimum time to enter a position is the third week of January, and the optimum time to exit a position is the first week of March.

September Soybeans/May Soybeans

This is an old crop/new crop spread, with the crop year beginning September 1 (old crop). As long as there is not a major upside breakout in price, the price of the May contract should lag that of the September contract due to uncertainty about the new crop. The optimum time to enter the position is the first week of January, and the optimum time to exit is the last week in February.

May Soybeans/May CBOT Wheat

The soybean supply, which is based on a September–October harvest, is known at the beginning of the year. Wheat harvest yields, based on a May–July harvest, are, on the other hand, unknown at that point in time. The outlook is an increase in the price of soybeans over the price of wheat on account of a widening of carrying charge differential between the two commodities due to the higher price per harvest for soybeans and estimations of the wheat crop size becoming more

1. Neal Weintraub, Barrett Fiske, and Lan Turner, *Trading Winter Spreads* (www.pitnewspress.com, 2007), PDF e-Booklet or CD format.

accurate as harvest time approaches. The optimum time to enter a position is mid-February, and the optimum time to exit is the first week of April.

Conclusion

Spreads are a sophisticated means of providing finer control of risk than outright positions afford, the latter being limited to stop-loss orders. Most option strategies utilize some type of spreading with a high degree of flexibility to allow taking advantage of all different types of market conditions. Spreads can be effectively used for both equities and derivatives markets.

Summary of Chapter 8

- Spreads provide a means of hedging your bet on market direction and thereby managing downside risk.
- With options there are myriad different strategies involving spreads.
- Futures can be spread across different months in the same market or across different markets within the same sector.

Putting It All Together

CHAPTER 9

A Cyclical Model of the Markets

When I began trading oats futures in the summer of 1983, it was under unusual market conditions. A severe drought had caused a big bull market in grain contracts, and many traders were racking up phenomenal profits on soybeans, in particular playing the long side of that market. Many floor traders cashed in on both the short and the long side of the market with the wild intraday price swings.

For the oats contract, I used a simple strategy of looking for prices to deviate by a significant amount from a single short-term moving average and then selling when they closed above the average by that amount and buying when they closed below the average by that amount. I was a complete novice, having to first find out how to call in orders to my discount broker. Nonetheless, I was able to make profitable trades, without a single losing position, for almost two months straight. My broker was amazed at my success, and he urged me to apply my technique to other markets when the oats market cooled off that autumn and I was not getting any more buy or sell indications with my strategy.

I investigated all of the actively traded futures markets at the exchanges in Chicago and New York to see if that was viable. After some close scrutiny and trying moving averages of various lengths, I came up empty-handed. I then spent the better part of a year searching for a good strategy based on technical analysis. Everything I studied was, to me, mediocre at best. It was at that point that I began to ponder market cycles. I looked into the work of the legendary analyst Burton Pugh, who theorized that phases of the moon could be used to predict price trends. Unfortunately, I did not find anything particularly useful about such an approach to analysis. I did not stop there, though. I was still in search of cycles that actually work well.

Why Cycles?

I first noticed a statistical correlation between cycles and prices as I was poring over some price charts of gold and silver futures from the 1970s and early 1980s. Two very long-term cycles matched up with major bull markets in those precious metals. In fact, they are such long cycles that analyzing a significant sampling of prices would require several centuries of price data. Granting that the statistical sampling is inadequately small, still, the recent long-term run up of prices in the spot and futures markets came right on schedule. What I would expect to find upon examining a long historical record of prices would be some rise in price trends matching up with those two cycles. They probably would not be as dramatic as those found in the past three bull metals markets, however.

I then proceeded to investigate cycles of shorter length, and major and minor tops and bottoms on daily Open/High/Low/Close bar charts of various commodity and financial futures that coincided with those cycles literally jumped right off the pages at me. I knew I was onto something very significant. I started to wonder if other market analysts had also discovered the same phenomenon. If they had, they had not written about it in any of the literature on market cycles. All of the research I had read about up to that point in time was on cycles that were totally different from the ones I was applying in my analysis. If any others had made the same discovery I had, they were definitely keeping it to themselves. Knowledge is power and loose lips sink ships. There is a general tendency for traders to keep their systems a secret. One reason for that is the belief that if too many other people know about a system and act upon it, then it will have a net effect on the market that could counteract the strategy being employed.

The next thing that came to mind was from one of the little voices that provide me with occasional reality checks. I am not sure whether it was the little virtual angel floating on my right shoulder or the little virtual devil perched on my left shoulder. Was my postulate even valid? What if the phenomenon I was seeing was just something imaginary, and there is really no cause-and-effect relationship between various cycles and price movement in markets? Was there some underlying force that caused price-trend reversals to occur according to some order that could be modeled via a timing mechanism? Certainly, it is an undeniable fact that market prices do not continue in one direction over time. Eventually there is either some type of correction on the way up or prices top out to fall back to their original levels or perhaps even lower levels. I then decided that all of that was not the most important thing. What mattered most was whether any money could be made in the markets with my approach.

Historical Credibility of Cycle Analysis

Although the technical efficiency of actual effective market performance is the proverbial and real bottom line, before the presentation of my own cyclical model insights it is in order to briefly discuss the existing body of work on market cycles.

Modern cycle theory and practice were invigorated by incentives well beyond mere financial market analysts seeking better trend assessment tools. At the behest of the Hoover administration in the early 1930s, government official Edward R. Dewey was recruited to the task of determining the causes of the Great Depression. His discovery that the type of economic decline seen in that decade had occurred before as a regular, cyclic phase of economic weakness that was merely the next phase in a series of seemingly endemic occurrences led to his extensive review of other cyclic activity as well, and ultimately to the establishment of the Foundation for the Study of Cycles with a host of other visionaries in 1941. They published their magnum opus of cyclical research on various market cycles in 1970 in a massive tome in three volumes.[1] Among many other phenomena, Dewey found cycles in stock market prices of many different lengths: 9.2 years, 18.2 years, 6.01 years, 3.83 years, 46 months, 17.166 weeks, 41 months, 7.94 years, 8.39 years, 5.91 or 5.92 years, 8.5 years, 6.41 years, and 6.33 years. He also found the following cycles in commodities prices: 9.2, 8.5, and 17.75 years for pig iron; 17.75, 5.91, and 5.5 years for cotton; 5.5 years for corn; 42 and 54 years for European wheat; and 54 years for copper.

In identification of cycles, Dewey had various criteria and approaches, including regularity of intervals, separation of multiple cycles into individual cycles, filtering out random ups and downs, and ample repetitions.[2] He also states that cyclical phenomena are defined by orderly cyclic patterns in time exclusive of patterns in space, which can be rhythmic or nonrhythmic, repetitive or nonrepetitive.[3]

---

1. Edward R. Dewey, *Cycles Classic Library Collection, Volume I–Cycles Selected Writings* (Foundation for the Study of Cycles, 1970).

2. Ibid., pp. 4–5.

3. Ibid., p. 35.

With respect to cycles in general, Dewey stated, "Cycles are meaningful, and all science that has been developed in the absence of cycle knowledge is inadequate," adding that "any theory of economics, sociology, history, medicine, or climatology that ignores non-chance rhythms is as manifestly incomplete as medicine was before the discovery of germs."[4]

In that regard, I agree. Although, of necessity, cycles are best used in conjunction with other forms of analysis and risk management, note that the type of cycle analysis that the most disciplined price trend analysts apply to this type of study conform to the highest level of Dewey's hierarchy of cycle studies: "Truly *periodic cyclic patterns in time*—and truly periodic recurrent events—are both ... necessarily special cases of recurrent cyclic patterns in time or recurrent events."[5]

Definitive Cyclical Market Analysis

Of necessity, the market analysts who are among the most aggressive on both a theoretical and practical basis have taken the classical cycle analysis approach a bit further than the historical luminaries. Although the Foundation for the Study of Cycles and Dewey's fellow travelers have made major contributions to the overall study of cycles, in many cases they tend to "average out" the net influence of concurrent cycle projections from different periods. This can be very effective when analyzing the anticipated net cyclical impact of broad trends. Yet, much as is the case with seasonal cycle "averaging" to establish the net effect of the general influence on price trends (which is not covered in this book), it is less than effective for highly defined trend reversal analysis, and does not contribute much to rigorous risk management due to that factor.

One of the folks among many who have extended that form of cycle analysis as a meaningful part of their overall multidisciplinary approach to trend analysis and timing is Alan Rohrbach, who authored the foreword for this book. His observations on the specific ways in which definitive cycle analysis must be refined for effective application are expressed in a simple yet meaningful manner in his training materials. The following is excerpted from the extensive technical analysis portion of his "macro" analysis seminar segment on "Cycle Parameter Tolerances":[6]

---

4. Edward R. Dewey, "The Case for Cycles," *Cycles* (July 1967), p. 30.

5. Dewey, *Cycles Classic Library Collection, Volume I* , p. 35.

6. Alan Rohrbach, Intensive Technical Analysis Seminar, Module IV: Cycles (Rohr International, Inc., 1988), p. M-46.

To assist in interpreting the "decision process" during projected cycles, it is most important to understand what price trend variance is acceptable before the attempted cycle must be considered to be unreliable for the current phase. As in bar chart formation Tolerances, there is usually some point in the price trend at which an attempted cycle parameter no longer represents a significant high or low. The specific conditions under which a market is conclusively above a Cycle High or below a Cycle Low to the degree that it is Negated (beyond its acceptable Tolerance) as a level of Trend Support or Trend Resistance can only be discerned by studying specific previous activity during cyclical intervals.

In the example in **Figure 9.1**, the Treasury Bills respected the 19-day Cycle High (arrows) unless the market Closed above the Cycle High shortly after the cyclical interval occurred. So, the Tolerance of the 19-day Cycle High in this example can be defined as "no Closing price above the Cycle High." If the Tolerance is violated (i.e., a Closing price occurs above the Cycle High parameter), then the Cycle High is "Negated" (no longer an effective level of Trend Resistance). Also, for the limited number of cycle attempts under study, it seems that a Negation of this particular Cycle High leads to a "directional" uptrend. Whether each cycle attempt succeeds or not, the projected cyclical interval represents a "decision process," which should render a

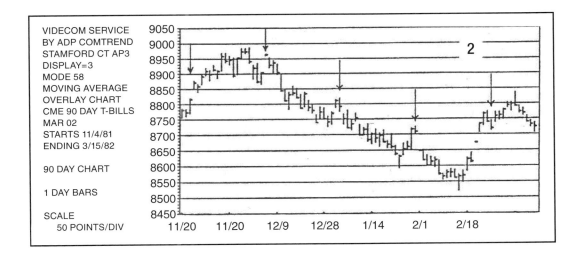

FIGURE **9.1**

19-Day Cycles on T-Bills

Source: ADP Comtrend

"directional" price trend. When a market exhibits this tendency of becoming "directional" when the cycle parameter is Negated, defining the Tolerance properly is even more important to analyzing the current price trend.

Rohrbach is highly focused on "directionality" being a primary consideration for this more rigorous and definitive analysis of cycle tendencies. It means that whether particular signals succeed or fail, there are still important implications to be drawn from the "decision." That substantially intensifies the need for technical analysts to discern the most reliable time periods for decisive price trend activity.

This is no different in its way for cycles from the need to properly assess the evolution of various forms of price activity as chart patterns form. It relates to the need to be patient once fledgling patterns are detected or price swings near the boundaries of channel trend lines and return lines. In the case of cycles, that just happens to occur as a function of waiting for prices to enter well-defined time periods, as opposed to the indeterminate passage of time while chart patterns evolve.

Developing a Proprietary Approach

The ironic part of this story is that I did not actually study all that extremely weighty historical cycle background and theory prior to developing a proprietary approach. Although that may sound a bit odd, sharing the extreme performance mentality that draws so many to active market analysis ensured that the immediate awareness of cycle activity and the obvious ways in which that implied an effective approach to risk management meant the method was more important than philosophy.

All theory of which I later became aware only confirmed my instincts. In essence, it became glaringly apparent that it was operating in the background as a foundation for my process without my even necessarily being aware of it. More important from the outset, and ultimately assisting my view of extended application of this analysis, was figuring out a general strategy for trades.

The first rule I devised was that on the day of an imminent price reversal, the place to enter a trade was on the opening of the trading session, but only if the market was within ten ticks either way of the previous session's settlement price (in other words, as long as there was not an appreciable gap up or down on the opening). A second rule I devised was to avoid trading against a very pronounced trend in which a trend line approaching 90 degrees up or down could be drawn on a daily bar chart. So, I had two filter conditions. Now, I just needed some exit strategies. For risk management, a protective stop was in order. I decided upon risking anywhere from ten to twenty ticks, depending on the particular market and levels of relative volatility. For taking profits, I established preset levels in discrete price increments. I then spent several months paper trading with that strategy and closely monitoring the markets using five- and ten-minute bar charts. I tabulated the results for several different futures markets including 30-year Treasury bonds, S&P 500 Stock Index, soybeans, wheat, sugar, silver, gold, crude oil, the Swiss franc, the German mark, the British pound, and the Japanese yen. From that hypothetical test, it appeared that my overall strategy was indeed sound.

I had what looked like a decent forecasting tool. With it I could predict with statistical reliability when a major or minor trend in price was about to reverse. The method does not work all the time, but it works significantly more than half the time. It is superior to throwing a dart or tossing a coin. The only thing it could not tell me is just how far the price would rise or fall, only the right direction in which to place a trade. If the analysis indicates a cycle ending on a downswing in price, the strategy is to take a long position. If the ending of a cycle comes on an upswing, the strategy is just the opposite: Take a short position. That may seem simple enough, but there are myriad other considerations when it comes to trading highly leveraged instruments like futures and options on futures (some of which are touched upon in earlier chapters).

Cycles and Changing Conditions

Over the past twenty years, the character of the futures markets has changed. The main causes are the nature of the participants and the impact of electronic trading. There are far fewer locals in the pits, which have shrunk dramatically. The days of locals making a market are now a bygone era, with program trading having taken over. Pit traders now mostly hang around attempting to participate in moves initiated by program trading. To borrow a phrase from well-regarded long-term macro and short-term technical analyst Aaron Reinglass, these have become "Terminator" markets.

Reinglass was among the first to notice (and adapt his analysis to) these changes. As he sees it, the long history of modern market analysis was accompanied by parallel developments that allowed people to take advantage of astounding leaps in computing power to achieve more in-depth technical and quantitative analyses. Then along came the algorithm masters and their ever more extensive development of effective trading programs, and it was time for "the revenge of the machines." Anyone temporarily attempting to engage in old-time tactics of "fading" (that is, taking positions opposite to) a seemingly overextended short-term price swing is soon provided an object lesson in exaggerated near-term price movement. The "cascade" effect of program trade swings creates self-fulfilling signals that trigger further momentum in the direction of the near-term price swing: more selling in weak markets and more buying in strong ones. The net effect is to viciously extend the near-term aggressive trend beyond that which had traditionally been the case.

This calls for more circumspection on when to assume near-term price swings are indeed exhausted, and that is much more relevant than the old days when locals were able to create reactions. Of course, there are now also far more funds and other money managers trading huge lots. Individual traders have generally become much more active in terms of employing short-term position and day-trading strategies, as well.

Trend Directionality and Cycles

In 2004, I decided to consider other strategies that might work with my cyclical model. I investigated the use of Market Profile charts as a potential tool to enhance profitability. I also considered the use of various technical studies. I discovered that I could obtain better precision with my entry and exit points than I had with my original strategy. One factor had changed over the course of twenty years: price gaps between the previous close and the opening price need to be filtered only if they occur in the direction opposite to the buy/sell signal. In other words, if there is a buy signal and the market gaps down, then do not buy the opening range—but if it gaps up, then the opening range is a good place to buy, as long as the gap is not more than fifty ticks.

Perhaps the most difficult aspect to communicate with respect to utilization of my cyclical model to generate buy and sell signals is the methodology behind determination of market direction. Sometimes it is obvious at a quick glance that a particular market has just had a significant swing up or down. At other time it takes some closer scrutiny and can boil down to a judgment call as to whether the market has any current direction at all or is simply a sideways market. There has to be at least some price bias, either bullish or bearish, to make a determination that at a cycle boundary there is some probability for a new countertrend on which to act. In the case of the blatantly obvious direction, it can be a dramatic price move of several days duration with a very steep trend line established along daily highs and/or lows, or it could be a rally or dip of several days' duration that is starting to lose momentum with the formation of a doji candlestick or two. In the case of direction that is somewhat obfuscated, it could be a daily session that stands on its own and closes on a high or low of an expanded range that is perhaps double or even triple the average daily range over several weeks or months.

Measurement of cycle amplitude is also a means to project potential future price levels based on the already established range for which a major top or bottom is heralded with a combination of cycle boundaries and chart analysis, including the width of channels. Simply put, amplitude is the distance between the extreme price bounces between in cyclical fashion. Just as the amplitude of a sound wave determines its decibel level (or volume)—as opposed to its frequency, which determines its pitch (high or low)—the amount of change in price over time from the beginning to the midpoint of a cycle should determine the amplitude.

Short-Term Trading Based on Cycle Analysis

The extensive examples of short-term cycle analysis that follow are meant to review both the effectiveness of the analysis across a range of markets, as well as how the use of relevant analyses from other forms of technical analysis support its implementation. Yet, this does not preclude the use of other complementary techniques for optimization of cycle analysis. The select group of other indicators combined with the cycle analysis below is intended to allow for clear examples of some of the best combinations, and preferences of other analysts will determine their view of which additional indicators are best for their personal trade timing and risk management. Additional examples of cycle analysis for long-term strategies are found later in this chapter.

S&P 500 E-Mini Futures

Figure 9.2 is a daily candlestick chart of the S&P 500 E-mini futures contract, on which are marked turning points that correlate with my multiple-cycle model. The dotted vertical lines are cyclical boundaries at which a turning point could occur.

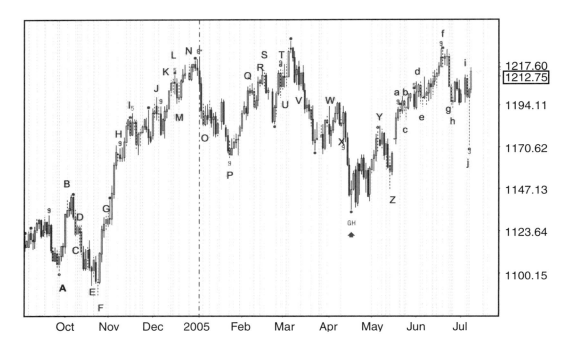

FIGURE 9.2

Daily Chart of S&P 500 E-Mini Futures

Source: Wave59

At the end of September 2004, the price had dropped for a couple of days and a buy signal was generated (A). The exhaustion bars (the dot below the candle) also yielded a buy indication at the same time. The market rose slightly for two days, stalled for a day with a doji candle on the chart, then had a dramatic rise the next day. The sell signal in early October (B) came two days before the actual turning point as the market generated signs of uncertainty with an evening star doji. The buy signal that came after a significant one-day drop in price (C) did not result in an actual trade, because the market opened below the previous session's low and dropped from there. However, the market did reverse and rally slightly the following session (D), only to sell off the next session (note the dotted lines indicating potential reversals—often the market will flip-flop when there are cyclical boundaries on consecutive days).

The next buy signal in October (E) is followed by a one-day rally, and the following buy signal two days later conjoined with a doji candle (F) is followed by a dramatic uptrend. The sell signal at the end of October (G) was a false signal, and would be a losing trade as was the sell signal five days later (H). Sometimes the market does seem to be affected by a cyclical boundary, although it may only result in some short-term sideways price movement (the market stalls but fails to reverse enough to make any profit). That was the case with the signal at H on the chart. The sell signal a few days later (I) in mid-November does see some slight downward price action for a few days, as does the one in early December (J).

The next sell signal comes a few days later, and is a false signal (K), but the turning point comes two days later (L) in conjunction with an exhaustion bar sell indicator (dot over the candle), a 5 on the 9-5 count indicator and a high wave candle. The buy signal two days after that (M), which is conjoined with a high wave candle, is followed by a decent rally. The sell signal following that in late December just after the Christmas holiday does not work well. That is fairly typical. The rule is to ignore signals that come just after holidays, as they are not reliable. The same goes for the buy signal right after the New Year's holiday (O). The buy signal in late January 2005 (P), which is conjoined with an exhaustion bar buy indication and a buy indication on the 9-5 count (a 9 below the candle), is followed by a several-day uptrend as predicted.

The sell signal in mid-February (Q), which coincides with a couple of spinning top candles, sees an ensuing one-day sell-off with some profit potential as a day-trade. The next turning point comes two days (S) after the false sell signal in late February (R). The next two consecutive cycle boundaries at the tail end of February (T, U) result in a flip-flop of the trend: A sell-off followed by a rally, as expected. The next buy signal in mid-March (V) sees a one-day rally with good opportunity to profit from a day-trade. The sell signal at the very end of March (W) sees a slight sell-off, although nothing to write home about. The buy signal a few days later in early April (X) in conjunction with a spinning top candle sees a very small rally ensue over two days.

The sell signal near the beginning of May (Y), which is in conjunction with a doji candle and an exhaustion bar sell indication (dot over the candle) correctly presages a several-day sell-off. The buy signal in mid-May (Z), which is in conjunction with a high wave candle, is followed by an impressive rally. The sell signal near the end of May (a) is a dud, but the flip-flop of direction at the next two reversal signals (b, c) two days later is true to form as is the next one in early June (d, e). The sell signal in mid-June (f), which is in tandem with a sell indication on the 9-5 count and exhaustion bar indicator, as well as with a high wave candle followed by spinning top candle and then a doji candle, is followed by a significant sell-off.

The next buy signal near the end of June (g) does not result in a trade, because the market opens lower and continues down from there, but the buy signal the next day (h), which is in conjunction with a spinning top candle, does yield a potential for profit on the long side over a two-day period. The sell signal in early July (i) sees a steep drop on that day and into the next session with the buy signal (j), as a support level is tested, and the market does an about-face to close higher for the day and rally into the next session.

10-Year Treasury Notes Futures

Figure 9.3 is a daily price chart of the 10-year Treasury notes futures contract. The sell signal at the end of August (1) is followed by a drop in price with a large gap the following day and then a rebound for that session, but failure to fill in the gap. The following day is another sell signal (2) along with a spinning top doji candle. A wild ride ensues as the market sells off the first day, then rallies midday the next and falls off precipitously to close much lower. The buy signal after Labor Day is disregarded according to the rule that says the signals following holidays are not reliable, although in this case it was a true signal. The sell signal in mid-September (3) sees a sell-off for one day, providing potential for a day-trade.

The sell signal in late September (4) sees a two-day sell-off followed by an accurate buy signal (5) preceded by a spinning top candle, and then an accurate sell signal comes the next day (6), presaging a large downswing in prices. The buy signal at the beginning of October (7) sees a support level tested and then a rebound in prices to close higher with a slightly higher close the next day. After a double bottom forms along with a spinning top candle, the next buy signal in mid-October (8) is followed by a significant rally for several days. Although cycle boundaries are falling on the next three consecutive days (9, 10, 11), there are no trades due to the market opening higher and rising from the opening on each of those sessions. A buy signal comes after a one-day sell-off (12), and it is followed by a continuation of the upward trend that was already under way.

The sell signal at the end of October (A) comes with a very slight sell-off for a single day, but the next sell signal two days later (13) in conjunction with a couple of spinning top candles marks a major top. A couple of days later, there is a flip-flop in prices as a buy signal is followed the next day by a sell signal (14, 15), an opportunity for a doubleheader winning-trade

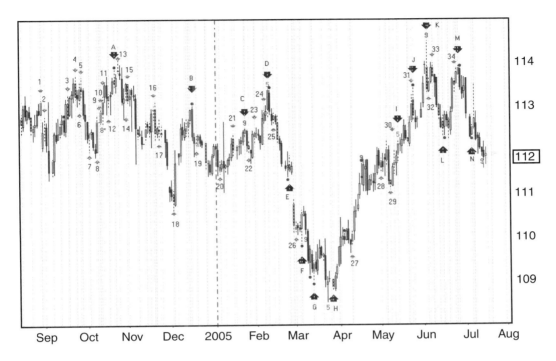

FIGURE 9.3

Daily Chart of T-Notes Futures

Source: Wave59

combination. The sell signal in mid-November (16) in conjunction with a doji candle is followed by a sharp decline the next session. A false buy signal comes a couple of days later (17), and then a buy signal at the beginning of December (18) is followed by a dramatic rebound in prices beginning with the following session.

The next top is indicated by the exhaustion bar sell signal (dot over the candle), but in the absence of falling on a cycle boundary (although there is one on the prior day). Sometimes, the combination of cycle boundaries with other indicators that correctly forecasts a reversal occurs over a couple of days or more, rather than on the same day. This was one of those instances. The following buy signal in mid-December (19) sees only a temporary stalling of the downtrend, with little or no opportunity for profit on the long side.

The buy signal after the New Year's Day holiday at the beginning of January 2005 (20) is ignored based on the holiday stand-aside rule. The sell signal in mid-January 2005 (21) sees a decent sell-off for a single session, and the next sell signal at the end of that month (C) in conjunction with a sell indication on the 9-5 count sees a three-day drop in prices. The buy signal two days later (22) sees only a very slight increase in price for a single session, yielding a very small opportunity for profit as a day-trade. The sell signal at the beginning of February (23) is followed by a couple of doji candles and then a sell-off. The sell signal several days later in mid-February (24) is a false signal that would result in a losing trade. A major top is marked by the cycle boundary a couple of days later (D)—no trade on that day because the market opens higher and rallies from there, which is conjoined with a sell indication on the 9-5 count (golden 5) followed by another sell indication on the exhaustion bars (dot over the candle).

The buy signal a couple of days into the downtrend (25) sees only a slight rise in price for a single session, making for only a small profit opportunity on the long side. At the end of February, a couple of reversal candles (a spinning top followed by a high wave candle) line up with an exhaustion bar buy indication (E), and then a cycle boundary is hit; however, due to the sideways price movement over two days following a holiday, it is a mixed signal, and the market gaps way down two days later. The buy signal at the beginning of March (26) is followed by a few days of uncertainty (three spinning candles in a row) and an exhaustion bar buy indication (F) and then a significant two-day rally.

The next buy signal in mid-March (G), which is in conjunction with an exhaustion bar buy indication, sees a one-day rally followed by a retracement to the downside the next day, then a two-day rally. The major bottom (the head of a head and shoulders bottom pattern) has a high wave candle with a golden 5 reversal indication on the 9-5 count followed two days later by coincidence with a cycle boundary (H). The next buy signal occurred mid-April (27), and a spectacular rally follows for several days. The buy signal in early May (28) sees only a small rise in prices for a single session and the market retraces to the downside the next day. The buy signal several days later (29) is followed by a strong rally. The sell signal two days later (30) is a dud signal. The next sell signal (31) does not result in any trade, since the market gapped higher on the opening and rallied from there. A cycle boundary in conjunction with a golden 5 on the 9-5 count (I) is a false reversal indication. (I reiterate that the model is not a crystal ball, and sometimes there will be a string of losses—it is the overall performance over time that is important.)

The sell signal in late May (J) in conjunction with an exhaustion bar (dot over the candle) sees a two-day drop in prices. The sell signal in early June (K), which follows a doji candle and is in tandem with a sell indication on the 9-5 count (the 9 above the candle), sees a sell-off after a spike up and prices retreating from the extreme high. The next day is a buy signal (32) with a two-day rally ensuing. Then a sell signal comes the next day (33) with a steep correction to the downside over several sessions. The buy signal in mid-June (L) is followed by an exhaustion bar buy indication (the dot below the candle), and a strong rally follows after the completion of a double-bottom formation. A couple of days into the rally, a sell signal (34) sees a minor correction with some profit potential for a day-trade. Then a couple of days later is a sell signal (M) followed by a significant downswing. The buy signal at the beginning of July (N) sees a strong two-day rally.

Euro Currency Futures

Figure 9.4 is a chart of the euro currency futures contract. The buy signal near the end of August 2005 (1) sees a two-day rally. Then, a sell signal (2) in conjunction with a spinning top candle is followed by a sell-off over the next two days. Then the market turns around again and rallies until the next sell signal in mid-September (3). There is a doji candle on the day of the signal and the following day and then a drop as predicted by the cyclical model. Often there are a series of dojis or spinning top candles at a market turning point, instead of just one of them. The next cycle boundary in mid-September (4) comes after a piercing candle, and the market does reverse again to the long side after two doji candles. The following cycle boundary after a piercing candle (5) fails to see a reversal to the short side, however. The reversal comes a couple of days later at the beginning of October (A), with a sell signal after a bearish harami candlestick pattern in conjunction with an exhaustion bar sell indication (dot over the candle).

The next buy signal in mid-October (B) is in conjunction with an exhaustion bar buy indication and a spinning top candle. The market rallies as predicted until the next sell signal a couple of days later (7) in tandem with a spinning top candle, and it is followed by a sell-off. The next buy signal (6) in mid-October is in tandem with an exhaustion bar buy indication and a hammer candle, and the market reverses to the long side as predicted. The sell signal in later October (C), which is in conjunction with a sell indication on the 9-5 count, is a false reversal signal, and the market continues its steep ascent. The next cycle boundary at the end of October (D) is followed the next day by a reversal with sell indications both on the exhaustion bars and the 9-5 count along with a piercing candle. The buy signal a couple of days

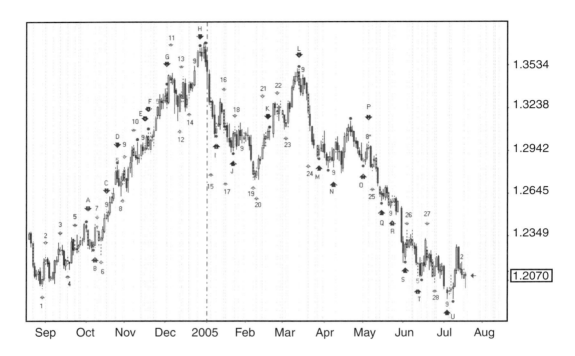

FIGURE 9.4

Monthly Chart of Euro Currency Futures

Source: Wave59

later (8) at the beginning of November, which follows a high wave candle, correctly predicts a reversal to the long side. The following day has a sell signal (9) in conjunction with a piercing candle and correctly predicts a two-day sell-off.

The sell signal several days later in mid-November (10), which is in conjunction with a piercing candle, is followed by only a slight drop in prices. The sell signal in late November (E) in conjunction with a sell indication on the 9-5 count and a bearish harami candlestick pattern followed by a spinning top candle is yet another false reversal signal. A couple of days later are two cycle boundaries in a row (F) that see a sell-off one day and a rally that begins the next day (the flip-flop described earlier in this chapter) as expected. A one-day sell-off comes with the sell signal at the beginning of December (G). The sell signal two days later (11), which is in tandem with a spinning top candle, correctly predicts a several-day decline.

The buy signal in mid-December (12) in conjunction with a bullish engulfing candle is followed by a one-day rally as predicted. There are cycle boundaries on the next two consecutive days (13) and the market does its flip-flop (decline followed by rally) as expected. The buy signal in late December (14) is in conjunction with a bullish harami candlestick pattern. It correctly predicts a rally, which breaks through a major resistance level from early December. A rounded market top begins to form a day after the next cycle boundary (H) in late December. There are two sell indications on the exhaustion bars along with a doji candle. A false buy signal occurs in early January (15). Three days later in early January is a good buy signal (I), and it is in tandem with a bullish harami candlestick pattern and a buy indication on the exhaustion bars.

The next sell signal in early January (16) is in conjunction with a bearish harami candlestick pattern, and it is followed the next day with a buy signal (17) with only a slight rally for one session. The buy signal in mid-January (J) is in conjunction with a tweezers bottom candlestick pattern and an exhaustion bar buy indication. A sell signal comes the next day (18), and the following session brings a reversal to the downside. A cycle boundary at the beginning of February (19) does not result in a trade to the long side due to the market opening lower and falling from there for that session.

The next day, on the other hand, is a buy signal (20) with the formation of a tweezers bottom candlestick pattern, and a rally occurs as expected. The sell signal in mid-February (21) is another false reversal signal. The exhaustion bar sell indication and doji candle that follow (K), which would ordinarily be confirmation of a reversal, similarly scream reversal in the absence of one. The sell signal in late February (22) is followed by a few days of uncertainty, but then a slight decline does occur. A buy signal in early March (23) in conjunction with a spinning top candle is followed by a significant rally. The sell signal in mid-March (L) in conjunction with an exhaustion bar sell indication and a bearish engulfing candle correctly predicts a decline. A false buy signal occurs a few days later (24), and the market continues its precipitous slide.

The market forms a double bottom following a cycle boundary in late March (M). A couple of exhaustion bar buy indications show up, as well as a buy indication on the 9-5 count indicator (N). The buy signal at the beginning of May (O), which is in tandem with a morning star doji candle, correctly predicts a rally. The sell signal a few days later (P), which is conjoined with a spinning top candle and a sell indication on the 9-5 count (8* above the candle), is followed by a decline in prices. The buy signal a couple of days later in early May (25) is followed by a slight rise in prices, and the market continues its slide to the downside. The buy signal in late May (R) is followed by only a very slight rise in prices, without much opportunity, if any, for profit on the long side. There is then an exhaustion bars buy indication with a piercing candles(s) and a cycle boundary (34), but there is a lack of follow-through to the long side.

A bottom takes three days to form in mid-June (T) with a cycle boundary and doji candle followed by a buy indication on the 9-5 count (golden 5 below the candle) and then a buy indication on the exhaustion bars (dot below the candle). The sell signal several days later (27) is followed by a four-day decline. The buy signal at the end of June (28) correctly anticipates a two-day rally. The buy signal in early July (U), in conjunction with a few spinning top candles, a buy in indication on the 9-5 count (9 below the candle), and an exhaustion bar buy indication, is followed by a significant rally.

Light Sweet Crude Oil Futures

Figure 9.5 is a chart of the light sweet crude oil futures contract. The buy signal near the end of August 2005 (1) is a day early. The reversal comes the following day in conjunction with a spinning top candle followed by an exhaustion bar buy indication (A) (dot under the candle). The buy signal in mid-September (2) correctly predicts a two-day rally. There is a false sell signal in late September (3) in conjunction with a spinning top candle. A couple of days later near the end of September (B), a top appears to be forming with a couple of cycle boundaries and sell indications on the exhaustion bars (dot over the candle) and on the 9-5 count, however the market continues its ascent. A false sell signal occurs in mid-October (4), but a reversal to the downside does occur with the next sell signal a couple of days later (C), which is in tandem with sell indications on the exhaustion bars and the 9-5 count. The expected flip-flop occurs the next day with a buy signal and a rise in prices (5). Following a two-day rally, a sell signal (6) in mid-October in conjunction with a spinning top candle sees a two-day price decline.

The next sell signal after a two-day rally (7) is a false signal. The next sell signal two days later (D) is a good indication in conjunction with a tweezers top candlestick pattern, an exhaustion bars sell indication, and a sell indication on the 9-5 count (8*). A flip-flop occurs with a buy signal (8) and a one-day rally followed by a sell signal at the end of October (E) in conjunction with a bearish engulfing candle followed by a significant decline in prices. The next reversal

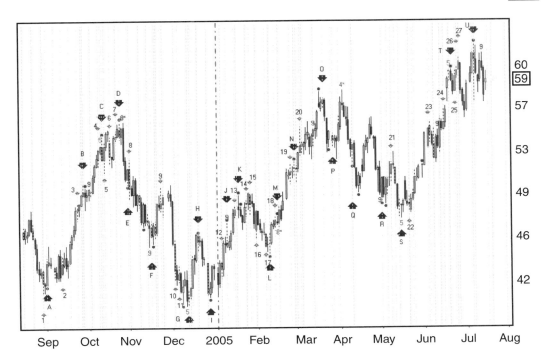

FIGURE **9.5**

Monthly Chart of Crude Oil Futures

Source: Wave59

signal (F), which is a buy indication on the 9-5 count followed by a cycle boundary followed by a buy indication on the exhaustion bars, correctly predicts a rise
in prices. The sell signal in late November (9), which follows a spinning top doji,
is the beginning of a double top formation, which is followed by a decline.

A false buy signal occurs at the beginning of December (10). The buy
signal two days later (11) sees a one-day rise in prices. The next buy signal in
mid-December (G) is with the formation of a double bottom, a spinning top
doji, and a buy indication on the 9-5 count. A sell signal in late December (H)
in conjunction with a bearish harami candlestick formation and a sell indication on the exhaustion bars (dot over the candle) is followed by a decline
over several days. The cycle boundary the day after the Christmas holiday (I)
is disregarded as a buy signal due to the after-a-holiday rule. A sell signal in
early January (12) sees a one-day decline. A couple of days later a false sell
signal occurs (J) and then another one several days later (14). There is a cycle

boundary (13) just before the holiday, but the rule is not to trade. A sell signal in late January (15) correctly predicts a decline, which lasts for three days. A buy signal at the very end of January (16) sees a one-day rally.

A buy signal in mid-February (17) does not result in a trade as the market opens lower and drops from there. Two days later a buy signal (L) in conjunction with a doji candle and a buy indication on the exhaustion bars (dot under the candle) are followed by a significant rally. A few days later a false sell signal occurs (18), and then another one at the end of February (19) and one at the beginning of March (20). A sell signal in mid-March (O), which is preceded by an exhaustion gap, a hammer candle, and a sell indication on the exhaustion bars, is followed by a significant decline. A buy signal in late March (P), which follows a bullish harami candlestick pattern and a buy indication on the exhaustion bars (dot under the candle), is followed by a significant rally over several days. A buy signal in early April (Q) sees a one-day rally. A buy signal at the end of April (R), which is accompanied by buy indications on the 9-5 count and exhaustion bars (dot under the candle), is followed by a rally as predicted.

A false sell signal in early May (21) is followed by a genuine one two days later preceded by an evening star doji candle. A buy signal in mid-May (S), which is accompanied by a bullish harami candlestick pattern, a doji candle, and a buy indication on the 9-5 count, correctly predicts a reversal to the long side. A buy signal in late May (22), which is accompanied by a couple of spinning top candles and a bullish engulfing candle, correctly anticipates a rally.

A sell signal in early June (23), which is accompanied by a piercing candle, is followed by a three-day decline with a false buy signal on the third day. A sell signal occurs in late June (T) accompanied by a doji candle and sell indications on the 9-5 count and exhaustion bars (dot over the candle), and it correctly anticipates a decline. The buy signal a few days later (25) correctly anticipates a reversal to the long side followed by two false signals in a row (26 and 27).

The sell signal at the beginning of July (U), which is accompanied by a bearish harami candlestick pattern and a sell indication on the exhaustion bars (dot over the candle), correctly anticipates a reversal to the short side.

100 Ounce Gold Futures

Figure 9.6 is a daily chart of the 100 ounce gold futures contract. A sell signal in late August 2005 (1) accompanied by a bearish harami candlestick pattern correctly anticipates a reversal to the short side. A buy signal at the end of August (2) forecasts a two-day rally. A sell signal at the start of September (3) accompanied by a bearish harami candlestick pattern portends a several-day decline. A buy indication (4) after the Labor Day holiday would be disregarded according to the holiday rule. The following cycle boundary (A) does not generate a signal, due to a lack of strong price direction. The cycle boundary mid-month (5) is in the middle of a sideways market, so there is no buy or sell signal generated. The sell signal at the beginning of October (B), which is preceded by a hammer candle, pinpoints a reversal to the short side, but it lasts for only a single session. The sell signal in early October (C) accompanied by a spinning top candle and a sell indication on the exhaustion bars (dot over the candle) correctly forecasts a reversal to the short side. The buy signal two days later (6) pinpoints a new bottom. A sell signal in mid-October (7), which is preceded by a spinning top candle, sees a one-day decline. There is a false sell signal in late October (8). A two-day flip-flop occurs at the end of October (9) with a buy signal following a high wave candle as part of a bullish harami

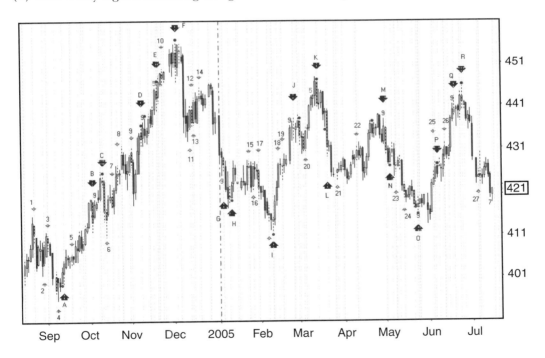

FIGURE **9.6**

Daily Chart of Gold Futures

Source: Wave59

pattern correctly predicting a one-day rally. A sell-off the next day was correctly predicted by a sell signal in conjunction with a bearish piercing candle.

A sell signal in early November (D) in conjunction with a sell indication on the exhaustion bars (dot over the candle) sees only a slight decline for a single session. The sell signal in late November (E) accompanied by sell indications on the exhaustion bars (dots over the candles) and 9-5 count sees a one-day decline, as does the next one three days later (10). A rounded top forms at the tail end of November and beginning of December, and there is the occurrence of a cycle boundary (F) and a bearish engulfing candle and sell indication on the exhaustion bars (dot over the candle).

A buy signal in mid-December (11) is followed by a sell signal the next day (12) and then a buy signal the following day (13), resulting in a flip-flop-flip in prices as expected—the opportunity for a triple play of winning day-trades. The following sell signal a few days later (14) is followed by a slight drop in prices over a few days. A false buy signal occurs at the beginning of January (G), but a couple of days later the next buy signal (H), which is accompanied by a spinning top candle and a buy indication on the exhaustion bars (dot under the candle), is followed by a sharp rally for two days. A sell signal occurs in late January (15) in conjunction with a hammer candle, and is followed by a one-day decline. A buy signal then occurs (16) with a one-day rally. Two days later comes a sell signal (17) after a high wave candle, and it presages a sharp decline over several sessions.

A bottom forms in early February with a couple of cycle boundaries (I), a couple of spinning top candles, and a buy indication on the exhaustion bars (dot under the candle). A couple of false sell signals occur in mid-February (18 and 19). A sell signal in late February (J), accompanied by a couple of spinning tops and a doji candle, eventually sees a two-day decline. A buy signal at the beginning of March (20) correctly predicts a rally, which lasts for several sessions. A sell signal in mid-March (K), which is accompanied by a sell indication on the 9-5 count and on the exhaustion bars (dot over the candle), pinpoints a market top. A false buy signal occurs in late March (L), as the market continues its steep descent. A buy signal near the end of March (21), which is accompanied by a morning star doji candle, marks the beginning of a triple-bottom formation.

A sell signal in early April (22) is followed by a decline beginning the next day. A sell signal in late April (M), which is accompanied by a sell indication on the 9-5 count predicts a two-day decline. A buy signal at the beginning of May (23) accompanied by a doji candle is followed by a slight rise in prices and then a sell signal two days later with a steep decline. (This is a variation on the flip-flop pattern wherein the signals are separated by a day in between rather than occurring on consecutive days.) A false buy signal occurs mid-May (24). The formation of a major bottom begins in later May (O) in conjunction with buy indications on the 9-5 count and exhaustion bars (dot under the candle) and a high wave candle. It is roughly a double bottom with the second low being slightly lower than the first.

A couple of false sell signals occur in early June (25, P), and then another one occurs a few days later (26). A sell signal in mid-June (Q) accompanied by a doji candle and sell indications on the 9-5 count and exhaustion bars sees a slight decline over two days. A few days later (R) a top forms with a sell signal accompanied by a high wave candle and a sell indication on the exhaustion bars. A buy signal in early July (27) accompanied by a series of three spinning top candles predicts a rally, which occurs over three days.

Money Management for Cycle Trading

There are a number of different approaches that can be taken to trading with the use of this cyclical model. Various factors to consider include stop-loss levels, profit targets, and time frame. I devised strategies for short-term and long-term position trades as well as for day-trades.

In the case of position trades, a suitable stop-loss level is used based on the market traded and its current level of volatility, combined with the amount of risk capital in the trading account. If the account size is $250,000, a wider stop may be in order than for an account size of $50,000. With futures markets, options are preferable for any position that potentially will be held overnight. There is no reason to take on unnecessary risk. The trade-off in less profit because of delta is worth the containment of risk with option strategies. The maximum risk on trading naked long puts or calls is limited to the premium on the option, which is vastly less risk than that of a naked futures position.

Risk can be further managed by option spreads. Because the positions involved will be one day to several weeks rather than much longer-term positions, the risk profile of certain option strategies involving spreads is not the same on the risk side of the equation as it would be for positions held for many months or years with the same strategies. Profit targets are based on present prices according to average daily ranges for the particular market traded, as well as on support and resistance levels. Trailing stops are used to lock in profits on a position. Multiple contracts are used to manage a position by liquidating at incremental profit objectives.

Because there is no crystal ball to tell a trader how far a price swing is going to go, there is no way for the trader to know whether he is exiting a position near the end of the move or prematurely. It is not realistic to attempt to always ride a price swing for its entirety, but the next best approach is to use the multiple contract strategy, which prevents giving up most or all of the profits achieved by overstaying a position.

Day-trading strategies with this cyclical model need tighter stops and smaller profit objectives. There may be more than one trade on any given day, depending on what the intraday price action looks like. I have found that using a fast and slow moving average (usually a four-bar and a nine-bar) on a one-minute chart is useful for providing entry and exit points. There are some rules for day-trading that need to be applied. First, if there is a buy signal and the market opens lower than the previous day's closing price, do not trade. Similarly, the strategy is to stand aside when there is a sell signal and the market opens higher than the previous session's close. Certain support and resistance levels may be tested and when the price trades back into the previous day's range, there may be a trade, but not otherwise. Second, if the market at opening gaps from the previous close, there will be an entry on the opening provided the gap is in the direction of the trade (in other words, if the market gaps up with a buy signal or down with a sell signal). Third, if it is not the first day of a price swing, there is no trade if the market has retraced the previous day's range by two-thirds or more.

The moving average crossings on day-trades are used to determine entry points when they occur at support or resistance levels as indicated on daily or intraday price charts. They also may provide entry points when the price returns to the opening range, which is another key level. The moving average crossings are used for exit levels as the trade has incrementally achieved more profit throughout the session. If, for example, ten contracts are traded, then the first crossing level may be where four contracts are liquidated, the next level where three contracts are liquidated, the next level where two contracts are liquidated, and the final level where the last open contract is liquidated. Because day-trading precludes holding positions after the regular close, any contracts not liquidated at moving average crossing levels will be exited at that time.

Two types of stops are employed with day-trading strategies using this model: protective (for catastrophic loss) and trailing (to lock in profit). A tight protective stop (usually only a few up to ten ticks' risk) is used on entering any trade, and it is moved to lock in two ticks' profit on remaining open contracts as soon as the first profit objective is reached. Obviously, there is a lot more work as well as close monitoring of intraday prices with a day-trading strategy than there is for position trades.

December 2006 S&P 500 E-Mini Futures

Figure 9.7 is an intraday chart of the S&P 500 E-mini December 2006 futures contract with four- and nine-bar moving averages plotted (simple average of the close). The low of the previous day was tested (coming within two ticks of that price) early in the day, as marked by the crosshairs on the chart. The entry of a trade on the opening results in a loss as the market drops from there. The second entry is determined by the four-bar moving average crossing above the

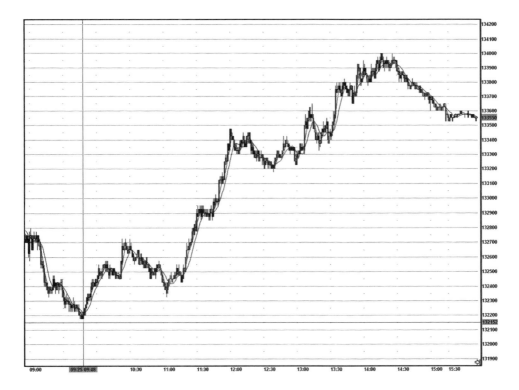

FIGURE **9.7**

One-Minute Chart for 9/25–December 2006 S&P 500 E-Mini Futures

Source: eSignal

nine-bar moving average, which occurred a few minutes after the key support level of the previous day's low was tested.

There are three types of orders that could be used to put on the long position: market, limit, and stop. Although limit and stop orders give a trader the ability to obtain a better fill price, only a market order guarantees an immediate fill (as long as the number of contracts is not something really huge).

Exits are at the four-bar moving average crossing under the nine-bar moving average at around 10:30 (for 4 points), 12:15 (for 10.5 points), 13:45 (for 12 points), 14:20 (for 17 points), and finally at the session close at 15:15 (for 13 points). With five contracts traded and one contract sold at each level, and accounting for slippage on market orders, the total profit potential is 4 + 10.5 + 12 + 17 + 13 = 56.5 points. If 1.5 points were risked on the first losing trade, the estimated hypothetical net profit for the day, exclusive of transaction costs, would be approximately 56.5 − 7.5 = 49 points. At $50 per point per contract, that equals $2,450 gross profit. (Realized net profit would factor in the brokerage commissions plus all other costs.)

For the S&P 500 E-minis to have that much daily range is unusual; therefore, average profits for a day-trading strategy with five contracts are going to be somewhat lower than that amount. As mentioned above, part of the day-trading strategy is to trail the protective initial stop to lock in a couple of ticks' profit (which also helps to cover commission costs) once the price rises to the first profit level.

Euro Currency March 2006 Futures

Figure 9.8 is a one-minute chart of the euro currency March 2006 futures contract for January 9, 2006, with four- and nine-bar moving averages plotted. There was a buy signal for that day. The foreign currency markets are sensitive to reports that come out at 7:30 a.m. CT on several days a month. Because of erratic behavior that often occurs at those times, it is best to wait until the dust settles rather than enter positions at the regular open at 7:20 a.m. CT. Although it may involve sacrificing entering the trade at the best price, this strategy has the advantage of not exposing the trader to a risk of the price trading through a protective stop. Entering on the regular session open at 7:20 a.m. CT (A) would require risking at least ten ticks, or $125 per contract, and clearly it was a losing potential trade. The crossing of the fast moving average under the slow moving average at 8:39 a.m. provided another entry point as the price tested a level of resistance established earlier in the day just above 1.2135.

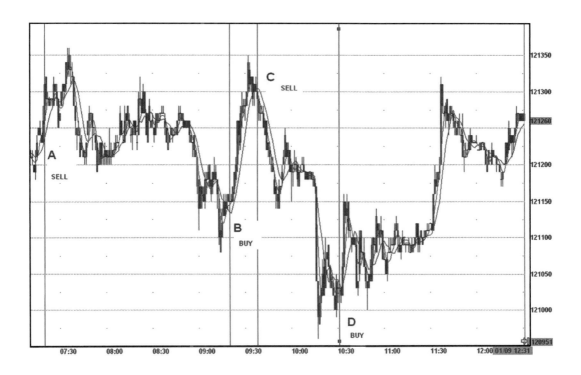

FIGURE 9.8

One-Minute Chart for March 2006 Euro Currency Futures

Source: eSignal

The first exit point (B) occurs as the fast moving average crosses over the slow moving average. The trailing stop to lock in a few ticks would be the closing of the position as the market reverses and rallies. The next entry (C) is where the price returns to the opening range of the regular session, and then the fast moving average once again crosses under the slow moving average. The initial exit point on the new position (D) occurs with a moving average crossing to take profits.

E-Mini S&P 500 March 2006 Futures

Figure 9.9 is a one-minute chart for the E-mini S&P 500 March 2006 futures contract for January 3, 2006, with four- and nine-bar moving averages. There was a buy signal for this date. The opening of the regular session at 8:30 a.m.

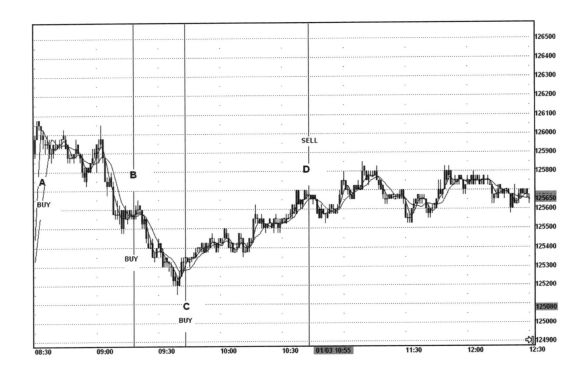

FIGURE 9.9

One-Minute Chart for March 2006 S&P 500 E-Mini Futures

Source: eSignal

CT (A) was followed by such a small rally it would be difficult to trade effectively, although it could be done by aggressively moving the initial protective
stop to lock in a couple of ticks. The next opportunity to play the long side
(B) is where the support (near 1254.75) established in prior sessions is tested
and the four-bar moving average crosses above the nine-bar average. Because
the price action was in the opposite direction from what was anticipated, that
trade would have resulted in a loss. With such trades, the stop-loss level is
critical to ensure a healthy risk/reward profile. Then, another support level is
tested (near 1252.50), and the buy signal is triggered with a moving average
crossover. That trade was a winner, as is evident from the chart. A level to take
profits is reached as the market rallies (D), and a moving average crossing

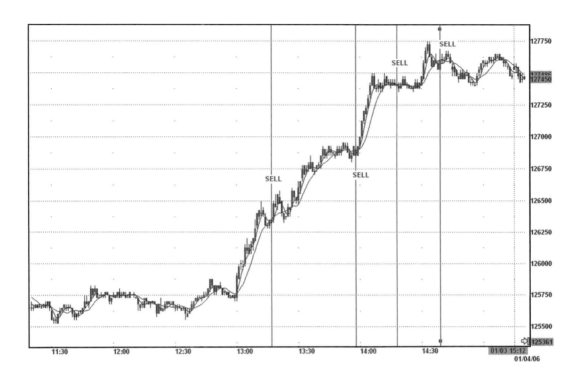

FIGURE **9.10**

One-Minute Chart for March 2006 S&P 500 E-Mini Futures (continued)

Source: eSignal

occurs (vertical lines marked on the chart in **Figure 9.10**, which is the chart for the remainder of the regular hours of the session).

The total extent of the upswing was more than twenty points, which is more than $1,000 per contract. Statistical analysis of that strategy on that market using a protective stop risking four to eight ticks ($50 to $100) per contract on 728 trades for the E-mini S&P 500 futures from June 2003 to December 2005 had 468 wins, 139 losses, and 121 break-even trades. That represents a win/loss ratio of 64.3 percent for all trades, and 77.1 percent after discarding break-even events. The average win per contract is $137.6 and the average loss per contract is $85.2. That results in a risk/reward ratio of 1:1.6.

In an equity curve based on the statistical analysis, there are some periods

TABLE 9.1 **Distribution of Discreet Data**

RANGE	<125	125–250	251–500	501–1000	1001–1500	>1500
Trades	85	112	63	48	14	3

where the curve is fairly flat, especially September 2004 through April 2005. Applying the strategy in several different noncorrelated markets, such as E-mini S&P 500, euro currency, 10-year Treasury notes, or light sweet crude oil and gold, would tend to result in a smoother equity curve over time.[7]

Statistical analysis of the day-trading strategy on the euro currency futures for 175 trades for one year yielded 126 winners, 36 losers, and 13 break-even plays. Based on that, the win/loss ratio is about 72 percent for all trades and 77.7 percent if the break-even trades are discarded. The average net profit per contract is $186.50 (assuming a trailing stop, locking in two ticks once the first profit target of a minimum of $100 per contract is achieved), and the average loss is $100. That gives a risk/reward ratio of 1:1.865. To achieve a higher risk/reward ratio would require setting a higher first profit target, which would negatively impact the win/loss ratio. **Table 9.1** shows discrete data distribution for the number of positions involving price swings of various dollar amounts.

Long-Term Trading Based on Cycles

Paying attention to the major landmarks on a price chart is important for using the cycle boundaries to plan longer-term trades. In Figure 9.2, a triple top formation coincides with the cycle boundary at (f). This was after a run-up of over 230 points in the S&P 500 futures, which is a substantial price swing, over the seven-and-a-half months it took to complete the pattern with the entire long-term bullish trend showing signs of losing its momentum. In Figure 9.3, the right shoulder of a head and shoulders bottom sees its extreme low at (27) on the 10-year Treasury notes futures, which gives the trader a heads-up before the later confirmation of breaking the neckline. The market had been in a tailspin, dropping six full basis points in a month. Expectation of 100 percent retracement was met and then some. At $1,000 a basis point, that is a nice intermediate-term swing trade in anyone's book.

---

7. Mark Tinghino, "Cycles and Technicals: A Profitable Pair," *Futures* magazine (October 2006): 41–42.

Of course, proper money management and addressing the need to respect time exposure calls for intelligent assessment of levels at which to take advantage of partial profit opportunities, even if you believe that the full pattern or trend objective will be achieved. As just one example, Fibonacci retracements at 38.2 percent and 61.8 percent would be levels to take profits for approximately $2,000 and $4,000 per contract, respectively. Assuming multiple contracts, the position could have been followed with some remaining open contracts to the full $6,000 per contract profit potential of the swing. Risking $500 to $1,000 per contract as a stop-loss level and averaging between $2,000 and $4,000 per contract partial profits, with some contracts possibly achieving the full $6,000 potential, should have averaged out to approximately $4,000 to $5,000 per contract on the best trades, which translates into a desirable risk/reward profile.

The same principles apply to trend-line support or resistance. In Figure 9.4, a projected trend line from the two descending highs on the euro currency futures in March and April is touched at a cycle boundary at (P). Major support levels are then broken in the succeeding six sessions as the market heads back to September's low, continuing its descent to make more than a 600-point downswing. At $7,500 maximum potential per contract (taking profits along the way as in the above example), a very respectable return relative to the initial entry risk for the trades that fail (and some certainly do) would have been achieved.

Of course, as is obvious from the range of overall technical approaches that are reviewed, the chart patterns are just one form of correlation that can be used to reinforce and clarify cycle analysis and trading. For those with the inclination to utilize a broader range of tools from the full kit, the extensive combination of support and resistance from moving averages, oscillators, Fibonacci, and other techniques that enhance the proper assessment and management of cyclic tendencies are limited only by the personal preference and expertise of the individual analyst or investor.

Risk/Reward Option Optimization

Executing position trades with options makes it possible to trade on the short side for sell signals and trade further on the long side on other buy signals at higher price levels. That can all be accomplished by trading puts and calls with various strike prices. A spread strategy could also be used as follows: Purchase of a call (or put if playing the short side) that is at-the-money or in-the-money while selling a call (or put) that is at least a few strike prices out-of-the-money. This has two advantages over a naked option position. First, it includes a hedge

TABLE 9.2 **Distribution of Discreet Data**

RANGE	5–9	10–14	15–20	21–30	31–50	51–80	81–150
Trades	14	22	9	21	8	9	10

for managing risk—the option that is sold provides some measure of downside protection, plus it has a lower delta (rate of change of premium with respect to the underlying instrument). Second, it can counter the negative impact of theta (erosion of time value), because it works in favor of the trade for the option sold despite working against the trade for the option that is bought. (Any of the direction-biased option strategies described in Chapter 8 could also be utilized for even more finely tuned risk management.)

Statistical analysis of such a position trade strategy on the S&P 500 E-mini futures from June 2003 through December 2005 resulted in 83 winning trades and 21 losing trades. The win/loss ratio for that data sample was 79.8 percent. If profits had been taken when the underlying futures price moved 5, 10, 15, 20, 30, 50, and 80 points, the average profit per option would have been $2,118.82. If the average amount risked per option is $200, the risk/reward ratio is 1:10. **Table 9.2** shows the discrete data distribution of the frequency of price swings in full points for that period.

Based on those statistics, a logical strategy for taking profits by trading options positions would be to set targets of 5-, 10-, 25-, 50-, 75-, and 100-point moves on the underlying futures contract, which with an average delta of 70 would translate into $175, $350, $875, $1,750, $2,625, and $3,500 increases in premium (before factoring in loss of time value due to theta) for each naked option purchased. For a position of twelve options, that is a total of $18,550 for a trade where the price swings at least 100 points in the direction of the trade.[8]

The Cycle Advantage

Applying a cyclical model such as the one described in this chapter can give a trader the additional edge that the use of standard popular approaches to analyzing chart patterns and using standard popular indicators does not

---

8. Ibid., p. 43.

provide. In addition to that, the power of volume analysis that Market Profile charts provide should bolster any such approach. The advantage is that such multidisciplinary innovations enhance what is already part of technical analysis tool sets that have been developed for several decades, and are now part of the technician's vernacular.

Conclusion

Even allowing that cycle analysis is best employed in conjunction with insights from other technical projections, it remains among the most powerful tools. It is useful in both its prediction of the turning points for some of the major intermediate- and long-term price trends, and the discipline it naturally provides by restraining the worst tendencies to overanalyze or overtrade in liquid, active markets. Whether broad or narrow, cycle analysis is an important part of any market approach that attempts to achieve a fully professional perspective.

Summary of Chapter 9

- Cyclical analysis of financial markets has been carried out for several decades.
- The unique cyclical model for timing market moves, which is explained in this chapter, is distinct from the work of others on cycles.
- The cyclical model can be utilized for trading strategies in various time frames, from day-trades to long-term positions.

CHAPTER 10

Backtesting and Planning Trading Strategies

The first step in the process of developing an effective trading system is the analysis phase. The prospective trader starts with an idea about what might work as a strategy. To evaluate the potential of that strategy involves applying it to a set of historical price data.

The concept here is that what has worked in the past has some statistically significant chance of continuing to work in the future. Of course, the obvious danger inherent in this procedure is the possibility that the market being analyzed may change behavior from that which is observed in the sample data set. One means of guarding against that is to take random samples of a long-term string of data. For example, if there is a ten-year history of prices, you might choose to alternate sets of two-year samples, such as the first two years, skip the third and fourth years, sample the fifth and sixth years, skip the seventh and eight years, and sample the ninth and tenth years.

So, starting with a hypothesis, you can then proceed to verify the validity of it with some real-world situations. If such a scientific attitude is not present, then you are merely rolling the dice willy-nilly with your money. Having a well-tested strategy also serves to build confidence. That is important, because without it you will find it near impossible to adhere to a trading plan with any mental discipline. Once doubt enters, fear will inevitably follow and thwart your efforts at every turn, and what should be a profitable strategy becomes a source of cumulative losses over time.

There are two approaches to backtesting a strategy: 1) doing analysis by hand with manual calculations and hard-copy paper charts, and 2) performing analysis using computer technology and software. In the case of the first strategy, you could construct price charts by hand or order historical charts from various vendors, such as Commodity Research Bureau (CRB), that sell such charts tailored to your specifications. Although it is more time-consuming and perhaps somewhat counterproductive, there is something to be said for charting by hand. It is a good exercise for someone who has never done it. Drawing out OHLC bar,

Japanese candlestick, point and figure, or Market Profile charts on a piece of graph paper can help educate you about how the charts work, in turn giving you a more in-depth understanding of charting software.

Most of the popular backtesting software on the market does not really lend itself to analysis that includes flexibility of applying customized techniques. If you happen to be an accomplished software developer with extensive programming skills, it gives you a distinct advantage. If, on the other hand, you don't already know how to program, it would be a wise investment to take a class at a local college or university in C#.NET or C++. One of the reasons is that being able to analyze prices only one bar at a time with one of the off-the-shelf backtesting software packages on the market imposes some serious limitations on what can be accomplished. At some point, you will probably want to analyze high-frequency data and, preferably, the raw data in terms of all price quotes that come out of the exchanges as time and sales data. Those data not only have prices in them, but share, lot, or contract sizes in them as well. It is a question of granularity of the data. At the level of finest granularity, there are the individual ticks for each trade made in a particular market. At the coarsest levels are thirty-minute bars, one-hour bars, daily, weekly, and monthly bars. Strategies based on analysis across multiple time frames will require the need to analyze price data at different levels of granularity as part of the backtesting process.

After having mastered programming, it is possible to move to the next level: accessing the APIs (application programming interfaces) that tap directly into the quote streams coming out of electronic exchanges such as Globex, eCBOT, and Forex and that also allow you to transmit orders directly to those exchanges. The exchanges at the date of this writing do not charge anything for their APIs, which are downloadable from their websites. The PATS API, which makes life a little easier, does cost money, however. If it is in your trading budget, you might consider purchasing the PATS libraries. After all, it is a legitimate business expense, along with all other computer hardware and software that is used for trading. Software to execute orders will need to be submitted to the exchange's testing and quality control processes. Those are in place for everyone's safety. Unintentional or corrupted orders are obviously undesirable. Bear in mind with respect to this approach of doing your own software development that programming tools and languages are designed for the person of average to above-average intelligence to use. You do not need to be a super genius or a rocket scientist to be able to effectively utilize such tools.

If, on the other hand, you have neither the inclination nor time to devote to writing your own software, you can always get yourself a hired gun to do the work. These people are generally known as software (or IT or computer) consultants. If you want the top talent, you are more likely to find it among independent consultants. Large consulting firms tend to send their senior-level people over to large corporate accounts of the Fortune 1000 genre. It may not pay to have them send over a junior-level person to work for you while charging premium hourly rates for services. A word of caution, though, when it comes to retail stores that offer technical services: *caveat emptor.* Quality can vary tremendously from provider to provider, especially when it comes to networking of multiple computers. Be sure to thoroughly evaluate service providers prior to considering them.

With full control over computerized backtesting at your disposal, you are free to set the parameters any way you want in order to fine-tune a financial model, as well as play various what-if games for any imaginable number of different trading strategies. Using Microsoft Excel to do statistical analysis of prices in a spreadsheet can be a useful tool, if you are not drilling down to time frames shorter than monthly, weekly, or daily duration. For high-frequency data analysis, however, it is not going to work as well as storing your price data in a database such as MySQL, SQL Server, Oracle, or Access and using ODBC (open database connectivity) from your custom analysis software.

The greatest pitfall of backtesting is curve fitting, which is essentially making the empirical data fit the theory rather than using that data to validate or invalidate the theory. It would behoove anyone with a trading strategy in mind to apply rigorous statistical measures of the performance of that strategy to a sufficient sampling of historical price data, while at the same time bearing in mind that markets can change literally overnight and cause unexpected results in real time.

Masterminding the Trading Plan

You may have heard the adage "plan the trade and then trade the plan." These seem like simple words to live by, but the reality is that it is much, much harder to actually carry that out than you would expect. It requires a type of mental discipline that is unlike any other form of discipline in any other endeavor. Deviation from rules in other arenas does not result in the instant karmic recoil and whiplash that failing to adhere to a carefully crafted trading system often unleashes. The main reason is that the market is a force far greater than any single trader, and there is always the danger of being financially annihilated by the market if you trade recklessly. You could get lucky and make a small fortune by being on the right side of a huge move, or you just as easily could get caught on the wrong side of such a move. Different types of traders have different approaches to risk management suitable to their strategy. Specialists on the New York Stock Exchange or market makers on the Nasdaq are obligated to take on huge risks as being the buyers and sellers of last resort, a responsibility they take on as being the ones to keep an orderly market by maintaining liquidity. On the other hand, they make their money not by forecasting big price moves but by pocketing the difference on the bid/ask spread, which historically has more than made up for the inherent risk they shoulder as their cost of doing business. A specialist or market maker has certain advantages as a market insider that those who are not in that position do not have. For the rest of the trading community, a different approach to both trading strategy and risk management are necessary. Whether you are a stock exchange specialist, a trader for a bank or hedge fund, or a private speculative investor, you need to have a sound plan that includes managing the risks involved in trading.

A sound trading plan should have three components: risk exposure, stop-loss levels, and profit objectives. Regardless of trades made, the exposure of a percentage of your overall portfolio to any one market needs to be considered. Just because there is 100-to-1 leverage in trading a Forex contract on a currency pair does not mean that using your entire block of investment capital to go long or short as many lots as you can is a very wise approach, any more than buying shares of stock in only a single company or single sector would be. That is true even if a trade has been backtested with a high probability such as 75 percent. No one likes to get margin calls from the brokerage firm, and the best way to avoid them is to minimize exposure to risk by not overleveraging your trading capital.

With respect to stop-loss levels and profit objectives, risk/reward ratio is the primary critical factor. Granted there may be varying risk/reward ratios over all trades for a fiscal quarter, due to changing market conditions that affect key levels like long-term and short-term support and resistance; still there should be a healthy average risk/reward ratio for all trades. Here is a hypothetical example: In one scenario, there is an average risk/reward ratio of 1:10 with only 30 percent profitable trades. In a second scenario, there is an average risk/reward ratio of 1:1 and 60 percent profitable trades. If you had ten trades with each scenario, risking $1,000 per trade, the net profit and loss (P&L) in the first scenario would be $30,000 minus $7,000 for a return of $23,000, whereas the net P&L for the second scenario would be $6,000 minus $4,000 for a return of $2,000. If $100,000 is the initial capital for the quarter, the better risk/reward ratio scenario results in a rate of return (before transaction costs) of 23 percent, and the scenario with the much weaker win/loss ratio results in a rate of return (before transaction costs) of 2 percent. With the superior risk/reward ratio, the rate of return is more than ten times better, despite the probability of winning trades only being half as high.

The term "drawdown" refers to cumulative net losses at any point in time. If, at the end of one quarter, there are profits that increase the initial capital invested (at the beginning of that quarter) by 5 percent, and then in the next quarter there are net losses that result in a decrease in the capital by 2 percent (from the beginning of that next quarter), there is quarterly drawdown of 2 percent, despite there being a return over two quarters of 3 percent. The profile of any trading strategy (whether that be a pro-forma hypothetical based on backtesting or tracking P&L based on actual trades) can be assessed by charting an equity curve.

Setting a level for a stop-loss should be handled with steadfastness. That level should always be determined prior to entering a position and entered as a stop order preferably immediately or simultaneously (and under some circumstances even prior to entering a position) with the buy or sell order to initiate the trade on the long or short side of the market. The stop should be moved (unless there was some miscalculation of the level prior to making the trade) only in the direction of the trade to risk less money, scratch the trade at breakeven, or to lock in profits already made on paper—and never wider to risk more capital on the position. Otherwise, there is really not much point to having the stop for risk protection. I am specifically referring here to stop orders that will serve to offset an open position when they are triggered and filled, rather than stop orders that are utilized to enter or add to a position.

Stop orders are just like any other type of order, except that they become market orders when the price is hit, which means they will be filled as soon as possible, unless they are effectively cancelled before getting filled. A buy stop order that is submitted at a price lower than the current market price will automatically be rejected. A sell order that is submitted at a price higher than the current market price will be automatically rejected. There are a couple of very good reasons for such constraints on stop orders: If they are submitted by mistake in the case of electronically matched markets, they will not automatically become market orders and either offset an open position or initiate a new position unintentionally. Also, the price on the stop order triggers the order whether the market merely trades at that level or actually has penetrated that level; in other words, with a sell stop, for example, the order is triggered to become a market order as soon as the market trades at the price of the order or at a lower price.

Test-Driving the Trading Plan

Paper trading is the next step in the process. It can be done either with pencil and paper or a demo version of an electronic trading platform. In the case of simulated trading on a demo account with an electronic trading platform, you need to realize that the software is merely simulating what is most likely to occur with actual trades made in real markets. It is not unlike the situation encountered by the legendary trader Jesse Livermore[1] when there were still bucket shops in existence. Those were trading arcades that allowed the public to literally wager on the rise or fall of stock prices without actually investing in shares on an actual stock exchange. An order was always filled in those shops at the price that was on the ticker tape, which was generated by actual orders filled at the stock exchange. Young Jesse became very proficient at reading the ticker tape and forecasting price movements, but when he later tried his approach making actual trades through the New York Stock Exchange, he had a rude awakening. He discovered that he was usually unable to get his orders filled at the price on the ticker tape as he had at the bucket shops. This literally threw a wrench in the works for him, and he had to completely overhaul his trading strategies to once again make them profitable.

Transitioning from simulated electronic trading to actual electronic trading with real money should therefore be done very, very cautiously. For those who have not yet traded except for on simulated versions of electronic trading platforms, there is going to be an additional learning curve for slippage and split fills and market conditions ranging from slow to normal to fast to insanely illiquid (typically in the wake of reactions to major reports).

---

1. Edwin LeFevre, *Reminiscences of a Stock Operator* (John Wiley & Sons, Inc. 1994).

Conclusion

Trading for profit is a business just like any other type of enterprise, whether you are a professional trader or private investor. A business needs a good plan in order to be successful. If you are depending on enough luck to tide you over through the spells of inevitable drawdown, then you are simply courting disaster. To develop a plan that is going to make you successful, you need to have a sound trading strategy that includes evaluation of risk versus reward and exit strategies for when the market goes against your positions.

Summary of Chapter 10

- Both research and paper trading are crucial for any professional or serious amateur trader.
- Mastering computer programming will give you a leg up on your competition via the ability you will have to do your own sophisticated analysis.
- After backtesting your strategy, it is essential for you to formulate a carefully thought out trading plan that best suits your situation and tolerance for risk.

CHAPTER 11

Mental Discipline and Risk Management

Of this great tree, my dear, if someone should strike at the root, it would bleed but still live. If someone should strike at its middle, it would bleed, but still live. If someone should strike at its top, it would bleed, but still live. CHANDOGYA UPANISHAD 11.1[1]

People, in general, are not hardwired for participation in financial markets. There are very good reasons for the tendency of the average trader to hesitate to enter a position when the time is ripe, to jump out of a position way too early, to overstay a position, to make trades impulsively that are not part of the established trading program, to skip trades after a losing streak, and to move stop orders that should not be moved: our emotional responses that govern our actions are a survival mechanism.

When our distant ancestors descended from tree branches to walk upright on the African savannahs that had suddenly become accessible due to climactic changes on the planet, they walked into not only a new opportunity but a set of extremely dangerous hazards as well. Large predators were waiting in the shadows and quick reflexes made the difference between being eaten and living to see the next day. The latest archaeological and DNA evidence has revealed that the first hominids were not actually predators but prey. The cause of a more advanced brain evolving was the need for cooperation and cunning. The hunting and farming activities of our ancestors came much later.

Psychologists refer to the human reaction to stressful situations involving some imminent danger as the flight-or-fight response. It is not unique to our species. Any creature must choose between running and defending, depending on whether they are cornered or have a viable escape route. Money for modern man carries quite a bit of emotional baggage. Access to food and shelter, among

---

1. *The Thirteen Principal Upanishads*, Translated by Robert Ernest Hume, 2nd ed. (Oxford University Press, 1977), p. 247.

other things, is dependent upon having money available. Access to luxury items is dependent upon having some in reserve. The prospect of financial gain as well as financial loss will inevitably trigger the adrenalin surge that comes with things that tend to excite us either out of fear or desire. Although out in the wilderness that is an asset, in the context of the markets it is an obstacle. A trader needs to be ruled by the head and not the heart in order to be successful.

So, in the face of that dilemma, what can you do? Psychologists who have studied traders of varying levels of success in action have observed that they carry on an internal dialogue, which sometimes also manifests itself as an external dialogue (for example, self-berating or directing comments at the markets themselves). The nature of that dialogue is vastly different in successful traders than it is in unsuccessful traders. The point is that a trader should not aim to become like a robot and simply execute orders mechanically. Suppression of your biology is not the key, but understanding it is essential to overcoming its deleterious effects with respect to making sound trading decisions.

Building confidence goes a long way toward getting the emotional roller coaster under control. What is essential to building confidence as a trader is comprehending that market strategies need to be predicated on probabilities rather than certainties. Traders should not be aspiring for prophecy, just for an acceptable rate of return.

Many professional traders have turned to trading coaches who help prepare them by getting them to develop a successful mind-set. This is not the same thing as positive thinking whereby you mentally repeat affirmations that everything will be rosy. That other approach will not give you the ability to deal with losses, which are inevitable. The saying goes, "You need to love your losses." That means taking any losing trades in stride and not being undermined by them to the point of deviating from a trading plan.

Assessing your character flaws is part of that process. It is not an easy task for anyone to be entirely objective about their own behavior. Traits and habits are so deeply ingrained in us by the time we reach adulthood that, even after reflecting upon them, it is no simple feat to overcome those flaws that thwart us as successful market participants.

Level of intelligence does not directly correlate with success in the markets. Being a genius can actually be a drawback, as it can exacerbate the tendency to overthink about a trade and to second-guess yourself. Success in other arenas does not necessarily translate into success as a trader. Studies have shown that many successful people in almost every field actually don't think of themselves as successful. They are plagued with self-doubt and may even consider themselves as frauds despite their clearly evident high level of achievement. For a trader, on the other hand, lack of confidence is a fatal flaw. Not only does it affect your judgment and execution of a trading plan, but it often also causes a trader to turn to outside authorities for validation, and reliance upon those sources is, for the most part, no better than throwing darts at a dart board.

Confidence for a trader is not about egotism or pride. Being able to admit that you are wrong when the market has moved against your position is a sign of maturity and genuine self-assurance. Falsely predicated confidence based on an inflated opinion of your self-worth and place in the universe will quite simply set you up for failure: Pride precedeth a fall. And the prouder they are, the harder they fall. Hanging on to a losing trade can quickly result in catastrophic losses that bring on financial ruin and bankruptcy. Once that occurs, your whole life can unravel, with potential for shattered personal relationships, divorces, alcoholism, depression, and possibly even suicide lurking right around the corner.

The first time I managed money for a large floor trader at CBOT, I was given some advice by that trader: no one should be trading out of ego and in pursuit of fame—the fabulous financial gain was reward enough. However, trading out of financial need is not a good idea; it will completely undermine your ability to be successful. That is a hard reality to swallow for any aspiring trader who hopes to rely on the markets for her livelihood. I once commented to a fellow trader about how frustrating it was to have even a slightly unprofitable trade, and his poignant reply was, "It's just money after all. It's not like losing fingers and toes." That very neatly put it all into the proper perspective.

Writers of books on trading psychology point out that if there is any sort of anxiety while trading, then something is seriously wrong and a self-overhaul is in order. Even with that knowledge, trading without stress does not come automatically. Losing money is not something the average person is accustomed to as a routine event. Most people have a job that comes with a guaranteed paycheck on a regular basis and some very conservative investments in addition to the one asset into which they sink most of their money, their house. How many people would show up for work if they did not know whether they would be paid for their time or if they would have to pay their employer instead? Their jobs tend to be stressful enough as it is without adding that dimension of risk to the equation.

In his book *Trading in the Zone*,[2] Mark Douglas defines a variety of problems that plague the trader who is not master of himself. One of them is an aversion to setting rules to trade by. Douglas describes it as an extremely subtle resistance characterized by a conscious acknowledgment of the need to have rules, while at the same time having a subconscious rebellion against them. It stems from past experiences wherein boundaries that were forced upon you have caused many a negative emotion including frustration, disappointment, disillusionment, rage, and animosity. Those experiences cause you to have a knee-jerk reaction towards anything perceived as being restrictive of freedom. One motivation for trading is financial freedom.

Another problem is accountability for your actions. It is always easier to blame your failures on outside factors rather than place the blame on your own shoulders where it belongs. This leads to chaotic trading rather than systematic trading. Markets may have some element of randomness to them, but by and large they follow certain repeatable patterns that technical analysts have identified. Granted, no single outcome in the markets is 100 percent predictable, but it is still often statistically predictable as a better than chance probability. Consistency in results is not going to come from haphazard approaches to trading. It will come only with a high level of discipline.

Elation from the unexpected is a third problem that Douglas cites. Random outcomes that produce rewards willy-nilly trigger a euphoric high, because they are unpredictable. This is an obstacle for a trader, for it can cause you to continue down a path that causes net losses, because of the possibility, however remote, that there just might be a huge payoff when you hit the jackpot on some huge price action. This is a type of addiction that is particularly insidious due to its ability to rob the trader of free will—the object of addiction takes control.

Finally, Douglas cites a problem that I have already discussed: caving to outside pressures. In other endeavors, having positive feedback and cooperation from others is a key to success. It is something that makes a good leader. Expecting that to help you succeed in the financial markets is irrational, because there is no possibility of influencing others to get the markets to behave as expected, and if something like that is accomplished, it will probably fall under the heading of illegal insider trading or market manipulation.

---

2. Mark Douglas, *Trading in the Zone* (New York Institute of Finance, 2000).

Douglas, as the title of his book implies, recommends achieving a state of mind conducive to trading success that he calls "the zone." It begins with fully comprehending that yielding consistent profits from trading depends on having a statistical edge based on the right probabilities. Those are a combination of win/loss and risk/reward ratios inherent in your trading program. Just having done the analysis does not necessarily mean that the trader is then going to have a probabilistic frame of mind. There is still the danger of reacting negatively to a losing trade or second-guessing the outcome of a winning trade. No event has any meaning in itself. It only matters as a cog in the wheel of hundreds or thousands of similar events on a continuum over time. For example, knowing that a random coin toss should come up heads half the time and tails the other half the time, getting a certain outcome of fifty/fifty heads/tails depends on the number of tosses. A mere two tosses could easily be 100 percent heads or 100 percent tails. Ten tosses could be five heads/five tails, but it could also be eight heads/two tails or eight tails/two heads, although a series of ten toss experiments is going to have a higher grouping of five heads/five tails, and an incident of ten heads or ten tails is going to be extremely rare, based on the law of averages. A million tosses is going to result in a number within a very small percentage deviation of half a million heads, and a trillion tosses is going to have an even smaller percentage of deviation from that statistic. If there is an infinite number of tosses, then theoretically exactly half of them should be heads. The higher the number of tosses, the smaller the percentage of deviation from the mean or fifty/fifty heads/tails in a 1:1 ratio.

So, with a trading program that has a genuine statistical edge, results should be more and more consistent the longer the period of time over which it is utilized due to the higher number of individual trades executed. Statistics from games of chance show clumping patterns of the same event occurring in consecutive streaks as opposed to alternating with the opposite event (for example, black or red on a roulette wheel). As a consequence, any systematic betting on such events will result in a cycle of cumulative wins alternating with cumulative losses around the net zero level, as opposed to a curve that is fairly flat. A successful trading program will have a similar cyclical profile, except with a positive slope instead of a flat one. (Conversely, an unsuccessful program will have a cyclical profile with a negative slant.) Optimization of a trading program has the aim of smoothing the equity curve to resemble an upward angle of ascent as closely as possible.

Being in a probabilistic frame of mind also means not falling into the trap of seeking the elusive consistency that the markets are never going to provide.

A pattern that occurred previously may appear to be in the process of being repeated, but it invariably turns out to be different in some way from what came before. The reason for that is the conditions are not identical to the conditions that occurred when the pattern emerged in the past. Trying to find an exact match is not realistic. You must be able to apply some type of fuzzy logic within which a certain degree of resemblance is what provides a match. Even with a matching condition, the outcome is still not certain beyond a shadow of a doubt. Being prepared for the unexpected is essential, and despite a particular trader's believing that he has mastered thinking in probabilities, he will not be so prepared if there is a lack of acceptance of all possibilities that allows taking them into account.

Being confident of the edge conferred by a successful strategy based on the probabilities enables a trader to be able to apply that edge indiscriminately and not resort to cherry-picking trades based on a waxing and waning level of confidence in that edge. Considering every trade as a unique event while trading based on the probability of it being a winning trade is the key to success. You must get past the mind-set of attaining the ideal of being right all the time. As much as that would be nice to achieve, it is like an infant trying to grab the moon upon seeing it for the first time.

Acceptance of loss as part of the game is also one feature of having a probabilistic mentality. If you are distressed by being wrong on a trade, it is a clear indication of treating a loss as unacceptable on account of the painful nature of that experience. Such a trader does not love his losses, he abhors them. Inability to take on the risk due to a potential loss being unacceptable can easily cause a trader to stand aside even though market analysis is telling him to make a trade.

In addition to being able to think in probabilities, a trader needs to be able to deal with expectations with respect to trading. Any given trader can have realistic expectations, but too often that trader will have quite unrealistic expectations. To expect the future to conform to an imagined ideal is extremely dangerous in the arena of financial markets, because the resultant disappointment from having any such expectations unfulfilled will destroy your mental and emotional equilibrium. A very deep-rooted pain-avoidance mechanism is at work, which puts the trader into a state of denial upon being wrong and therefore unable to perceive that the market is moving in the opposite direction from what was expected. What would ordinarily be plainly apparent becomes obscured from vision while in such a state of mind. That whole dynamic is completely natural, and it must be overcome for you to succeed as a trader.

Emotional and mental distress caused by price action is not due to any intrinsic menace from those phenomena. For someone who never trades, any particular chart pattern or price swing causes neither pleasure nor pain. It has no negative connotations whatsoever, except for the trader who has some financial stake in what that price activity is going to do to the trading account balance. It is not the same as the pain experienced when stepping on a thorn, which will be felt by anyone regardless of one's attitude towards thorns in general. The result of having unrealistic expectations is that unexpected behavior is threatening to a trader who is a participant in a particular market. That same behavior occurring in a market in which that the same trader has no financial stake will not be threatening. In the case of managing expectations, it is flexibility that is needed, as opposed to trading rules wherein flexibility is fatal and rigidity is a necessity.

Douglas deftly provides his five fundamental truths underlying a probabilistic mind-set:

1   Anything can happen.
2   You don't need to know what is going to happen next in order to make money.
3   There is a random distribution between wins and losses for any given set of variables that define an edge.
4   An edge is nothing more than an indication of a higher probability of one thing happening over another.
5   Every moment in the market is unique.[3]

Mastering the various concepts on which a probabilistic mind-set is based is accomplished via a process of self-assessment and a shoring up of the various chinks in the armor of your psyche that cause deviation from that frame of mind. You can attempt to do that on your own or find a trading coach to help with the effort.

W.D. Gann, the legendary trader, also gave some sage advice to the traders of his era with respect to risk management: "Accumulated profits over a long period of time are lost because traders have not protected themselves with STOP

---

3. Ibid., p. 121.

LOSS ORDERS. A STOP LOSS ORDER is much better protection for traders because it works automatically."[4]

Entrepreneurs are much like traders, because they have to take on a measure of risk to embark on a new business enterprise, often financing the effort out of their own savings. The difference is that the risks and potential rewards are far more concrete. Given enough potential customers and a product or service that is competitive in quality and price, there is a reasonable prospect for success, despite no absolute guarantees. Barring something cataclysmic such as severe economic recession affecting the industry or some natural disaster, the risks are usually quite clear: the amount of money they invest may only be partially recovered, and they may never operate in the black; and in the event they fail to do so within a year or two (depending on their staying power based on available capital), the business will be shut down, and they will move on with their lives. Most entrepreneurs are not reckless individuals. They take calculated risks and have a bankroll to tide them over for a while before starting up a new business.

Trading as a business pursuit is really no different from any other profession. The same factors come into play: Profit and loss from the principal activity of the business, costs associated with conducting business, and operating capital to run the business. For the professional trader, the P&L component is trading wins and losses. The costs are commissions, subscriptions to real-time price quotes, computer hardware and software, and trading literature. Operating capital is the trading account balances. Instead of employees, unless you are running a floor operation or managing a fund, there is a team of experts with whom the trader allies himself. Those include brokers, bankers, tax accountants, IT help-desk personnel, authors of market letters, and so forth.

A good trading plan also should include a well-constructed business plan. How much profit from trading is required to make it worthwhile as a full-time (or even part-time) pursuit should be figured out at the beginning. How much in net losses that will dictate when the plug should be pulled should also be calculated. If you see that the ship on which you stand is sinking, how long are you going to wait to either jump ship to swim to safety or look for life preservers and lifeboats? The management of the costs of doing business is also crucial for the trader. If the commissions end up offsetting the majority

---

4. W.D. Gann, *How to Make Profits in Commodities* (Lambert-Gann Publishing Co., 1951), pp. 10–12.

of the gross profits from trades, then that could spell the difference between success and failure.

Any businessman who spends all his operating capital is just plain foolish. Without money to run the day-to-day operations, failure is immediate. Employees are not going to show up for work on Monday morning if they have not been paid on Friday. Suppliers are not going to extend credit for very long if bills are not paid. The utility companies are not going to continue to supply electricity, water, and natural gas for offices and plants if they are not paid in a timely manner. Bankers are not going to lend the business money when there is nothing on hand for operating capital—it makes for a very pathetic balance sheet. For a trader to take too big a risk on trades that end up wiping out the trading account is the equivalent of any other type of business letting all its capital on hand go out the door without enough revenue coming in at the same time to offset the drain on its finances. Any single trade should not put more than a small fraction of the total capital in the trading account at risk. Ideally, only up to 1 or 2 percent should be at risk, and never more than 5 percent. If 20 percent is risked and there are a string of five losses, that adds up to the entire amount in the account. Although such a losing streak may be a rare occurrence with a good trading program, the possibility still needs to be considered and preparations must be made to weather the storm.

A trader who does not have sound risk management principles is no different from an out-of-control compulsive gambler who puts all his chips on black or red at the roulette wheel on a single turn. Although most people would simply laugh at the gambler, they would not think twice about investing all their money on shares in a single company or sector. I once asked a venture capitalist friend of mine what kind of odds most investors in start-up companies look for, and he said that they are hoping to have just one in ten of the companies they buy become a success. So, obviously they are not going to invest everything they have in fewer than ten start-up companies, and probably they are going to invest in at least fifty to one hundred or more of them. VCs are an extremely shrewd and savvy crowd, especially if they have been in that arena for any length of time without going bankrupt.

As mentioned in earlier chapters, managing risk on individual trades is accomplished with well-placed stop orders and hedging strategies like spreads. Managing the risk for the entire portfolio also needs a comprehensive strategy involving diversification and keeping an eye on drawdown (the net percentage of loss at any given point in time) of capital.

Conclusion

Good risk management is even more crucial to consistent overall success than having a profitable trading strategy. With even the most outstanding system, a reckless approach that does not include that key component will inevitably cause the program to unravel when one huge loss wipes out the net sum of many net gains. To practice effective management of risks requires a high level of mental discipline and mastery of your emotions. That is easier than it looks at first glance, and it behooves you to achieve the necessary self-mastery to be able to execute your trading program prudently in the face of the inherent dangers of a volatile (and oftentimes explosive) marketplace.

Summary of Chapter 11

- Humans are biologically at a disadvantage when it comes to trading, on account of the traits necessary for survival our species developed as a result of being faced with many potentially fatal hazards in our natural environment. You need to overcome that weakness to be successful.
- We need to overcome our aversion to discipline as well.
- We need to take responsibility for our trading decisions.
- We need to become independent of and immune to outside influences that serve only to sway us from our trading plan.
- It is necessary to think in terms of probabilities rather than certainties.
- Sound money management as a key component of your trading plan is what makes the difference between success and failure as a trader.

APPENDIX A

Commonly Used Technical Indicators

LIST OF INDICATORS (*continued*)

Lagged Line Weighted Moving Average

Lagged Line Weighted Moving Averages Difference

Lagged Moving Average

Lagged Moving Averages Difference

Lagged Value

Line-Weighted Moving Average

Line-Weighted Moving Averages Difference

Linear Regression Indicator

Linear Regression Slope

Linear Regression Squared

Lomb Periodogram

Lowest Value

MACD Indicator

Market Facilitation Index (MFI)

Market Facilitation Index 1 (MFI x 100)

Martin Pring KST Filtering System

McClellan Oscillator

McClellan Summation Index

Median Price

Momentum

Money Flow Index (MFI)

Morris Daily Pressure

Morris Intraday Accumulator

Moving Average

Moving Average Convergence-Divergence (MACD)

Moving Average Difference

Multivote OBV

Negative Changes Count

Negative Changes Sum

Nicoski Index

OBV Midpoint

OBV Oscillator

OBV—Raw

OBV with Average Volume

On-Balance Volume (OBV)

On-Balance Volume with Variable Smoothing

Percent Change

Percentage Price Oscillator (PPO)

Percentage Volume Oscillator (PVO)

Performance Indicator

Period Volatility Percentage

Positive and Negative Changes Counts Difference

Positive Changes Count

Positive Changes Sum

Price Action Indicator (PAIN)

Price Oscillator Indicators

Price Rate-of-Change (ROC)

Price Rate-of-Change Points Indicator

Price Volume Rank

Price Volume Trend

Qstick Indicator

Rainbow Band Lower

LIST OF INDICATORS (*continued*)

Rainbow Band Upper	Variable Length Average
Rainbow Maximum	Velocity
Rainbow Minimum	Vertical Horizontal Filter (VHF)
Rainbow Oscillator	Volatility (annualized, dispersion changes, percent changes)
Range Difference	
Range Expansion Index	Volume percentage +/– Average
Rate of Change (ROC) Oscillator	Volume (number of standard deviations)
Rate of Change (ROC) Indicator	
Relative Strength Index (RSI)	Volume Accumulator
RSI Crossover Indicator	Volume and Price Accumulator
Smart Money Index	Volume Line Variation
Smooth Acc/Dist	Volume Oscillator Percentage
Standard Deviation	Volume Oscillator Points
STIX	Volume Rate-of-Change Percentage
Stochastic Oscillator	Volume Rate-of-Change Points
Stochastic Oscillator Alert	Volume Rating
Stochastic Oscillator and RSI Alert	Volume Reversal
Swing Index (High and Low)	Volume Reversal Alerts
TEMA21	Volume-Weighted RSI-MFI
TEMA26	Weighted Close Indicator
TEMA26—MACD	Whipple Volume Average
Total Volatility	Whipple Volume Plot
Trade Volume Index	Wilder RSI Indicator
TRIX Indicator	Williams %R
Typical Price Indicator	
Ultrasmooth Momentum Curve	
Up/Down Volume	
Up Volatility—Down Volatility	

Details of Selected Indicators

Arms Index (TRIN). A measure of market breadth and strength.
  Formula to calculate:

(Number of advances/Number of declines) ÷ (Advancing volume/Declining volume)

Average Directional Index (ADX). Trend continuation/reversal detection.
  Formulas to calculate:

Calculation of positive and negative directed movement
(Directional Movement, or DM) = $+DM_j$ and $-DM_j$.

If

$High_j$ *(a maximum of a current bar)* > $High_{j-1}$ *(a maximum of the previous bar)*,

that

$+DMj = High_j - High_{j-1}$, *differently* $+DM_j = 0.$

If

Low_j *(a minimum of a current bar)* < Low_{j-1} *(a minimum of the previous bar)*,

that

$-DM_j = Low_j - Low_j$, *differently* $-DM_j = 0.$

If

$$+DM_j > -DM_j,$$

that

$$-DM_j = 0.$$

If

$$-DM_j > +DM_j,$$

that

$$+DM_j = 0.$$

If

$$+DM_j = -DM_j,$$

that

$$+DM_j = 0, \ -DM_j = 0.$$

Determination of the true range = TR_j, TR = maximal module of three values

$$|High - Low|, \ |High - Close_{j-1}|, \ |Low - Close_{j-1}|.$$

$Close_{j-1}$ = the close price of the previous period.

Note: In most cases module $|High - Low|$ will be maximal on Forex in absence of price breaks.

Determination of the indicator of a positive direction and the indicator of a negative direction = $+DI_j$ and $-DI_j$ [Directional Movement Index (DMI)].

$$+DI_j = \textit{exponential moving average}_j \; (+SDI, N) \; - DI_j = \textit{exponential moving average}_j \; (-SDI, N)$$

where, if

$$TR_j \text{ not} = 0,$$

that

$$+SDI_j = +DM_j \div TR_j; \; -SDI_j = -DM_j \div TR_j$$

if

$$TR_j = 0,$$

that

$$+SDI_j = 0, \; -SDI_j = 0$$

Determination of the average directional index = ADX_j, ADX_j = exponential moving average$_j$ (DX, N), where DX_j it is calculated under the formula:

$$DX_i = \frac{"+"DI - "-"DI}{"+"DI + "-"DI} \times 100$$

Average True Range. Volatility detection.
   Formulas to calculate:

$$ATR = \textit{moving average} \; (TR_j, n),$$

where

$$TR_j = \textit{maximal modules from three values} \; |High - Low|, \; |High - Close_{j-1}|, \; |Low - Close_{j-1}|.$$

Bollinger Bands. An envelope of bands plotted above and below the price bars on the chart.

Formulas to calculate:

$$UpperBand = MA + \left[D \times \sqrt{\frac{\sum\limits_{j=1}^{n}(Closej - MA)^2}{n}} \right]$$

$$LowerBand = MA - \left[D \times \sqrt{\frac{\sum\limits_{j=1}^{n}(Closej - MA)^2}{n}} \right]$$

where *MA* is a simple moving average

$$MA = \frac{\sum\limits_{j=1}^{n} Close_j}{n}.$$

Parameters: D = standard deviation, n = number of days.

Chande Momentum Oscillator (CMO). An overbought/oversold indicator.
    Formulas to calculate:

$$diff = P_i - P_i - 1,$$

where P_i = the price (usually closing price) of the current period; $P_i - 1$ = the price (usually closing price) of the previous period.

If $diff > 0$, then $cmo_{1i} = diff$, $cmo_{2i} = 0$.

If $diff < 0$, then $cmo_{2i} = -diff$, $cmo_{1i} = 0$.

$sum_1 = Sum(cmo_1, n)$ — summary value of cmo_1 within n periods.

$sum_2 = Sum(cmo_2, n)$ — summary value of cmo_2 within n periods.

$CMO = ((sum_1 - sum_2) \div (sum_1 + sum_2))\ 100.$

Daily High/Low Differential Ratio. A momentum and overbought/oversold indicator.

Formula to calculate:

Daily High/Low Differential Ratio = (Number of new fifty-two-week highs − Number of new fifty-two-week lows) ÷ Total number of issues traded during the day

DeMark Range Projections. Used to predict range, high, and low of next bar.

Formulas to calculate:

If the close of the most recent bar is less than the open, then the calculations are:

(Current High + 2 × Current Low + Current Close) = X

Projected High = X − Current Low

Projected Low = X − Current High

If the close of the most recent bar is greater than the open:

(2 × Current High + Current Low + Current Close) = X

Projected High = X − Current Low

Projected Low = X − Current High

If the close of the most recent bar is equal to the open then:

(Current High + Current Low + 2 × Current Close) = X

Projected High = X − Current Low

Projected Low = X − Current High

Ease of Movement. Measures volume level in relation to price movement.

Formula to calculate:

$$[\{(H + L) \div 2\} - \{(Hp + Lp) \div 2\}] \div [V \div (H - L)]$$

where:

H = today's high

L = today's low

Hp = the previous day's high price

Lp = the previous day's low price

V = current day's volume

Envelopes. Same concept as Bollinger bands.

Formulas to calculate:

$$UpperBand = \left(1 + P\right)\sum_{j=1}^{n}Close_j$$

$$LowerBand = \left(1 - P\right)\sum_{j=1}^{n}Close_j$$

Parameters: n = number of days, P = percentage shift.

Exponential Moving Average (EMA). A simple moving average weighted towards the most recent data in the set.

Formula to calculate:

$$EMA = Close\frac{2}{n+1} + \frac{\sum_{j=1}^{n}Close_j}{n}\left(100 - \frac{2}{n+1}\right)$$

Exponential Moving Average Difference. Used to detect the potential reversal of a *trend*.

Formula to calculate:

$$EMA_{difference} = EMA(n_1) - EMA(n_2)$$

Parameters: n_1, n_2 = number of days; $n_1 < n_2$.

Keltner Channel. Another envelope band around prices.

Formulas to calculate:

$$KC_{Middle} = MA(Price, n, Type),$$
$$KC_{Upper} = KC_{Middle} + MA(TR, n, Type) \times Dev,$$
$$KC_{Lower} = KC_{Middle} - MA(TR, n, Type) \times Dev,$$

where
Price = the price in the current period (*Close*, *Open*, etc.), *TR* = true range,
Dev = deviation factor.

Lomb Periodogram. Method of spectral analysis for unevenly sampled series. Astrophysicist N.R. Lomb[1] modified the definition of periodogram, obtaining the following expression for a zero-mean time series $x(tn)$:

$$P(\omega) = \frac{1}{2\sigma^2} \left\{ \frac{\left[\sum_{n=1}^{N} x(t_n) \cos \omega(t_n - \tau(\omega)) \right]^2}{\sum_{n=1}^{N} \cos^2 \omega(t_n - \tau(\omega))} + \frac{\left[\sum_{n=1}^{N} x(t_n) \sin \omega(t_n - \tau(\omega)) \right]^2}{\sum_{n=1}^{N} \sin^2 \omega(t_n - \tau(\omega))} \right\}$$

where σ^2 is the variance of $x(tn)$ and

$$\tau(\omega) = \frac{1}{2\omega} \arctan \left\{ \frac{\sum_{n=1}^{N} \sin 2\omega t_n}{\sum_{n=1}^{N} \cos 2\omega t_n} \right\}$$

is an offset that makes the periodogram invariant to time translation.[2]

McClellan Oscillator. An overbought/oversold indicator that measures flow of new money into or out of the market.

Formulas to calculate:

10% Trend – 5% Trend,

where the 10% Trend = the exponential moving average (EMA) of the daily number of advancers minus number of decliners with a 10% smoothing constant (or the nineteen-day EMA), and the 5% Trend = the EMA of the daily number

---

1. N.R. Lomb, "Least-Squares Frequency Analysis of Unequally Spaced Data." *Astrophysics and Space Science* 39 (1976): 447–462.

2. http://www.cbi.dongnocchi.it/glossary/Lomb.html

of advancers minus number of decliners with a 10% smoothing constant (or the thirty-nine-day EMA).

Momentum. The strength of a trend (used to detect trend reversals).
Formula to calculate:

$$Momentum_j = 100 \times \left(\frac{Close_j}{Close_{j-n}} \right)$$

Parameter: n = number of days.

Money Flow Index (MFI). An overbought/oversold oscillator.
Formulas to calculate:

$$MoneyFlowIndex = 100 - \left(\frac{100}{1 + MoneyRatio} \right)$$

$$MoneyRatio = \frac{\sum_{j=1}^{n} PositiveMoneyFlow_j}{\sum_{j=1}^{n} NegativeMoneyFlow_j}$$

$$PositiveMoneyFlow_j = \begin{cases} TypicalPrice_j \times Volume_j \\ if...TypicalPrice_j > TypicalPrice_{j-1} \\ 0...otherwise \end{cases}$$

$$NegativeMoneyFlow_j = \begin{cases} TypicalPrice_j \times Volume_j \\ if...TypicalPrice_j < TypicalPrice_{j-1} \\ 0...otherwise \end{cases}$$

$$TypicalPrice_j = (High_j + Low_j + Close_j) / 3$$

Parameter: n = number of days.

Moving Average Convergence-Divergence (MACD). Calculated by subtracting a longer-term simple moving average from a shorter-term simple moving average. The signal line is usually calculated as a nine-day simple moving average of MACD. Convergence-divergence is the difference between MACD and the signal line.

Formulas to calculate:

$$MACD = SMA(n_1) - SMA(n_2)$$

$$SignalLine = SMA(nSig, MACD)$$

Parameters: n_1, n_2, n_sig = number of days; $n_1 < n_2$.

On-Balance Volume. Detects trends in increases or decreases in trading volume.

Formulas to calculate:

$$OBV_{starting\ date} = 0$$

$$OBV_j = \begin{cases} OBV_{j-1} - Volume_j...if(Close_j < Close_{j-1}) \\ OBV_{j-1}...if(Close_j = Close_{j-1}) \end{cases}$$

Percentage Price Oscillator (PPO). An overbought/oversold and momentum indicator. Momentum is deemed to be positive while the shorter-term is above the longer-term average (or negative when vice-versa).

How it is calculated:

Subtract the longer-term moving average of prices from the shorter-term moving average and then divide the result by the longer-term moving average.

For example, six-week exponential moving average and twelve-week exponential moving average (twelve-day EMA and twenty-six-day EMA on the daily charts).

$$(x\text{-}period\ EMA - y\text{-}period\ EMA) \div y\text{-}period\ EMA$$

Parameters: x = short-term EMA length, y = long-term EMA length, period = daily/weekly/monthly, and so on.

Percentage Volume Oscillator (PVO). A volume trend indicator.

Formula to calculate:

$$PVO = ((Vol\ twelve\text{-}day\ EMA - Vol\ twenty\text{-}six\text{-}day\ EMA) \div Vol\ twenty\text{-}six\text{-}day\ EMA) \times 100$$

QStick. A price reversal indicator.

Formula to calculate:

A simple n-periodic moving average for the difference of the opening and closing prices.

$$QStick = MA(n, (Close - Open))$$

Parameter: n = period length.

Range Expansion Index. An overbought/oversold indicator.

Formula to calculate:

(current day's high minus high from two days ago) + *(current day's low minus low from two days ago)*

You can find details on the use of this indicator in DeMark's book on options.[3]

Rate of Change Oscillator (ROC). A short- to intermediate-term overbought/oversold indicator.

Formulas to calculate:

The **Rate of Change (ROC) Indicator** is the difference between the price of the current period and the price of the previous period, which is located n periods back from the current one:

$$ROC = P_i - P_{i-n},$$

$$P_i = \textit{the price of the current period,}$$

$$P_{i-n} = \textit{the price of the period,}$$

which is located n periods back from the current one.

As usual, they use the relative (in percentage) value of the velocity of the ROC:

$$ROC\% = 100\% \times (P_i - P_{i-n}) \div P_{i-n}$$

A ten-day ROC tends to oscillate in a fairly regular cycle. Often, price changes

---

3. T.R. DeMark and T.R. DeMark, Jr., *DeMark on Day Trading Options* (McGraw-Hill, 1999).

can be anticipated by studying past cycles of the ROC and applying the predicted pattern to the current market.

To construct a ten-day rate of change oscillator, the latest closing price is divided by the close ten days ago:

$$ROC = [(Close - Close\ ten\ periods\ ago) \div (Close\ ten\ periods\ ago)] \times 100$$

Relative Strength Index (RSI). The measure of the strength of a trend as a numeric value.

Formulas to calculate:

$$SMA = 100 - \left(\cfrac{100}{1 + \cfrac{UpTrend(n)}{DownTrend(n)}} \right)$$

where

$$UpTrend = \frac{\sum\limits_{j=1}^{n} Change_{j+}}{n} \qquad DownTrend = \frac{\sum\limits_{j=1}^{n} Change_{j-}}{n}$$

and

$$Change_{j+} = \begin{cases} (Close_j - Close_{j-1}) if(Close_j - Close_{j-1}) > 0 \\ 0\ otherwise \end{cases}$$

$$Change_{j-} = \begin{cases} Abs(Close_j - Close_{j-1}) if(Close_j - Close_{j-1}) < 0 \\ 0\ otherwise \end{cases}$$

Parameter: n = number of days.

STIX. A short-term trading oscillator that measures volume of advances/declines.

Formulas to calculate:

$$A/D\ Ratio = (advancing\ issues \div advancing\ issues - declining\ issues) \times 100$$

Stochastic (Fast). An oscillator to detect trend reversal.

Formulas to calculate:

$$\%K = \left[\frac{Close_j - Lowest..Low..In..n_1..periods}{Highest..High..in..n_1..periods - Lowest..Low..In..n_1..periods} \right] \times 100$$

$$\%D = SMA(\%K, n_2)$$

%D is a simple moving average of %K

Parameters: n_1 = number of days (for %K), n_2 = number of days (for %D)

Stochastic (Slow). An oscillator to detect trend reversal.

Formulas to calculate:

$$\%K =$$

$$\left[\frac{Close_j - 3..Day..Average..of..Lowest..Low..In..n_1..periods}{3..Day..Avg..of..Highest..High..in..n_1..periods - 3..Day..Avg..of..Lowest..Low..In..n_1..periods} \right] \times 100$$

$$\%D = SMA(\%K, n_2)$$

%D is a simple moving average of %K

Parameters: n_1 = number of days (for %K), n_2 = number of days (for %D).

Swing Index. Used to determine fair value.

Formula to calculate:

Swing Index = $50 \times [\{C_y - C + 0.5(C_y - O_y) + 0.25(C - O)\} \div R] \times (K \div T)$

where:

C = today's closing price

L = today's lowest price

O = today's opening price

C_y = yesterday's closing price

L_y = yesterday's lowest price

O_y = yesterday's opening price

H_y = yesterday's highest price

K = the larger of either $(H_y - C)$ or $(L_y - C)$

R = a variable based on the relationship between today's closing price and yesterday's high and low

T = the limit move value

Trade Volume Index. Detects surge in buying or selling activity.
Formulas to calculate:

The Trade Volume Index is calculated by adding each trade's volume to a cumulative total when the price moves up by a specified amount, and subtracting the trade's volume when the price moves down by a specified amount. That specified amount is known as the "Minimum Tick Value." To calculate the TVI, you must first determine whether prices are being accumulated or distributed:

$$Change = Price - Last\ Price$$

$$MTV = Minimum\ Tick\ Value$$

$$Accumulation\ when\ Change > MTV\ or\ Distribution\ when\ Change < MTV.$$

With direction determined, calculate the TVI:

$$Accumulation:\ TVI = TVI + Today's\ Volume$$

$$Distribution:\ TVI = TVI - Today's\ Volume$$

Volatility. Relative rate of price change over time.
Formulas to calculate:

$$HLAverage = EMA(High - Low, n_1)$$

in other words, *HLAverage* is an exponential moving average of the daily high/low difference:

$$Volatility = \left[\frac{HLAverage_j - HLAverage_{j-n^2}}{HLAverage_{j-n^2}}\right] \times 100$$

Parameters: n_1, n_2 = number of days.

APPENDIX B

Futures Products with High Daily Volume

Exchange codes:

CME—Chicago Mercantile Exchange

CBOT—Chicago Board of Trade

NYMEX—New York Mercantile Exchange

COMEX—Commodity Exchange (Division of NYMEX)

NYBOT—New York Board of Trade

Products:

CME E-Mini S&P 500

Trade unit: $50 times the Standard & Poor's 500 Stock Index

Minimum tick size: 0.25 = $12.50

Delivery months: March, June, September, December

CME E-Mini Nasdaq-100

Trade unit: $20 times the Nasdaq-100 Index

Minimum tick size: 0.25 = $5.00

Delivery months: March, June, September, December

CME E-Mini Russell 2000

Trade unit: $100 times the Russell 2000 Index

Minimum tick size: 0.10 = $10.00

Delivery months: March, June, September, December

CME Eurodollar

Trade unit: Eurodollar Time Deposit having a principal value of $1,000,000 with
a three-month maturity

Minimum tick size: Regular – 0.01 = $25.00, months 11 through 40; half tick
– 0.005 = $12.50, months 2 through 10; quarter tick – 0.0025 = $6.25 for
nearest expiring month

Delivery months: March, June, September, December (out to forty months)

CME Australian Dollar
Trade unit: 100,000 Australian dollars
Minimum tick size: 0.0001 = $10.00
Delivery months: March, June, September, December

CME British Pound
Trade unit: 62,500 pounds sterling (British pounds)
Minimum tick size: 0.0001 = $6.25
Delivery months: March, June, September, December

CME Canadian Dollar
Trade unit: 100,000 Canadian dollars
Minimum tick size: 0.0001 = $10.00
Delivery months: March, June, September, December

CME Euro FX
Trade unit: 125,000 euro
Minimum tick size: 0.0001 = $12.50
Delivery months: March, June, September, December

CME Japanese Yen
Trade unit: 12,500,000 Japanese yen
Minimum tick size: 0.000001 = $12.50
Delivery months: March, June, September, December

CME Swiss Franc
Trade unit: 125,000 Swiss francs
Minimum tick size: 0.0001 = $12.50
Delivery months: March, June, September, December

CME Live Cattle
Trade unit: 40,000 pounds
Minimum tick size: 0.00025/pound = $10.00
Delivery months: February, April, June, August, October, December

CME Lean Hogs
Trade unit: 40,000 pounds
Minimum tick size: 0.00025/pound = $10.00
Delivery months: February, April, May, June, July, August, October, December

CBOT Corn
Trade unit: 5,000 bushels
Minimum tick size: 1/4 cent/bushel ($12.50/contract)
Delivery months: December, March, May, July, September

CBOT Soybeans
Trade unit: 5,000 bushels
Minimum tick size: 1/4 cent/bushel ($12.50/contract)
Delivery months: September, November, January, March, May, July, August

CBOT Soybean Oil
Trade unit: 60,000 pounds
Minimum tick size: 1/100 cent ($0.0001)/pound ($6/contract)
Delivery months: October, December, January, March, May, July, August, September

CBOT Soybean Meal
Trade unit: 100 tons (2,000 pounds/short ton)
Minimum tick size: 10 cents/ton ($10/contract)
Delivery months: October, December, January, March, May, July, August, September

CBOT Wheat
Trade unit: 5,000 bushels
Minimum tick size: 1/4 cent/bushel ($12.50/contract)
Delivery months: December, March, May, July, September

CBOT 30-Year U.S. Treasury Bonds
Trade unit: One U.S. Treasury bond having a face value at maturity of $100,000 or multiple thereof
Minimum tick size: 1/32 point per 100 points ($31.25 per contract)
Delivery months: March, June, September, December

CBOT 10-Year U.S. Treasury Notes

Trade unit: One U.S. Treasury note having a face value at maturity of $100,000 or multiple thereof

Minimum tick size: One-half of 1/32 point per 100 points ($15.625 rounded up to the nearest cent per contract)

Delivery months: March, June, September, December

CBOT Mini-Sized Dow

Trade unit: $5 times the Dow Jones Industrial Average Index price

Minimum tick size: One index point (equal to $5 per contract)

Delivery months: March, June, September, December

NYMEX Light Sweet Crude Oil

Trade unit: 1,000 U.S. barrels (42,000 gallons)

Minimum tick size: $0.01 (1¢) per barrel ($10.00 per contract)

Delivery months: All twelve months

NYMEX Natural Gas

Trade Unit: 10,000 million British thermal units (mmBtu)

Minimum tick size: $0.001 (0.1¢) per mmBtu ($10.00 per contract)

Delivery months: All twelve months

NYMEX Heating Oil

Trade Unit: 42,000 U.S. gallons (1,000 barrels)

Minimum tick size: $0.0001 (0.01¢) per gallon ($4.20 per contract)

Delivery months: All twelve months

NYMEX RBOB Gasoline

Trade unit: 42,000 U.S. gallons (1,000 barrels)

Minimum tick size: $0.0001 (0.01¢) per gallon ($4.20 per contract)

Delivery months: All twelve months

COMEX Gold

Trade unit: 100 troy ounces

Minimum tick size: $0.10 (10¢) per troy ounce ($10.00 per contract)

Delivery months: Trading is conducted for delivery during the current calendar month; the next two calendar months; any February, April, August, and October falling within a twenty-three-month period; and any June and December falling within a sixty-month period beginning with the current month.

COMEX Silver

Trade unit: 5,000 troy ounces

Minimum tick size: ½ of one cent (0.5¢ or $0.005) per troy ounce, equivalent to $25.00 per contract

Delivery months: Trading is conducted for delivery during the current calendar month; the next two calendar months; any January, March, May, and September falling within a twenty-three-month period; and any July and December falling within a sixty-month period beginning with the current month.

COMEX Copper

Trade unit: 25,000 pounds

Minimum tick size: 5/100 of one cent (0.05¢ or $0.0005) per pound, equivalent to $12.50 per contract

Delivery months: Trading is conducted for delivery during the current calendar month and the next twenty-three consecutive calendar months.

NYBOT Cocoa

Trade unit: 10 metric tons

Minimum tick size: $1.00/metric ton, equivalent to $10.00 per contract

Delivery months: March, May, July, September, December

NYBOT Coffee

Trade unit: 37,500 pounds

Minimum tick size: 5/100 of one cent (0.05¢ or $0.0005) per pound, equivalent to $18.75 per contract

Delivery months: March, May, July, September, December

NYBOT Cotton No. 2

Trade Unit: 50,000 pounds net weight

Minimum tick size: 1/100 of one cent (one "point") per pound below $0.95 per pound, 5/100 of a cent (or five "points") per pound at prices of $0.95 per pound or higher

Delivery months: March, May, July, October, December

NYBOT Sugar No. 11

Trade Unit: 112,000 pounds (50 long tons)

Minimum tick size: 1/100 of one cent per pound, equivalent to $11.20 per contract

Delivery months: March, May, July, October

Single Stock Futures as of April 6, 2007

Margins: Margin requirements are generally 20 percent of the cash value of the contract, although this requirement may be lower if the investor also holds certain offsetting positions in cash equities, stock options, or other security futures in the same securities account.

Trade unit: 100 shares of underlying security

Minimum tick size: $0.01 x 100 shares = $1.00

UNDERLYING SECURITY	TICKER SYMBOL	OneCHICAGO BASE SYMBOL
3M Co.	MMM	MMM1C
Abbott Laboratories	ABT	ABT1C
Abercrombie & Fitch Co.	ANF	ANF1C
Abraxis BioScience, Inc.	ABBI	ABBI1C
ADC Telecommunications, Inc.	ADCT	ADCT1C
Adobe Systems Incorporated	ADBE	ADBE1C
Advanced Medical Optics, Inc.	EYE	EYE1C
Advanced Micro Devices Inc.	AMD	AMD1C
Aetna Inc.	AET	AET1C
Affiliated Computer Services Inc.	ACS	ACS1C
Agilent Technologies, Inc.	A	A1C
Air Products and Chemicals Inc.	APD	APD1C
Akamai Technologies Inc.	AKAM	AKAM1C
Alcoa Inc.	AA	AA1C
Allegheny Technologies Incorporated	ATI	ATI1C
Allstate Corp.	ALL	ALL1C
Alltel Corporation	AT	AT1C
Altera Corp.	ALTR	ALTR1C
Altria Group Inc.	MO	MO1C
Amazon.com Inc.	AMZN	AMZN1C
Amerada Hess Corporation	HES	HES1C

UNDERLYING SECURITY	TICKER SYMBOL	OneCHICAGO BASE SYMBOL
Ameren Corp.	AEE	AEE1C
America Movil SA de CV	AMX	AMX1C
American Eagle Outfitters, Inc.	AEOS	AEOS1C
American Electric Power Co. Inc.	AEP	AEP1C
American Express Co.	AXP	AXP1C
American International Group	AIG	AIG1C
American Standard Companies Inc.	ASD	ASD1C
American Tower Corporation	AMT	AMT1C
Amgen Inc.	AMGN	AMGN1C
AMR Corporation	AMR	AMR1C
Amylin Pharmaceuticals Inc.	AMLN	AMLN1C
Analog Devices Inc.	ADI	ADI1C
Anadarko Petroleum Corporation	APC	APC1C
Anheuser-Busch Inc.	BUD	BUD1C
Ann Taylor Stores Corporation	ANN	ANN1C
AON Corp.	AOC	AOC1C
Apache Corporation	APA	APA1C
Apartment Investment and Management Co.	AIV	AIV1C
Applied Materials Inc.	AMAT	AMAT1C
Apple Inc.	AAPL	AAPL1C
Arch Coal Inc.	ACI	ACI1C
Archer-Daniels-Midland Company	ADM	ADM1C
Archstone-Smith Trust	ASN	ASN1C
AT&T Corp.	T	T1C
Autodesk	ADSK	ADSK1C
Automatic Data Processing Inc.	ADP	ADP1C
Autozone, Inc.	AZO	AZO1C
Avalonbay Communities Inc.	AVB	AVB1C
Avery Dennison Corporation	AVY	AVY1C
Avis Budget Group Inc.	CAR	CAR1C
Avon Products Inc.	AVP	AVP1C
Baker Hughes Incorporated	BHI	BHI1C
Bank of America Corp.	BAC	BAC1C
Bank of New York Co. Inc.	BK	BK1C
Baxter International Inc.	BAX	BAX1C
Bausch & Lomb Incorporated	BOL	BOL1C
BB&T Corp.	BBT	BBT1C

UNDERLYING SECURITY	TICKER SYMBOL	OneCHICAGO BASE SYMBOL
Beazer Homes USA Inc.	BZH	BZH1C
Bed Bath & Beyond Inc.	BBBY	BBBY1C
BellSouth Corp.	BLS	BLS1C
Bemis Company Inc.	BMS	BMS1C
Best Buy Company Inc.	BBY	BBY1C
Biogen Idec Inc.	BIIB	BIIB1C
Biomet, Inc.	BMET	BMET1C
BJ Services Company	BJS	BJS1C
Boeing Co.	BA	BA1C
Boston Properties Inc.	BXP	BXP1C
Boston Scientific Corp.	BSX	BSX1C
Boyd Gaming Corporation	BYD	BYD1C
Bristol-Myers Squibb Co.	BMY	BMY1C
Broadcom Corp.	BRCM	BRCM1C
Brocade Communications Sys	BRCD	BRCD1C
Brunswick Corp.	BC	BC1C
Burlington Northern Santa Fe Corp.	BNI	BNI1C
CA Inc.	CA	CA1C
Cablevision Systems Corporation (Class A)	CVC	CVC1C
Campbell Soup Co.	CPB	CPB1C
Capital One Financial Corporation	COF	COF1C
Carnival Corp.	CCL	CCL1C
Carpenter Technology Corporation	CRS	CRS1C
Caterpillar Inc.	CAT	CAT1C
CBOT Holdings, Inc.	BOT	BOT1C
CBS Corporation (Class B)	CBS	CBS1C
CDW Corporation	CDWC	CDWC1C
Celgene Corp.	CELG	CELG1C
CenterPoint Energy, Inc.	CNP	CNP1C
Centex Corporation	CTX	CTX1C
Cephalon Inc.	CEPH	CEPH1C
Cerner Corporation	CERN	CERN1C
Check Point Software Tech	CHKP	CHKP1C
Cheniere Energy, Inc.	LNG	LNG1C
Chesapeake Energy Corporation	CHK	CHK1C
ChevronTexaco Corp.	CVX	CVX1C
Chicago Mercantile Holdings Inc.	CME	CME1C

UNDERLYING SECURITY	TICKER SYMBOL	OneCHICAGO BASE SYMBOL
Chubb Corp.	CB	CB1C
CIGNA Corporation	CI	CI1C
Cincinnati Financial Corp.	CINF	CINF1C
Circuit City Stores, Inc.	CC	CC1C
Cisco Systems Inc.	CSCO	CSCO1C
CIT Group Inc.	CIT	CIT1C
Citigroup Inc.	C	C1C
Citizens Communications	CZN	CZN1C
Citrix Systems Inc.	CTXS	CTXS1C
Clear Channel Communications Inc.	CCU	CCU1C
Clorox Co.	CLX	CLX1C
Coach, Inc.	COH	COH1C
Coca-Cola Co.	KO	KO1C
Cognizant Technology Solutions Corporation	CTSH	CTSH1C
Colgate-Palmolive Co.	CL	CL1C
Comcast Corporation	CMCSA	CMCX1C
Comcast Corp.	CMCSK	CMCS1C
Comerica Inc.	CMA	CMA1C
Commerce Bancorp Inc.	CBH	CBH1C
Compass Bancshares Inc.	CBSS	CBSS1C
Comverse Technology Inc.	CMVT	CMVT1C
ConAgra Foods Inc.	CAG	CAG1C
ConocoPhillips	COP	COP1C
CONSOL Energy Inc.	CNX	CNX1C
Consolidated Edison Inc.	ED	ED1C
Constellation Energy Group	CEG	CEG1C
Continental Airlines Inc.	CAL	CAL1C
Corning Incorporated	GLW	GLW1C
Costco Wholesale Corporation	COST	COST1C
Countrywide Financial Corp.	CFC	CFC1C
Coventry Health Care Inc.	CVH	CVH1C
Cree, Inc.	CREE	CREE1C
Crown Castle International Corp.	CCI	CCI1C
Crown Holdings, Inc.	CCK	CCK1C
CSX Corporation	CSX	CSX1C
Cummins Inc.	CMI	CMI1C
CVS Corporation	CVS	CVS1C

UNDERLYING SECURITY	TICKER SYMBOL	OneCHICAGO BASE SYMBOL
Cypress Semiconductor Corporation	CY	CY1C
Darden Restaurants Inc.	DRI	DRI1C
Deere & Co.	DE	DE1C
Dell Inc.	DELL	DELL1C
Devon Energy Corporation	DVN	DVN1C
Diamond Offshore Drilling Inc.	DO	DO1C
Dominion Resources Inc.	D	D1C
Dover Corporation	DOV	DOV1C
Dow Chemical Co.	DOW	DOW1C
D.R. Horton Inc.	DHI	DHI1C
DTE Energy Co.	DTE	DTE1C
Duke Energy Corp.	DUK	DUK1C
DuPont (E.I. Du Pont de Nemours)	DD	DD1C
E*TRADE Financial Corporation	ETFC	ETFC1C
Eagle Materials Inc.	EXP	EXP1C
Eastman Chemical Co.	EMN	EMN1C
Eastman Kodak	EK	EK1C
Eaton Corp.	ETN	ETN1C
eBay Inc.	EBAY	EBAY1C
EchoStar Communications Corp	DISH	DISH1C
Edison International	EIX	EIX1C
Elan Corp. PLC	ELN	ELN1C
Electronic Data Systems Corp.	EDS	EDS1C
Electronic Arts Inc.	ERTS	ERTS1C
Eli Lilly and Co.	LLY	LLY1C
EL Paso Corporation	EP	EP1C
Embarq Corp.	EQ	EQ1C
EMC Corp.	EMC	EMC1C
Emdeon Corporation	HLTH	HLTH
Emerson Electric Co.	EMR	EMR1C
Emulex Corp.	ELX	ELX1C
ENSCO International Incorporated	ESV	ESV1C
Entergy Corp.	ETR	ETR1C
EOG Resources Inc.	EOG	EOG1C
Equity Residential	EQR	EQR1C
Exelon Corporation	EXC	EXC1C
Expeditors Intnl. of Washington Inc.	EXPD	EXPD1C

UNDERLYING SECURITY	TICKER SYMBOL	OneCHICAGO BASE SYMBOL
Express Scripts, Inc.	ESRX	ESRX1C
Exxon Mobil Corp.	XOM	XOM1C
F5 Networks Inc.	FFIV	FFIV1C
Federal National Mortgage Association	FNM	FNM1C
Federated Department Stores Inc.	FD	FD1C
Federated Investors Inc.	FII	FII1C
FedEx Corporation	FDX	FDX1C
Fifth Third Bancorp	FITB	FITB1C
First Data Corporation	FDC	FDC1C
First Energy Corp.	FE	FE1C
First Horizon National Corp.	FHN	FHN1C
Foot Locker, Inc.	FL	FL1C
Ford Motor Co.	F	F1C
Forest Laboratories Inc.	FRX	FRX1C
Fortune Brands Inc.	FO	FO1C
FPL Group Inc.	FPL	FPL1C
Freeport-McMoRan Copper & Gold Inc.	FCX	FCX1C
Frontier Oil Corporation	FTO	FTO1C
Gannett Co., Inc.	GCI	GCI1C
Genentech Inc.	DNA	DNA1C
General Dynamics Corporation	GD	GD1C
General Electric Co.	GE	GE1C
General Mills Inc.	GIS	GIS1C
General Motors Corp.	GM	GM1C
Genuine Parts Co.	GPC	GPC1C
Genzyme Corp. (Genl. Division)	GENZ	GENZ1C
Gilead Sciences Inc.	GILD	GILD1C
Goldman Sachs Group Inc.	GS	GS1C
Goodrich Corporation	GR	GR1C
Google Inc.	GOOG	GOOG1C
H&R Block Inc.	HRB	HRB1C
Halliburton Co.	HAL	HAL1C
Harley-Davidson Inc.	HOG	HOG1C
Harrah's Entertainment Inc.	HET	HET1C
Hartford Financial Services Group Inc.	HIG	HIG1C
Hasbro Inc.	HAS	HAS1C
Hewlett-Packard Co.	HPQ	HPQ1C

UNDERLYING SECURITY	TICKER SYMBOL	OneCHICAGO BASE SYMBOL
H.J. Heinz Co.	HNZ	HNZ1C
Home Depot Inc.	HD	HD1C
Honeywell International Inc.	HON	HON1C
Humana Inc.	HUM	HUM1C
Huntington Bancshares Inc.	HBAN	HBAN1C
IAC/InterActiveCorp	IACI	IACI1C
Illinois Tool Works Inc.	ITW	ITW1C
ImClone Systems Incorporated	IMCL	IMCL1C
Ingersoll-Rand Co. Ltd.	IR	IR1C
Intel Corp.	INTC	INTC1C
IntercontinentalExchange, Inc.	ICE	ICE1C
International Business Machines	IBM	IBM1C
International Game Technology	IGT	IGT1C
International Paper Co.	IP	IP1C
Intersil Corporation	ISIL	ISIL1C
Intuit Inc.	INTU	INTU1C
Intuitive Surgical Inc.	ISRG	ISRG1C
Jabil Circuit, Inc.	JBL	JBL1C
J.C. Penny Company Inc.	JCP	JCP1C
J.P. Morgan Chase & Co.	JPM	JPM1C
JetBlue Airways Corp.	JBLU	JBLU1C
Johnson & Johnson	JNJ	JNJ1C
Joy Global Inc.	JOYG	JOYG1C
Juniper Networks	JNPR	JNPR1C
KB Home	KBH	KBH1C
Kellogg Co.	K	K1C
KeyCorp.	KEY	KEY1C
Keyspan Corp.	KSE	KSE1C
Kimberly-Clark Corp.	KMB	KMB1C
Kimco Realty Corporation	KIM	KIM1C
Kinetic Concepts Inc.	KCI	KCI1C
KLA-Tencor Corp.	KLAC	KLAC1C
Kohl's Corp.	KSS	KSS1C
Kraft Foods Inc.	KFT	KFT1C
L-3 Communications Holdings	LLL	LLL1C
Lam Research Corp.	LRCX	LRCX1C
Las Vegas Sands Corp.	LVS	LVS1C

UNDERLYING SECURITY	TICKER SYMBOL	OneCHICAGO BASE SYMBOL
Leahman Brothers Holdings Inc.	LEH	LEH1C
Legg Mason, Inc.	LM	LM1C
Leggett & Platt, Inc.	LEG	LEG1C
Lennar Corp.	LEN	LEN1C
Level 3 Communications, Inc.	LVLT	LVLT1C
Lexmark International Inc.	LXK	LXK1C
Limited Brands, Inc.	LTD	LTD1C
Lincoln National Corp.	LNC	LNC1C
Linear Technology Corp.	LLTC	LLTC1C
Lockheed Martin Corp.	LMT	LMT1C
Loews Corporation	CG	CG1C
Louisiana-Pacific Corp.	LPX	LPX1C
Lowe's Companies Inc.	LOW	LOW1C
M&T Bank Corp.	MTB	MTB1C
Marathon Oil Corp.	MRO	MRO1C
Marriott International, Inc.	MAR	MAR1C
Marshall & Ilsley Corp.	MI	MI1C
Marsh & McLennan Cos.	MMC	MMC1C
Masco Corp.	MAS	MAS1C
Massey Energy Company	MEE	MEE1C
Mattel Inc.	MAT	MAT1C
Maxim Integrated Products Inc.	MXIM	MXIM1C
MBIA Inc.	MBI	MBI1C
McAfee, Inc.	MFE	MFE1C
McCormick & Co. Inc.	MKC	MKC1C
McDonald's Corp.	MCD	MCD1C
MeadWestvaco Corp.	MWV	MWV1C
MedImmune, Inc.	MEDI	MEDI1C
Medtronic Inc.	MDT	MDT1C
Mellon Financial Corp.	MEL	MEL1C
MEMC Electronic Materials Inc.	WFR	WFR1C
Merck & Co. Inc.	MRK	MRK1C
Merrill Lynch & Co. Inc.	MER	MER1C
MetLife Inc.	MET	MET1C
MGIC Investment Corp.	MTG	MTG1C
MGM Mirage	MGM	MGM1C
Micron Technology Inc.	MU	MU1C

UNDERLYING SECURITY	TICKER SYMBOL	OneCHICAGO BASE SYMBOL
Microsoft Corp.	MSFT	MSFT1C
Mirant Corporation	MIR	MIR1C
Monsanto Company	MON	MON1C
Morgan Stanley	MS	MS1C
Motorola Inc.	MOT	MOT1C
Murphy Oil Corporation	MUR	MUR1C
Mylan Laboratories Inc.	MYL	MYL1C
Nabors Industries Inc.	NBR	NBR1C
National City Corp.	NCC	NCC1C
National Oilwell Varco, Inc.	NOV	NOV1C
NAVTEQ Corporation	NVT	NVT1C
Network Appliance Inc.	NTAP	NTAP1C
New Century Financial Corporation	NEW	NEW1C
Newell Rubbermaid Inc.	NWL	NWL1C
Newmont Mining Corp. Hldg. Co.	NEM	NEM1C
New York Times Co.	NYT	NYT1C
Nicor Inc.	GAS	GAS1C
NiSource Inc.	NI	NI1C
Noble Corporation	NE	NE1C
Nokia Corp. (ADR)	NOK	NOK1C
Norfolk Southern Corp.	NSC	NSC1C
North Fork Bancorp Inc.	NFB	NFB2C
Northrop Grumman Corporation	NOC	NOC1C
Novellus Systems Inc.	NVLS	NVLS1C
Nucor Corporation	NUE	NUE1C
NutriSystem Inc.	NTRI	NTRI1C
NVIDIA Corp.	NVDA	NVDA1C
NYMEX Holdings, Inc.	NMX	NMX1C
NYSE Group Inc.	NYX	NYX1C
Occidental Petroleum Corp.	OXY	OXY1C
Oceaneering International, Inc.	OII	OII1C
Odyssey HealthCare Inc.	ODSY	ODSY1C
Office Depot, Inc.	ODP	ODP1C
OfficeMax Incorporated	OMX	OMX1C
Omnicare, Inc.	OCR	OCR1C
Oracle Corp.	ORCL	ORCL1C
OSI Pharmaceuticals Inc.	OSIP	OSIP1C

UNDERLYING SECURITY	TICKER SYMBOL	OneCHICAGO BASE SYMBOL
Panera Bread Company	PNRA	PNRA1C
Parker-Hannifin Corporation	PH	PH1C
Patterson-UTI Energy Inc.	PTEN	PTEN1C
Paychex Inc.	PAYX	PAY1C
Peabody Energy Corporation	BTU	BTU1C
PepsiCo Inc.	PEP	PEP1C
Pfizer	PFE	PFE1C
PG&E Corp.	PCG	PCG1C
Pinnacle West Capital Corp.	PNW	PNW1C
Pioneer Natural Resources Company	PXD	PXD1C
Pitney Bowes Inc.	PBI	PBI1C
Plum Creek Timber Co. Inc.	PCL	PCL1C
PMC Sierra Inc.	PMCS	PMCS1C
PNC Financial Corp.	PNC	PNC1C
PPG Industries Inc.	PPG	PPG1C
PPL Corp.	PPL	PPL1C
Praxair, Inc.	PX	PX1C
Pride International, Inc.	PDE	PDE1C
Procter & Gamble Co.	PG	PG1C
Progress Energy Inc.	PGN	PGN1C
ProLogis	PLD	PLD1C
Prudential Financial Inc.	PRU	PRU1C
Public Service Enterprise Group Inc.	PEG	PEG1C
Public Storage, Inc.	PSA	PSA1C
Pulte Homes Inc	PHM	PHM1C
QLogic Corp.	QLGC	QLGC1C
QUALCOMM Inc.	QCOM	QCOM1C
Qwest Communications International Inc.	Q	Q1C
RadioShack Corp.	RSH	RSH1C
Rambus Inc.	RMBS	RMBS1C
Raytheon Co.	RTN	RTN1C
Red Hat Inc.	RHT	RHT1C
Regions Financial Corp.	RF	RF1C
Research In Motion Ltd.	RIMM	RIMM1C
Reynolds American Inc.	RAI	RAI1C
Rohm & Haas Co.	ROH	ROH1C
Rockwell Automation Inc.	ROK	ROK1C

UNDERLYING SECURITY	TICKER SYMBOL	OneCHICAGO BASE SYMBOL
Rockwell Collins Inc.	COL	COL1C
Rowan Companies, Inc.	RDC	RDC1C
RR Donnelly & Sons	RRD	RRD1C
Salesforce.com, Inc.	CRM	CRM1C
SanDisk Corp.	SNDK	SNDK1C
Sara Lee Corp.	SLE	SLE1C
Schering-Plough Corp.	SGP	SGP1C
Schlumberger Ltd.	SLB	SLB1C
Sears Holdings Corporation	SHLD	SHLD1C
Sempra Energy	SRE	SRE1C
Sepracor Inc.	SEPR	SEPR1C
Sherwin-Williams Co.	SHW	SHW1C
Silicon Laboratories Inc.	SLAB	SLAB1C
Simon Property Group Inc.	SPG	SPG1C
Sirius Satellite Radio Inc.	SIRI	SIRI1C
SLM Corporation	SLM	SLM1C
Smith International, Inc.	SII	SII1C
Spectra Energy Corp.	SE	SE1C
Stryker Corporation	SYK	SYK1C
Southern Co.	SO	SO1C
Southern Copper Corporation	PCU	PCU1C
Southwest Airlines Co.	LUV	LUV1C
Southwestern Energy Company	SWN	SWN1C
Sovereign Bancorp.	SOV	SOV1C
Sprint Nextel Corp.	S	S1C
St. Jude Medical Inc.	STJ	STJ1C
St. Paul Travelers Cos. Inc.	STA	STA1C
Starbucks Corp.	SBUX	SBUX1C
Starwood Hotel & Resorts Worldwide	HOT	HOT1C
Steel Dynamics, Inc.	STLD	STLD1C
Sun Microsystems	SUNW	SUNW1C
Suncor Energy Inc.	SU	SU1C
Sunoco Inc.	SUN	SUN1C
SunTrust Banks Inc.	STI	STI1C
Supervalu Inc.	SVU	SVU1C
Symantec Corp.	SYMC	SYMC1C
Synovus Financial Corp.	SNV	SNV1C

UNDERLYING SECURITY	TICKER SYMBOL	OneCHICAGO BASE SYMBOL
SYSCO Corp.	SYY	SYY1C
Target Corp.	TGT	TGT1C
TD Ameritrade Holding Corporation	AMTD	AMTD1C
TECO Energy Inc.	TE	TE1C
Telefonos de Mexico SA de CV	TMX	TMX1C
Tellabs, Inc.	TLAB	TLAB1C
Temple-Inland Inc.	TIN	TIN1C
Tenet Healthcare	THC	THC1C
Terex Corporation	TEX	TEX1C
Tesoro Corporation	TSO	TSO1C
Texas Instruments Inc.	TXN	TXN1C
Textron Inc.	TXT	TXT1C
The AES Corporation	AES	AES1C
The Bear Stearns Companies Inc.	BSC	BSC1C
The Charles Schwab Corporation	SCHW	SCHW1C
The Gap Inc.	GPS	GPS1C
The Goodyear Tire & Rubber Company	GT	GT1C
The Hershey Company	HSY	HSY1C
The McGraw-Hill Companies, Inc.	MHP	MHP1C
The Nasdaq Stock Market, Inc.	NDAQ	NDAQ1C
The PMI Group, Inc.	PMI	PMI1C
The Ryland Group Inc.	RYL	RYL1C
The Stanley Works	SWK	SWK1C
The St. Joe Company	JOE	JOE1C
Time Warner Inc.	TWX	TWX1C
Titanium Metals Corporation	TIE	TIE1C
TJX Companies Inc.	TJX	TJX1C
Toll Brothers Inc.	TOL	TOL1C
TODCO	THE	THE1C
Transocean Inc.	RIG	RIG1C
Tribune Co.	TRB	TRB1C
TXU Corp.	TXU	TXU1C
Tyco International Ltd.	TYC	TYC1C
UAL Corporation	UAUA	UAUA1C
U.S. Bancorp (New)	USB	USB1C
Union Pacific Corp.	UNP	UNP1C
Unisys Corporation	UIS	UIS1C

UNDERLYING SECURITY	TICKER SYMBOL	OneCHICAGO BASE SYMBOL
UnitedHealth Group Incorporated	UNH	UNH1C
United States Steel Corporation	X	X1C
United Technologies Corp.	UTX	UTX1C
United Parcel Service Inc.	UPS	UPS1C
UnumProvident Corporation	UNM	UNM1C
US Airways Group Inc.	LCC	LCC1C
USG Corporation	USG	USG1C
UST Inc.	UST	UST1C
Valero Energy Corp.	VLO	VLO1C
Verizon Communications Inc.	VZ	VZ1C
VeriSign, Inc.	VRSN	VRSN1C
Vertex Pharmaceuticals Incorporated	VRTX	VRTX1C
V.F. Corporation	VFC	VFC1C
Viacom Inc. (Class B)	VIAB	VIAB1C
Virgin Media Inc.	VMED	VMED1C
Vishay Intertechnology Inc.	VSH	VSH1C
Vornado Realty Trust	VNO	VNO1C
Vulcan Materials Company	VMC	VMC1C
Wachovia Corp.	WB	WB1C
Walgreen Co.	WAG	WAG1C
Wal-Mart Stores Inc.	WMT	WMT1C
Walt Disney Co.	DIS	DIS1C
Walter Industries, Inc.	WLT	WLT1C
Washington Mutual Inc.	WM	WM1C
Waste Management Inc.	WMI	WMI1C
Weatherford International Ltd.	WFT	WFT1C
WellPoint Inc.	WLP	WLP1C
Wells Fargo & Co.	WFC	WFC1C
Wendy's International, Inc.	WEN	WEN1C
Western Digital Corporation	WDC	WDC1C
Weyerhaeuser Co.	WY	WY1C
Whirlpool Corporation	WHR	WHR1C
Whole Foods Market Inc.	WFMI	WFMI1C
Williams Companies Inc.	WMB	WMB1C
William Wrigley Jr. Co.	WWY	WWY1C

UNDERLYING SECURITY	TICKER SYMBOL	OneCHICAGO BASE SYMBOL
Windstream Corporation	WIN	WIN1C
WW Grainger Inc.	GWW	GWW1C
Wyeth	WYE	WYE1C
Wynn Resorts Limited	WYNN	WYNN1C
Xcel Energy Inc.	XEL	XEL1C
Xilinx Inc.	XLNX	XLNX1C
XM Satellite Radio Holdings Inc.	XMSR	XMSR1C
XTO Energy Inc.	XTO	XTO1C
Yahoo! Inc.	YHOO	YHOO1C
YRC Worldwide Inc.	YRCW	YRCW1C
YUM! Brands Inc.	YUM	YUM1C
Zimmer Holdings, Inc.	ZMH	ZMH1C
Zions Bancorp.	ZION	ZION1C

Forex Currency Pairs

Symbols:
USD—U.S. Dollar
EUR—Euro
GBP—British Pound
JPY—Japanese Yen
AUD—Australian Dollar
CAD—Canadian Dollar
CHF—Swiss Franc

Base/Counter Pairs for Dominant Base Currencies:
- Euro—EUR/USD, EUR/GBP, EUR/CHF, EUR/JPY, EUR/CAD
- British Pound—GBP/USD, GBP/CHF, GBP/JPY, GBP/CAD
- U.S. Dollar —USD/CAD, USD/JPY, USD/CHF

APPENDIX C

Educational Resources

A little learning is a dangerous thing; drink deep, or taste not the Pierian spring: there shallow draughts intoxicate the brain, and drinking largely sobers us again.

ALEXANDER POPE, *AN ESSAY ON CRITICISM*, 1709

Beware of the many high-priced trading seminars available. Despite all of the hype and slick brochures, they are almost always not any better than a good book on technical analysis or a course for a few hundred dollars at one of the futures exchanges. The worst thing a trading educator can do is arm a student with a little knowledge—that is extremely dangerous. Someone ill equipped to trade with sound strategies and stop-loss orders is, for the most part, a person on a suicide mission. His hard-earned money is destined to be fodder for market sharks.

Some reliable seminars, however, are available. The following certainly do not constitute an exhaustive list of good resources out there. You should be able to find others by shopping around:

- *Chicago Board of Trade* has free webcasts (webinars) from its website (http://www.cbot.com/cbot/pub/page/0,3181,1058,00.html).

- *Chicago Mercantile Exchange* also offers free webinars, as well as reasonably priced classes at its learning center (http://www.cme.com/edu/).

- *Online Trading Academy* is another organization that provides quality classroom education with hands-on trading exercises (www.onlinetradingacademy.com). The basics of technical analysis and electronic order entry are taught by qualified instructors who are not out to pick your pockets or sell you their latest get-rich-quick book about the markets. Actual money is provided for making real-time trades on equities (not available for derivatives due to regulatory restrictions and risk factors). The academy offers a spectrum of trading styles and instruments, from day trading, swing trading, position trading, and investment theory for stocks, options, futures (e-minis and commodities), and currencies. Courses in actively trading stocks, options, futures, Forex, exchange traded funds (ETFs), and general investing strategies are offered. Instructors emphasize understanding the risks involved in various markets and money management skills, which is something many overpriced seminars may gloss over.

At Online Trading Academy, the entire cost of tuition and other related expenses are rebated to students in the form of discounted tickets from the academy's affiliated broker/dealers. Most of their broker/dealer affiliates will discount their tickets 10 to 20 percent from their "per ticket" published rate until the discount saved equals the full class cost.

Online Trading Academy is headquartered in Irvine, California. At the time of this writing it has locations in the following cities: Los Angeles; Des Plaines, IL; Houston; Irving, TX; Norwood, MA; Secaucus, NJ; Orlando, FL; Toronto; London; Dubai; and Riyadh, Saudi Arabia.

APPENDIX D

Trading Reports and Other Forms
of News Service

There are a number of different sources of fundamental news a trader can access to help trade futures. Besides the usual collection of government economic reports (a list of which is provided at the end of this appendix), there also are specialty pit, local community, radio, and television sites that provide the trader with valuable information. The question is, of course, how this information can be used and how strong an effect the news or information will have on the underlying community.

Many of the trading pits at the exchanges have small websites set up for their little community. These websites are not private; they are just little known. For example, let's say you trade rice. By simply searching the Web under "rice futures" or "rice commodities," not only will you get sites put together by locals in the trading pits but you may find sites set up by producers, processors, and retailers. As a sample exercise, I searched "rice futures" and not only got brokerage and exchange listings, but, more important, I got www.Firstgrain.com and www.oryza.com. Both these websites have news content related to the rice market.

Alternative Information: Looking for Specialized Information in an Open Marketplace

In the commodities market, technically, there is no such thing as insider information. Information gathered regarding the commodities market is not privileged because it is openly available information that does not affect a particular company and is not kept behind closed company doors. For instance, say I have a client who calls the docks where a great deal of crude enters the United States. He finds out whether there are any problems with shipments coming in or the loads are light or heavy. Now, because this isn't the only point of entry for crude, and because there are many other factors at any given moment, and because a plethora of other factors could influence the price of crude, this information doesn't give him a particularly unfair advantage over any other trader in the market. Nevertheless, it does give him a better advantage than someone less informed.

Let me illustrate with another example involving energies. Say I have a client who happens to know the fire chief at a major refinery. The fire chief, in turn, is in contact with the other refineries throughout the country as well as many abroad. Every year as the refineries change their seasonal grade of gasoline produced, many fires and low-scale explosions occur as a natural part of wear and tear on the refineries. These accidents have direct relation to the unleaded market and sometimes even the crude market. So, when this client hears of a fire or explosion or leakage in a refinery, he takes a related course in the market. Often, it turns out in his favor. The knowledge isn't confidential; the client just has quicker access to it than someone without that relationship.

List of Economic Reports That Have an Impact on Prices

Many of the following are announced upon their release on financial television shows such as those found on Bloomberg Television and CNBC. Some are weekly reports, whereas others are monthly or come at other intervals. A number of these reports can be found through CBOT, Nasdaq, and other exchanges and markets, as well. Also, the government publishes some of the reports at www.census.gov and www.economicindicators.gov.

The reports listed below provide information on prices:

Acreage	Crop Production
Advance Durable Goods	Dairy Products Prices
American Petroleum Institute, Energy Information Administration (API/EIA) Energy Stocks	Employment Cost Index
	Employment Situation
	Export Inspections
Business Inventories	Export Sales
Cattle on Feed	Factory Orders
Capacity Utilization	Fats and Oils
Cold Storage	Federal Open Market Committee (FOMC) Meeting
Construction Spending	
Consumer Confidence	Grain Stocks
Consumer Price Index (CPI) and Real Earnings	Gross Domestic Product (GDP)
	Hogs and Pigs

Housing Starts and Permits

Industrial Production

Institute for Supply Management (ISM)
Manufacturing Index

ISM Non-Manufacturing Index

Jobless Claims

Milk Production

New Home Sales

National Oilseed Processors Association
(NOPA) Crush

Personal Income

Producer Price Index (PPI)

Prospective Plantings

Retail Sales

Unemployment

U.S. Department of Agriculture (USDA)
Baseline Projections

U.S. Trade Balance

World Agricultural Supply and Demand
Estimates (WASDE)

Wholesale Trade

APPENDIX E

Software Products

For those who have a healthy amount of "snow on the roof," it may seem like yesterday; however, the time is long passed since we operated in an environment where armies of young people were employed to keep paper up to date. They did the calculations and prepared the basic analysis that would then be passed on to the older and wiser members of the team who would actually make the decisions. Gone is the graph paper, the tablets of spreadsheet paper, the rulers and compasses, the protractors and drafting tables, which were the tools of the business. Gone are the armies of secretaries, replaced with Microsoft Word, the armies of young drafters who drafted and redrafted plans, replaced with AutoCAD, the armies of accountants who were there to add numbers in columns all day, replaced with Excel. The progress of raw computing power on the desktop, the sophistication of the software that is available to automate business tasks, and the pressure to increase the margins of profitability demand increasing efficiency.

We have been discussing trading. The last thirty years have created as much technical revolution in the trading industry as in any other industry. Every step in the process that leads from acquiring information, analyzing that information, buying, monitoring, selling and, completing the circle, back to information gathering, has been touched by technology—for better and for worse.

The sheer amount of information that is generated, the speed at which that information must be analyzed, the speed at which the decisions must be made, the number of decisions that must be made—buy, sell, hold—can be traced to and must be managed by the technological advances that we have seen. Instead of a ticker tape pushing out a single ribbon of tape, we now have ways to receive hundreds or thousands of parallel information feeds. Analytical graphs on any one of those feeds are available at the push of a button. Hundreds of positions can be monitored simultaneously with or without the push of a button. Alerts can be set up so our systems will let us know when we need to pay attention to significant changes in our positions. These are wondrous advances for the trading community. Because they are available, in order to keep up with the rest of the trading community and the volume they have themselves created, these advances are no longer optional.

In this appendix are tips for evaluating and choosing technology that will help to automate your trading activities. There are also cautionary notes when evaluating technology. The adoptions of technologies can both advance your endeavors or hinder them. Given the choice, we would rather choose advance.

Tails and Dogs, Carts and Horses

"Go out and get a trading system," comes the cry from the corner office. Whether that corner office is at the top of fifty-two gleaming glass and steel floors or at a small desk in the corner of the master bedroom, the process is pretty much the same. The first task—not undaunting—is to decide and document what you want. "We want a trading system," you guffaw.

Not good enough.

Like nearly any business process, the process of trading, although it contains quite a number of standard pieces, is as much art as it is science. How do you do trading? What kinds of analyses are important for your decision-making process? What level of visibility do you need on your analyses, decisions, and transactions? Who needs what kinds of reports? Who needs to sign off on what and how does that happen? Before you go out and get a trading system, you need to fully understand how it is you do trading—the good and bad, what you do well and what needs improvement.

Not engaging in this first task, explicitly, in detail, usually creates the classic condition of the tail wagging the dog for two reasons. First, you find yourself letting the system dictate your particular process rather than the other way around. Second, you run the risk of wrestling with a lack of clarity for the standards by which you will evaluate and choose from the products available on the market.

The first case is that of not fleshing out a set of requirements at all. Trading system components are purchased on a recommendation or after a C level person attends a seminar whose evening keynote is from a trading system provider. This is classic dog wagging. The directive from the corner office includes the name of a particular product and the product, if it ever is successfully integrated into your operation, dictates your process instead of augmenting your process. Even if you have no current process, it is always best for you to determine what your software should do, rather than for your software to determine what you should do.

The second case is when you do start to evaluate various components of a trading system and you haven't created an independent standard against which to assess the systems you are evaluating. The decision of buying one set of components over another has less to do with what you need, than it does with the charisma of a particular salesperson or presentation. Having an external set of metrics particular to your operation gives you a template to place alongside every tool set you evaluate. Each tool set under consideration then can be judged against your requirements and how well it meets them. Yes, I realize this sounds incredibly obvious, but it doesn't take too many years in the software business to collect a painful number of projects whose chief problem is: We didn't fully flesh out our requirements.

Until we are able to see the future, fleshing out how you do your particular business, in as much detail as is practical, will go a long way to reducing the number of surprises you experience as you adopt new trading system components into your business.

Fleshing Out Requirements

Before investing much time in looking at particular products, spend the time to define what your process is and what parts of that process you want to improve. The following questions are by no means the full extent of what you will need to know, but a beginning:

- What analysis is important to you? What graphing, reports, news feeds?
- Do you prefer fundamental or technical analysis?
- Do you trade frequently or buy and hold?
- Do you have preferred vendors for data feeds, trades, or information?
- What exchanges, markets, commodities are your targets?
- How much do you expect to budget for software licensing, external feeds of data, and trading services?
- What level of support do you need?
- How close to real time do you need your data feed(s) to be?
- What software infrastructure does this new system need to fit into?
  - What operating system?
  - Are there any other office automation systems that it needs to talk to? Microsoft Office, OpenOffice.org, a particular accounting system?

- What does the hardware infrastructure look like?
  - Is everybody in one office or multiple offices?
  - Are you buying a stand-alone system?
  - What desktops do you have, and will you need to purchase more or new ones to accommodate what you buy?
- How many users?
- What is your workflow of processing a trade from beginning to end and back?
  - Who is touched by the work?
  - Who needs to communicate with whom?
  - Who needs to know what when?
  - What reports need to be generated?
  - What approvals need to be granted?
  - Do those approvals need to happen in order, AVP to VP to SVP and above?
- Do you have any proprietary practices that set you aside from the rest of the industry that you want to maintain and enhance?
- Do you have any pain points that restrict your efficiency that you would like to mitigate?
- Is there a part of the process that is a better candidate for automation than another?
- How much of your process do you want to automate?

Ask everyone about his role in the process. Everyone. From the people at the top of the food chain getting the reports to the analysts who create them. While doing this work, you may learn things about what you do that may surprise you, for good or for ill.

Once this has been done, create a list of questions and metrics that you take to every product under consideration. How do they answer your requirements? Does their solution offer you capabilities that you didn't think of before? Does a particular solution offer you more than you need or want?

Am I Too Small to Worry About This?

If you are part of a large enough organization, the need to analyze your processes and create metrics and requirements is probably a no-brainer (although this is not necessarily so). But if you are the guy that occupies the corner office of your master bedroom suite, defining requirements is no less important or necessary for you. As with many tool purchases, just buying the tool does not make you the professional. Buying a trading system without first understanding what it is you want to do with it and if it has the capabilities that you will need may saddle you with an investment that is either more, less, or off center to what you find you need. First, find out what you need. Then, using your list of requirements, judge the products that are available, the costs, the capabilities, and then buy.

What Are Some of the Choices?

So, you wanted to cut to the chase and turn right here for our recommendations. Sorry. No can do. Your particulars and processes, while having many of the basics of any trading activity—analyze, buy, analyze, sell, and back again, your size, target market, staffing, and all the details—insure that one size does not fit all. We will however in the following section discuss enough about the capabilities of some of the products on the market to help distinguish between products and capabilities.

Pieces of the Puzzle

The act of trading is an act of coordinating a grouping of different yet related components to a common end, a trade. This is yet another obvious statement but one that is helpful to remember when evaluating software. Products receive data from various exchanges and markets; they display that data in ways to help a trader evaluate what the market is doing and where he should enter or exit; they actually enter trades and communicate with the exchange or broker to have those trades executed; and finally they keep track of what you have active and your current position. Each product has its own strengths in that process, and you should match your focus against the software strength.

One of the changes in technology that has made this conversation possible is that now that broadband digital communications have become more and more ubiquitous and much less expensive. Access to the necessary data feeds to trade in real time becomes possible in a way it wasn't a few years ago. The increasing power in desktop software and hardware also gives users access to the kind of computing power that is necessary for managing these kinds of transactions at far less cost than in the past.

This is not an exhaustive overview of trading packages. What we will present here is a brief portrait of the offerings of a few of the packages we have seen. The ultimate work will be done as you reflect on your requirements and ask and answer questions as you review and evaluate. Some software vendors position their product vertically and do all the required tasks associated with trading, soup to nuts. Some vendors position their product horizontally, and do one part of the process well, across a broad spectrum of markets. Your requirements will best decide how these different approaches might help your trading.

Create for yourself a matrix of features and requirements that are important to you so that as you go through packages you will have places to make your notes and check marks and put down values. When all is said and done, you will be able to remember the first package you looked at after you've evaluated the seventh and come closer to a decision.

Another tendency you will have as you move through packages is a little reminiscent of that catchy Sesame Street song, "Which of These Things Is Not Like the Other?" Once you've examined your first package, you will find yourself saying as you look at package B, "Gee, this is like package A," or "Package A did it this way." That is perfectly all right because you are in the process of differentiation. As long as you have made enough notes, so that when you go back to review your different evaluations, you can remember what you were talking about, then the comparisons will help you make your decisions.

Trading Technologies (http://www.tradingtechnologies.com)

Trading Technologies' core product is called X_Trader. X_Trader's focus is in commodities trading and is one of the granddaddies in the electronic trading industry. Historically, its focus has been in the making and tracking of the trade itself. As development has continued, additional functionality has been added to the tool. As new capabilities have been created, these have been added on and integrated into the original product. In the version current as of this writing, they have added a tool called X_Study, which shows real-time graphing of the market that you are currently working, as another view on the market activity. This would be important if real-time technical analysis is part of your requirements.

X_Trader has been architected to allow for personal preference. We all like to arrange the papers on our desktop a little differently than the next person. X_Trader provides a number of different ways to view and interact with the market. It provides a Market window where you monitor the market and place orders, an Order Book window that provides information on your current open orders, a Fill window that gives information about the current day's activity, a Trade Book window that is used to present aggregate information for a single order, an Autotrader window that allows you to create and execute complex trades, a Market Depth trader window that displays current activity for a market and allows you with a few mouse clicks to execute sells and buys and keep a close eye on the activity. Configurability is key. A trader can configure all these windows on the desktop the way that works best for him and then save the positioning so that he can quickly restore the desktop at the start of a session. In the latest version, they have added a new X_Study component that adds real-time technical analysis, which can be docked to other trading windows and give additional visual representation to help the trader make decisions. All the windows update in real time and reflect the market and your activity as is appropriate.

As of this writing, X_Trader runs on Microsoft Windows 2000 SP3 and above, as well as Windows XP Professional SP1 and SP2. You may be a trader who knows Windows Vista has been released and wonder if it will run on Vista. If that is important to you, make sure you continue to check with Trading Technologies as testing is still underway. Any time a major revision of an operating system is released, it is wise to not upgrade until you know your critical applications are compatible with the new operating system version. If you are a trader and make your living with your trading software, don't update immediately. As I prepared for this writing, I installed the demo that Trading Technologies provides of X_Trader, and it would not install on my Vista machine.

The list of market feeds that X_Trader provides is extensive with more coming online soon. U.S., European, Asian, Australian, and New Zealand exchanges are represented.

Trading Technologies also provides an application programming interface (API) that allows you to create your own custom screens or algorithms to the data feed and markets. This can add to your own decision-making capabilities, tailor the graphical user interface (GUI) to your own requirements or other needs that you might imagine. Not for the faint of heart, it is an offering that might be important to you.

X_Trader also allows you to feed data into Excel so you can manipulate, study, or report in whatever way is most helpful to you. This platform is available from Trading Technologies, as well as through a host of distributors.

When I started this review, I looked at X_Trader first. We've discussed earlier the need to establish your requirements before you begin to examine software products. While that is true, that is not the end of requirements. As you examine how different vendors approach the tasks involved in trading, it is good to keep your eyes open for new ideas that might generate new requirements. Don't be afraid to expand the breadth of what you are looking at as you move through your evaluations, but at the same time don't lose sight of the original requirements that you started with.

Patsystems (http://www.patsystems.com)

The core product for Patsystems is J-Trader. When considering Patsystems, it is interesting to understand what they mean when they say "customers." Patsystems does not work directly with end users. For them, customers are the brokerages, banks, and financial institutions that offer J-Trader for their customers to use to access services. Patsystems maintains an extensive list of partners through whom you can trade and access the J-Trader system.

While J-Trader is their core product, appropriate for retail and general trading and is extensively available through a wide list of customers, they have continued to improve and expand their offerings, adding products such as IQ-Trader and Pro-Mark, which incorporate technological advances or are optimized for higher volumes of trades.

Here in the evaluation process, I began to find myself entering the comparison and differentiation mode I spoke of earlier. As I looked at screens and windows and descriptions, I found myself saying, "Gee, that is like product A," or "Gee, that is not like product A."

As the trading process has a pretty standard set of operations, many of the same kinds of basic operations are available through their product as is available through X_Trader. You will find an order book, customizable charts, a market-depth window with mouse-click selling and buying, a spread-matrix window, a position window that displays your position in real time among others.

Patsystems provides an API, too, so that your team can interact with the data in your own unique ways.

It is clear that one way Patsystems differentiates itself is through working with providers rather than end users. Their system is built to be rebranded, so you may find their system being marketed under a number of different provider's names. In this case, part of your evaluation becomes learning what value the provider brings to the table and adding that information to your matrix.

This system, as is suggested by the name, is written in Java. This gives providers the ability to deploy in a number of different ways. Depending on whom you work with, you can gain access to their systems over a LAN, VPN, secured Web page, leased lines, etc. When we discussed the Trading Technologies products, it was important to discuss operating system versions and hardware. Because Patsystems products are written in Java, those considerations become less important, as long as your machine can run the appropriate Java Virtual Machine (JVM) fast enough to trade effectively.

RCG Onyx (http://www.rcgonyx.com)

We've seen it before. It has all the views that the others have. Windows for quotes, contracts, positions, all current orders, trade tickets, filled orders, and a couple of windows called "ABV" and "ABV2," which stands for ask, bid, and volume. This ABV window performs the same functionality as the market-depth window of the products above, and version two is a new revision of the original that some traders might find more intuitive. This product is one that you would install on your desktop and like X_Trader requires either Microsoft Windows 2000 or XP. Vista is not yet supported. But again, as above, stay tuned.

There are no graphs in the package to support your technical analysis, but there is a separate functionality for printing and exporting reports. All in all, the functionality is similar to the preceding products but the interface looks slicker. It uses a nonstandard font and, in a tip of the hat to the name, the background of most of the main windows is a deep black with some colors fading in and out—nice to look at. The different approach they have made toward the interface has enabled them to add some nice features to make understanding the movement of the market a little more intuitive. This is worth a look.

CQG (http://www.cqg.com)

CQG has a modular system allowing a trader to decide if he just wants to trade or if he wants the technical analysis side by side with his trading functionality. CQG Integrated Client has all the standard windows, an order window, and a market-depth display with integrated trading functionality much like the others above. It also has integrated graphing to help with on-the-spot technical analysis in real time. They offer a choice of products. For those traders who don't need to have the real-time technical analysis graphs as part of their trading desktop, one version of the software called the CQG Trader has all the functionality of the full version without the graphs, just the trading. They also have an API so that you creative traders can interface with Excel, create Web applications, desktop applications, and automated trading applications, as well.

WINdoTRADEr (http://www.windotrader.com)

WINdoTRADEr is presented here as an example that could very well meet your requirements in ways similar products do not. From its own materials, it claims that it is a "state-of-the-art charting application for futures, commodities, stocks, single stock futures, and Forex contracts." What you will find with WINdoTRADEr is attention to graphics. The cumulative volume bars for the Market Profile charts are unsurpassed in the industry. It is extremely user-friendly with respect to zooming Market Profile charts and merging profiles together and breaking out TPO tracks as individual bars for analysis purposes. WINdoTRADEr has recently merged with Photon, and plans to offer a full trading platform as part of the package.

Summary

Remember your requirements. Don't be afraid to expand upon them during your research, but don't forget your core needs. As I've said this is far from an exhaustive list. You can go to a place like the Chicago Board of Trade (http://www.cbot.com/cbot/pub/page/0,3181,1183,00.html) for other vendors. Go to your favorite search engine—Google, MSN, Yahoo!—and search for electronic trading or trading platforms and look through the lists. Don't skip over the advertising in industry tabloids either, since good leads can be found there as well. Don't believe the hype. Evaluate, take it for a test drive, and (repeat after me) remember your requirements.

Index

About Bloomberg

Bloomberg L.P., founded in 1981, is a global information services, news, and media company. Headquartered in New York, the company has sales and news operations worldwide.

Serving customers on six continents, Bloomberg, through its wholly-owned subsidiary Bloomberg Finance L.P., holds a unique position within the financial services industry by providing an unparalleled range of features in a single package known as the Bloomberg Professional® service. By addressing the demand for investment performance and efficiency through an exceptional combination of information, analytic, electronic trading, and straight-through-processing tools, Bloomberg has built a worldwide customer base of corporations, issuers, financial intermediaries, and institutional investors.

Bloomberg News, founded in 1990, provides stories and columns on business, general news, politics, and sports to leading newspapers and magazines throughout the world. Bloomberg Television, a 24-hour business and financial news network, is produced and distributed globally in seven languages. Bloomberg Radio is an international radio network anchored by flagship station Bloomberg 1130 (WBBR-AM) in New York.

In addition to the Bloomberg Press line of books, Bloomberg publishes *Bloomberg Markets* magazine.

```
London:  . . . . . . . . . +44-20-7330-7500
New York:  . . . . . . . . +1-212-318-2000
Tokyo:  . . . . . . . . . .  +81-3-3201-8900
```

SUBSCRIBE TO *BLOOMBERG MARKETS* & GET A FREE ISSUE

The magazine for and about people who move markets.

• Free issue plus 12 more for $19.95
• Save more with two years for $29.95

To subscribe to *Bloomberg Markets*, go to:
www.bloomberg.com/news/marketsmag/

About the Author

Mark Tinghino is a commodity trading adviser based in the Chicago area. His work on technical analysis, electronic trading, and cycles has appeared in Neal Weintraub's *Tricks of the Active Trader*, and his articles have been published in *Futures* and *TraderSOURCE* magazines. He has taught online seminars on technical analysis at the Chicago Board of Trade and Chicago Mercantile Exchange. Tinghino has spent the past twenty-five years developing and refining a unique model for market timing that utilizes a combination of several hundred separate cycles. The results of this ongoing research are available to subscribers of his market letter (details may be found at www.Tinghino.net). In addition to his involvement in financial market analysis, he owns an information technology consulting business. He is also an accomplished musician.

Bloomberg
PRESS

"Features a number of approaches that challenge conventional wisdom and are sure to form an invaluable part of your trading arsenal."

Jason Perl   Global Head of Fixed Income, Foreign Exchange and Commodities Technical Strategy, UBS Investment Bank

BREAKTHROUGHS IN TECHNICAL ANALYSIS
NEW THINKING FROM THE WORLD'S TOP MINDS

Bloomberg brings together top technicians, such as Bernie Schaeffer, Tom DeMark, Constance Brown, and other global leaders, to reveal groundbreaking approaches—in some cases for the first time in print—that have been key to their success. Broaden your approach as you incorporate their techniques into your own successful investment strategy.

In stores now or visit www.bloomberg.com/books

© 2007 Bloomberg L.P. All rights reserved. 27157763 1207